The Modern Stranger

Contributions to the Sociology of Language

47

Editor
Joshua A. Fishman

Mouton de Gruyter
Berlin · New York · Amsterdam

The Modern Stranger

On Language and Membership

by
Lesley D. Harman

Mouton de Gruyter
Berlin · New York · Amsterdam 1988

Mouton de Gruyter (formerly Mouton, The Hague)
is a Division of Walter de Gruyter & Co., Berlin.

Library of Congress Cataloging in Publication Data

Harman, Lesley D., 1956 –
The modern stranger.

(Contributions to the sociology of language ; 47)
Revision of thesis (doctoral)--York University, Toronto, Ont.
Bibliography: p.
1. Margnality, Social.   2. Alienation (Social psychology)
3. Home--Psychological aspects.   4. Sociolinguistics.
I. Title.   II. Series.
HM291.H158   1987   302.5'44   87-24845
ISBN 0-89925-324-5 (alk. paper)

CIP-Titelaufnahme der Deutschen Bibliothek

Harman, Lesley D.:
The modern stranger : on language and membership / by
Lesley D. Harman. – Berlin ; New York ; Amsterdam : Mouton
de Gruyter, 1988
(Contributions to the sociology of language ; 47)
ISBN 3-11-011235-3
NE: GT

Printed on acid free paper.

Typesetting: Asian Research Service, Hong Kong. – Printing: Gerike GmbH, Berlin.
Binding: Dieter Mikolai, Berlin. – Printed in Germany.

Preface

Growing up in a foreign service family, I learned at an early age that the worlds of "home" and "away" were constantly in flux; and that the entire taken-for-grantedness of one's authentic culture could never be assumed. In many ways, this awareness drew me to sociology, and theorizing about strangeness has characterized much of my scholarly life.

Writing about the stranger began with some early essays, and the idea that strangeness and familiarity were inextricably tied up with language and membership began to dawn on me during my graduate courses at York University. *The Modern Stranger* is a substantially revised version of my doctoral dissertation of the same name.

I would like to acknowledge the support of the Social Sciences and Humanities Research Council of Canada, and to thank my friends and teachers who encouraged me in this project: at Bethune College, where I was a fellow during my graduate school years; and in York University's Graduate Programme in Sociology, especially Ioan Davies, Thelma McCormack, Ray Morris, Gottfried Paasche, and Judith Posner. Bill Ramp was a great help with proofreading and providing insightful comments. Special appreciation goes to Orrin Klapp for his generous comments on the manuscript, and to Malcolm Blincow for his conscientious reading. Joshua Fishman took an interest in the project and encouraged me to revise it for his series. H. T. Wilson, a true teacher, I thank for allowing me to discover my path, yet always in the knowledge that *he was there*. James Côté has been with me from the beginning. This work would not exist without these valued contributions, but for the end product I bear full responsibility.

I dedicate this book to Margaret and Gary Harman, who showed me through their shining example that there is nothing wrong with being a stranger, and who gave me the emotional and material support so that some day I might find the words to write it down.

May 1987   Lesley D. Harmann

Contents

Introduction

1. Several years ago, while I was riding a Toronto subway, I witnessed an event which caused me to rethink assumptions about sociology, myself as a sociologist, the city, membership, and what members and sociologists mean by the word "stranger".[1]

The subway car was well filled; at the tail end of rush hour, heading out of the downtown core, it was likely that most passengers were on their way home from work or other business. They appeared to be regular subway riders, occupying themselves studiously: reading, knitting, gazing vacantly out of a window, dozing; coactors in a still and silent scene.

A man swaggered into the car and, in a loud Maritime voice, inquired "Anyone here from St. John's?". It was as if he had shouted in a vacuum. Glancing up, I seemed to be the only one responding to the "intrusion". Silence restored, the answer given, the man glared about, stating his name and repeating his question. Met again by no response, he found a seat and fell silent as well.

Observing as a sociologist, I had taken the stony silences, the self-conscious avoidance of eye contact, and the studied engagement in autonomous activities to indicate that the subway, microcosm of the city, is peopled by strangers determined to avoid community, to have nothing to do with one another beyond getting from one personal world to another. Looking around, I saw the most "heterogeneous" group imaginable, by ascribed indicators at least. Men and women of all ages and racial origins, for all intents and purposes in their own worlds, pursuing any number of thoughts and daydreams. Yet I saw that *they* were not the strangers at all. In that frame there were only two strangers: the man who had spoken, and myself.

It occurred to me, in one of those rare moments of astonishment in which one's assumptions reveal themselves to be completely without validity, that these "strangers" were acting collectively, as members, to *exclude* the poor man who was clearly *not one of them*. Moreover, at the same time I realized that I, by taking a sociologist's lens, had placed myself outside of that consensus.

How did I see this? Is sociological observation by its very nature a removal of the sociologist from the world being observed? Can one observe from *within* a world of which one is a part, or must the sociologist always be somewhat marginal to that world?

What has the stranger become? Is strangeness a norm unto itself? Has the city produced new rules of membership where the stranger has become the one who displays a desire for familiarity?

This book is as much about the former set of questions as the latter. Each chapter, in the process of trying to come to terms with various bodies of literature and their implications for the concept of "the stranger", struggles even more deeply with how I as a sociologist can even begin to make assertions, as if from the inside, about a world that I have come to call my own, when even beginning to ask about the stranger makes me one as well – on the outside. That this struggle is never entirely resolved I shall admit at the outset; yet to hope that it could would be to obviate the very need of sociology to continually reassess its role as both within and without society.

Distinctions have been made between *social problems, sociological problems,* and *sociologists' problems* (Boughey, 1978). It is an implicit theme of this book that these distinctions lose relevance as the modern actor becomes the modern stranger *qua* trained observer. A social problem has been designated as that which members perceive to be an impediment to ongoing, uninterrupted social order. A sociological problem is the construct of sociology: formulated by the sociologist, it is perceived as that phenomenon which requires study by sociological means and tools. It follows that all apparatuses associated with the sociological problem, including the "problem" itself, are constructs of sociology. Finally, a sociologist's problem has to do with the extent to which sociological problems conform with social problems, and the ability of the sociologist to fulfil the mandate of greater understanding of the mechanisms of social order and disorder.

The example of the man on the subway suggests that the distinctions between the three modes are far from discrete. Beginning with the last, the sociological lens, clearly implicated in the "seeing" of the man as a "stranger", created my "sociological problem" in which questions as to the faithfulness of my perception to sociology *as well as* to common-sense membership were raised. Yet this tension is intimately related to the other two modes. The sociological problem was invoked only after there was a distinct challenge to my common-sense view – a challenge, then, to my sensibility of social order which was grounded in my capacity as a member. Every member in the car was aware of the intrusion posed by this man. The mode of response taken, one in which I might have participated had my sociological problem-solving lens not been aroused, involved a clear maintenance of boundaries between "him" and "us" in the form of silent exclusion. I, however, in *observing* this, became marginal to "us" and closer to "him".

The problem of the modern stranger is precisely one of mediating between participating in collective events, and "groping" (Klapp, 1969) for the signals which inform him as to the norms governing propriety in those situations. This in turn is precisely the dilemma, of being "in between", which confronts the trained observer. One of the objectives of this book is to show in the practice of writing that the distinctions between the three modes of problem construction are vague at best; and it is this vagueness which gives the modern stranger his unique character of being both "within" and "without".[2]

2. In his pathbreaking article, "Urbanism as a Way of Life", Louis Wirth wrote:

The distinctive feature of the mode of living of man in the modern age is his concentration into gigantic aggregations around which cluster lesser centers and from which radiate the ideas and practices that we call civilization.

The degree to which the contemporary world may be said to be "urban" is not fully or accurately measured by the proportion of the total population living in cities. The influences which cities exert upon the social life of man are greater than the ratio of the urban population would indicate, for the city is not only in ever larger degrees the dwelling-place and the workshop of modern man, but it is the initiating and controlling center of economic, political, and cultural life that has drawn the most remote parts of the world into its orbit and woven diverse areas, peoples, and activities into a cosmos. (1938: 2)

Today, the west has evolved such that urbanism is no longer a new and problematic phenomenon. City living has become the norm, and with it the social relations enabling its continuance as the prevalent sensibility.

It is to these social relations produced by urbanism as a way of life that I intend to turn in the following pages. Even the most cursory glance at the literature on modernity reveals that the central feature of these relations entails the fact that by and large they occur among strangers. This view has continued despite the fact that the concept of "the stranger" has long been in need of re-examination.

"The stranger" has by and large been constructed by sociologists to account for an actor who is self-contained: he has an origin which is complete and separate from that of the group to which he is strange.[3] Its history has entailed a further assumption that the group approached has a definable, integrated, shared and self-contained identity. The stranger has always been formulated as the one who could not "pass" as a member, in turn implying a homogeneous group constituted of rigid rules for membership only available to those "inside". This view of the stranger has served sociology well until recently. As long as the dominant modes of social organization continued to make "the stranger" a logical and visible category, the prevalent definition could remain unchallenged. It is the claim of this book, however, that the time has come to seriously reconsider this version of the stranger as a self-contained outsider, in light of recent empirical and theoretical developments.

The principal empirical development is one of *cosmopolitan "mass culture"*, the consequence of three escalating forces in North American society: urbanization; mobility; and sophisticated global communications.

These changes have seriously altered conditions of membership in the modern world, and demand that questions of strangeness and familiarity be reopened.

The principal theoretical development is the increasing importance in sociology of the study of *language and meaning.* Work in the areas of socio-linguistics, phenomenology, symbolic interactionism, semiotics, and cultural proxemics has produced a rich reserve of theoretical approaches which are lacking in much of the literature to be reviewed.[4]

The subdiscipline of sociolinguistics, led by scholars such as Fishman, Gumperz, Hymes, Labov and Schegloff, emerged in the 1960s and 1970s in response to the growing recognition of the link between language and social behavior, and of the need to provide a firm grounding for the study of language within sociology. Although the field has mushroomed, it is safe to say that there are several assumptions which unite various forms of sociolinguistic research. Of these, we may identify the following as particularly salient to the current project. First, it is assumed that all language is *contextual.* For Hymes (1972a), this is demonstrated by contrasting sociolinguistics with linguistics:

Whereas linguists deal with dictionary meanings (denotation, or meaning abstracted from context), sociolinguists deal with what Sacks calls situated meaning (meaning mediated and sometimes transformed by rules of speaking) which reflects speakers [sic] attitudes to each other, and to their topics. (p. 37)

A second assumption of sociolinguistics is that of the *speech community* as a basic unit of society. While the concept of speech community has undergone considerable transformation since its introduction, Fishman's (1972b) broad use of the term is appropriate for the current usage. Simply, "a speech community is one, all of whose members share at least a single speech variety and the norms for its appropriate use" (p. 22). In his foreword to Fishman, Hymes endorses this wider use of speech community:

The old equation of speech community with language community, such that a common language implied, and indeed defined, the notion of speech community, hopefully is gone for good. (Hymes in Fishman, 1972b: vii)

Speech or language *varieties* constitute modes of socially differentiating within and between speech communities:

Regardless of the linguistic differences among them, the speech varieties employed within a speech community form a system because they are related to a shared set of social norms. Hence, they can be classified according to their usage, their origins, and the relationship between speech and social action that they reflect. They become indices of social patterns of interaction in the speech community. (Gumperz, 1971: 116)

This leads to a third assumption, namely that the social structure of a group is reflected in its language. Individuals possess *language repertoires* which constitute the set of varieties in which they are conversant. For

Bernstein (1972), repertoires are far from accidental. His influential distinction between elaborated and restricted codes indicates that members are socialized, in large part by their social class position, to speak particular codes. Language repertoires, then, reflect role repertoires. Fishman (1972b) has noted that the complexity of social organization of a speech community is also reflected in the language repertoires of its members.

This thumbnail sketch of some of the major tenets of sociolinguistics is important, for many of the concepts introduced are seminal, both implicitly and explicitly, to the remainder of this book. At the very least, the claim that we must go to language to discover fundamental relations of familiarity and strangeness within a group, requires that sociolinguistics be addressed.

At the same time, however, the approach taken is not strictly sociolinguistic for it borrows from other interpretative approaches — particularly those of phenomenology, symbolic interaction, semiotics, and cultural proxemics. This is necessitated in part because it will be argued that *language* is more than the verbal mode of communication. Gumperz (1972b) claims that

Although not all communication is linguistic, language is by far the most powerful and versatile medium of communication; all known human groups possess language. Unlike other sign systems the verbal system can, through the minute refinement of its grammatical and semantic structure, be made to refer to a wide variety of objects and concepts. At the same time, verbal interaction is a social process in which utterances are selected in accordance with socially recognized norms and expectations. (p. 219)

While strictly speaking this may be the case, it will be made clear that the verbal use of language is not the prevalent one among strangers. In urban settings, nonverbal communication achieves remarkable sophistication and often may be said to be more important than verbal communication. It becomes necessary, then, to push beyond the strictly verbal definition of language. For Wardaugh (1986), the three main criteria for language are standardization, codification, and recognition. These criteria apply to the language of membership, as will be shown through the appropriation of the contributions of phenomenology, symbolic interaction, semiotics and cultural proxemics.

From phenomenology is taken the notion that individuals experience the world as a "stream of consciousness". The world into which we are thrown precedes us historically and will continue after we are gone. The collectivity known as society is composed of biographically unique individuals who seek to share their experiences through "we-relationships" with others (Schutz, 1967). Understanding is accomplished through arriving at shared meanings.

For symbolic interaction, shared meanings are arrived at through "significant symbols" (Mead, 1934). These may be in spoken, written, gestural, sartorial, or material form. Interaction occurs when individuals respond to each others' symbols and thus share meaning. Symbolic interaction is concerned, then, with how social interaction is communicative; how meaning is diachronically achieved. In contrast, semiotics, the "science of signs", is concerned with codes in a synchronic way. Focusing at the level of mass culture and imagery, as in the work of Roland Barthes, this approach examines how meaning is culturally encoded and can therefore be shared by large groups, most members of which may in fact be strangers to each other.[5] The area of cultural proxemics, characterized by the work of Edward T. Hall, deals with the "silent language" of cultural clash. Nonverbal messages are produced when the taken-for-granted worlds of strangers do not coincide, as with the case of travellers, immigrants, and bilinguals (Fishman, 1965, 1972a & b), often producing misunderstanding.

In the pages that follow, the reformulation of the concept will draw freely upon the contributions of these interpretative disciplines. It is the objective of this book to arrive at a reconceptualization of the stranger that will respond to the empirical and theoretical trends identified, and that ultimately will serve as a framework for subsequent investigations into ways in which, as Wilson (1977) implies, the stranger has indeed become the norm.

3. The observations that follow are limited to the "modern world" at its most "advanced" stage: urbanized, postindustrial North American society in the 1980s. It is of this world that the question, "How is it possible for humans to adapt socially to changing conditions of membership?", must be posed. One hears daily of the "breakdown" of the family, of the phenomenal appeal of such epics as Haley's *Roots* (1976) and more recently Buscaglia's *Living, Loving and Learning* (1982) − appealing to a generalized sense of loss and lack of direction in a world which appears bent upon minimizing the individual's autonomous sense of self and instructing members on what it is that constitutes authentic being-in-the-world. Yet we survive. And culture, the barometer of members' sense of the need to mold their environment, to dispute the external government of experience, continues to take on new forms in response to change. So, too, the conditions of membership, and the criteria for being an insider or an outsider, have changed.

The rules determining membership and exclusion in modern society have been assumed by much of sociology to be rigid and self-evident to both insiders and outsiders. Such a view is made explicit in the now-famous definition of culture suggested by Goodenough: "A society's culture consists of whatever it is one has to know or believe in order to operate in a manner acceptable to its members" (1957: 167). As Geertz (1973) has pointed out, however, criteria for membership can not be listed by a society's members; rather, they are assumed. So, although one of the major tenets of the present reformulation of "the stranger" is that criteria of membership are ultimately determinate of strangeness, I take with Geertz that such rules must be seen as produced and sustained at the level of common-sense knowledge. The analytical perspective which grounds this work is therefore one which focuses upon the assumed nature of the rules of membership; and which looks to the embedded significations which serve to produce and sustain them.

In Chapter One, the sociological literature on the concept of "the stranger" will be reviewed with an eye to evaluating the applicability of the construct to modern society. In an attempt to suggest how new modes of social organization have produced the adaptive actor that I will call the "modern stranger", it will be argued that rather than being a self-contained outsider, *the modern stranger is an inside actor with an outward glance.*

In Chapter Two, it will be maintained, against those who call for an absolute definition of "authentic being-in-the-world" rooted in traditional modes of social organization, that authenticity can only be experienced when there is a clear, unimpeded communicative relation between the individual and the world to be experienced. Impediments to such a relation, such as mythologies, hegemony, and false consciousness, make it increasingly impossible for the individual to exercise choice and a degree of control over his environment. They produce, instead, nostalgia, alienation, and a widespread sense of helplessness.

In Chapter Three, the modern stranger will be posited as an expert navigator who is "in between" others, separated by the translucent wall of potential conversation; of otherness lying in wait. It will be shown that the modern stranger adapts only by taking the view that social situations are problematic and in need of mapping, and that mapping becomes the primary tool of membership orientation. The expert navigator is the one for whom the ever changing becomes a constant; the adaptable member is one who demonstrates his competence by being able to take for granted the unaccounted for.

In Chapter Four, it will be put forward that the key factor in this adaptability is one of language. As verbally articulated, gesturally conveyed, or culturally expressed through hegemonic signs and images, it transcends changes in spatial and social conditions of membership and remains the paramount tool of mapping and of sociability. As such it is to language that I will turn as the tool which enables the modern stranger to understand and communicate familiarity and strangeness in the face of the erosion of traditional recipes for doing so. It will be suggested that mapping is a reflexive form of speech that must be employed in order to manage membership in the modern world; and as such it normalizes what might have been problematic in another era where spatial and social criteria for membership and strangeness were more clearcut.

In Chapter Five, some of the implications of the reformulation of "the stranger" will be addressed in terms of its applicability to more specific types of social actors, in particular those whose spatial rootedness is precarious and who are forced to engage in cultural mapping as a way of "grounding" their social existence.

4. This book is informed by many diverse areas of interest in sociology. It is an attempt to theorize about some fundamental changes which have occurred in our society, and the topic has implications for the study of concepts ("the stranger", marginality, membership), as well as the structures (the city, the family, the community) which produce interactive relationships (inclusion and exclusion; reflexivity and reflectivity) between members. As such, the bodies of literature to be addressed, and the perspective to be taken, will inevitably raise questions for the reader as to their appropriateness to the topic. Concern may be voiced as to the lack of reference to the existential literature, in which strangeness is seen as inherent in life itself. The choice to leave this tradition to other authors reflects a sense that the question of membership, being a key element in the discipline of sociology, must take precedence in a sociological analysis of the stranger.

A second argument will be made against the apparently "apolitical" nature of this piece. There are a great many issues in the life of the modern stranger which may be seen to arise only by virtue of the powerless and hegemonically influenced position of the anonymous actor in the metropolis. While this is recognized and taken as axiomatic throughout the work, specific discussion is reserved for Appendix A.

Finally, I will be criticized by those who object to my use of a vast and variable literature as the primary source of "data" for arriving at conclusions that form the basis for my redefinition of "the stranger". As in any attempt at theory construction, the proverbial chicken-and-egg of theory and data looms problematically. This project conforms to Glaser and Strauss' (1967) agenda for "formal" theory generation.[6] It is hoped that the theoretical framework suggested here will help to spur subsequent empirical research leading to both the refinement of the formal theory, and the generation of "substantive" theory. Some implications for future research, and suggested directions, are provided in the conclusion.

The strength of the approach taken lies in its self-conscious tentativeness. To call for a fundamental rethinking of one of sociology's time-honored constructs is to call for an opening of the construct to other interpretations and critiques. My hope is to contribute in some small way to the liveliness of this debate.

Notes

1. Where the distinction between the sociological type, "the stranger", and the actor who is perceived/perceives himself as strange is unclear, the sociological type will be set off by quotation marks.
2. In writing this book, the stylistic question regarding gender has not been ignored. Current efforts to introduce nonsexist language in academic writing stress "problems of designation" and "problems of evaluation", both involving ambiguity of referent and stereotyping (American Psychological Association, 1977). Both sets of problems, however, are detected when oversight or hidden biases emerge in the writing up of material which may be oriented to androgynous situations. In the interests of readability and consistency, however, the various forms that nonsexist writing may take may not always be satisfactory:

Attempting to introduce nonsexist language at the cost of awkwardness, obscurity, or euphemistic phrasing does not improve scientific communication....
Any endeavor to change the language is an awesome task at best. Some aspects of our language that may be considered sexist are firmly embedded in our culture, and we presently have no acceptable substitutes. In English, the use of third-person singular pronouns is one example: the generic use of *he* is misleading; *it* is inaccurate, *one* conveys a different meaning, and *he or she* can become an annoying repetition. Nevertheless, with some rephrasing and careful attention to meaning, even the generic *he* can be avoided most of the time. The result of such efforts is accurate, unbiased communication ... (American Psychological Association, 1977: 8)

The choice to write this book in the male gender results from considerable thought, and several attempts in previous drafts to use alternative formulae. I feel, however, that the final choice deserves some explanation. There are three concerns which have been considered: responsibility to the literature; responsibility to the subject matter; and consistency.

The literature to be reviewed on "the stranger" has all been written in the male gender. There are two reasons for this. First, the emphasis on nonsexist writing has emerged only recently, while sociologists have been writing on the topic of "the stranger" for most of the century. Second, empirically speaking, "the stranger" has by and large been constructed and used as an ideal type to denote men. In Simmel's world, women were not "potential wanderers", as a rule. Even Margaret Mary Wood (1934) and Lyn H. Lofland (1973) saw only men in their writings on strangers in the city.

A responsibility to the subject matter demands that I exercise consistency with this fact. To introduce the androgynous stranger is to beg the question: how is woman now implicated in "the modern stranger"? Such an excursus is beyond the limits of the present work, although of considerable importance for future research.

The point is that the ideal type which I present represents an effort to make "the stranger" contemporary. In this sense it is assumed to apply to the social actor — male or female — in the city. Yet the particularities affecting the different sexes, also of importance, must be left to subsequent research.

The mandate of consistency in writing style requires that I choose one format in which to write throughout. The choice of the male gender which is made necessary by Chapters One and Two must consequently apply for the rest of the piece. It is hoped that the readability of the book will thereby be maximized; and that the reader will sympathize with the solution, unsatisfactory as it must be, to the dilemma of "nonsexist writing".

3. The recognition and negotiation of strangeness is assumed to occur at the level of culturally produced symbols. It is possible that the recognition of the stranger may occur at a precultural, sociobiological level at which the principle of species-recognition prevails; and that this instinctual awareness of fundamental similarities and differences has been adapted to our cultural forms but remains a fundamentally *human* activity. Leslie White's (1959) four stages in the evolution of minding suggest that language evolves from a need to respond symbolically to the environment. It follows that what the stranger is may also change with the shift from nonsymbolic (nondiscursive, denotative) communication to symbolic communication (discursive and connotative) — however what the stranger represents — a fundamental threat to the integrity of the group — may remain constant.
   Although the sociobiological origins of the social response to the stranger should be explored, they have not been dealt with in this book. Instead, the analysis is limited to what happens *within* a context of culturally-produced conditions for membership and exclusion.

4. Schutz (1944) is a notable exception; and MacCannell (1976), whose work on the tourist emerges from the new theoretical tradition, comes closest to the kind of direction to which I refer. Hall (1977) also touches on some extremely important issues relating to the intercultural communication and the beginnings of a science of cultural proxemics. Fishman has written extensively about language and culture; of particular interest is his work on bilingualism (1965, 1972a & b). However his work may relate implicitly to questions about the stranger, he is representative of much of the work in sociolinguistics by inviting application of the diverse contributions in the field to areas such as the one currently under investigation. Frake (1964) specifically identified the applicability of sociolinguistics to the dilemma of the stranger.

5. For a detailed study of the relationship between semiotics and symbolic interaction, see Harman (1986).

6. In their call for more theory generation in sociology, Glaser and Strauss distinguish between "substantive" and "formal" theory:

   By substantive theory, we mean that developed for a substantive, or empirical, area of sociological inquiry .... By formal theory, we mean that developed for a formal, or conceptual, area of sociological inquiry, such as stigma, deviant behavior, etc.... (p. 32)

   The present analysis falls in the latter category, in attempting to reformulate the concept of "the stranger". Grounded formal theory emerges from the constant comparative method as applied to data such as other studies, direct observation, and "lived experience":

   Grounded theory ... may take different forms. And although we consider the *process* of generating theory as related to its subsequent use and effectiveness, the *form* in which the theory is presented can be independent of this process by which it was generated. Grounded theory can be presented either as a well-codified set of propositions or in a running theoretical discussion, using conceptual categories and their properties. (p. 31)

Chapter I
Sociology and "The Stranger"

1. Sociology and "The Stranger"

> *O voyagers, O seamen, You who come*
> *to port, and you whose bodies will*
> *suffer the trial and judgement of the sea,*
> *Or whatever event, this is your real*
> *destination.*
>
> *T.S. Eliot, Four Quartets*

In an excellent critique of the sociology of the stranger, McLemore (1970) points to the faithfulness with which theorists call upon the authority of Georg Simmel, who is widely regarded as the father of "the stranger":

Simmel's "stranger" has enjoyed from the beginning a remarkable immunity to criticism. The "stranger" always is invoked as if its meaning were clear and as if its analytic power were obvious. The comparatively long and illustrious history of the "stranger", combined with its continued utilization and its freedom from criticism, has created the impression that "There is a special and well-developed sociology of the stranger" . . .[1] (pp. 86-87)

The literature on "the stranger", which both recognizes Simmel's authority and occasionally attempts to reformulate "the stranger", may be reduced to a series of articles "applying" Simmel's stranger to specific types of actors. These have led to new appellations (the marginal man, the newcomer, the sojourner, the dual man, the cosmopolitan) which draw their characteristics from particular case studies. All of these types rely on certain exclusionary rules which produce strangeness; rules implicit in Simmel which have remained largely unquestioned for over seventy-five years. There has been no serious effort made to update the concept along the various directions the stranger has taken, in the interests of discovering key indicators of social life which inform these directions. The question has not been asked: What are the fundamental conditions of membership that would produce "stranger" relationships? Instead, it has been assumed that Simmel's stranger is the timeless model which may be used.

The literature on "the stranger" falls into two categories: work on reformulating "the stranger"; and work on applying "the stranger" and its derivative categories to social groups, individuals, and perceived social problems. Because the work in the first category has been so poorly organized and inconsistent, the usefulness of the applications of the concept has been limited, generally resulting in confusion. The confusion over the definition of "the stranger" has sprung not only from theoretical carelessness but from the perceived pervasiveness of the "sociological problem" of the stranger in social life. The concept is needed by sociology and the uses to which it may be put are varied. Consequently, demands have been placed upon the concept which it has been unable to meet, and it has been weakened as a result.

1.1. "The Stranger" as an Ideal Type

Theorists of "the stranger" have tended to view Simmel's stranger as the ideal typical "outsider", produced by virtue of being on the outside of existing homogeneous groupings. Such an exercise has seriously impeded the further development of the concept. In this essay, I will attempt to reconstruct "the stranger" in a different light: by suggesting that the stranger is only produced in relation to what constitutes a member. This reformulation will take the form of drawing out the axes upon which the conditions of membership are established, and attempting to build ideal types of the various manifestations taken by "the stranger".[2] There are two such axes: that of *proximity* and that of *membership orientation.* The construction of the ideal types of the stranger will involve generating a changeable set of criteria for membership based upon the interaction of these two axes.

(i) *Proximity.* Proximity, or closeness, is an integral factor in determining and maintaining membership. Proximity may be identified at several levels, and these levels may be recognized as conforming to changes in modes of social organization and consequently modes of membership determination. Proximity coupled with distance, as perceived by both actor and other, forms a basis for strangeness and familiarity. Although a relationship between proximity and membership has been assumed throughout the literature, it has neither been explicitly examined apart from other factors, nor perceived as a *changeable* condition and one which may affect the ideal type of the stranger as the dominant mode of proximity has changed. The three types of proximity to be examined are the spatial, the social, and the cultural.

Spatial proximity deals with the dimension of space. One's "nearness" and "remoteness" in terms of geography have been central during some of the epochs in the history of "the stranger", particularly in Simmel's pioneering work. However, changes in mobility patterns and demographic makeup have had an immense impact on the exclusive determination of "the stranger" on the basis of spatial proximity, which has gone unrecognized to date.[3]

Social proximity refers to within-group distanciation, usually on the basis of built-in structural inequality between dominant and subordinate groups. Distance may be encoded in many ways, although most authors focus on visible, nondiscursive indicators such as physical appearance (both that which is ascribed, such as skin color; and that which is achieved, such as dress and material appurtenances). Social distance is peculiar within a culture and it is only upon achieving membership in a particular culture that one is privy to the "inside knowledge" necessary to navigate social distance.

Cultural proximity refers to elements concerning communicative competence between cultures. One's facility with language, customs, beliefs, and habits is one of the first criteria for determining strangeness/familiarity. Cultural indicators were introduced primarily in the literature on immigrants; however, empirical changes in the hegemony of culture and the generation of a mass communications network have been influential in altering the boundaries between cultural and social proximity, as well as minimizing the importance of spatial proximity. These developments have gone largely unrecognized in the literature on the stranger, yet seem to account, in retrospect, for much of the confusion surrounding the various attempts at redefining the concept.

(ii) *Membership Orientation.* The second axis which will be introduced in drawing together the various forms of the stranger is that of *membership orientation.* This addresses the interests of actor (stranger) and other (host) in establishing familiar and strange relationships. Is the stranger content to remain peripheral to the group and culturally autonomous? Is assimilation the goal? What kind of member, in short, does he wish to be? Concurrently, the motivations of the host group are also in question. To what extent is the stranger welcomed, and what place is he expected to take *vis-à-vis* the group? It is only through examining both the motivations of actor and other that the meaning that strangeness has may be established. Much of the literature, with the exceptions of the work of Simmel (1971b), Schutz (1944), and Levine (1979), tends to neglect the interactive element as it particularly serves to mutualize perceptions, expectations, and definitions.

Together, the different forms the stranger has taken may be collected according to these determinants of membership. Proxemically, is membership conditional upon spatial proximity, social proximity, cultural proximity, or a combination of the above? In terms of membership orientation, what effect does an actor's desire to join or remain autonomous have upon his and his host's perceptions of membership/strangeness? How does the attitude of the host toward membership orientation affect the stranger? Each manifestation that "the stranger" has taken should be able to fit these measures and thus to be typified along lines of membership criteria.

It is my intention to trace the major works on the stranger with an eye to establishing their position in relation to the two concerns of proximity and membership orientation. This is done for three reasons. First, if we are ever to emerge from the mire of inconsistency with a useful application of "the stranger", there must be established some fundamental indicators by which strangeness/familiarity may be determined and ideal types created. Second, the works reviewed all exemplify, to a certain extent, implicit attention to the two categories to be employed. It is the present task to use the two categories in order to reconstruct the tradition of "the stranger", by drawing together common threads on the one hand, and by pointing toward the need for a reformulation of the concept on the other. This mode of analysis offers a flexible approach to rearticulating what has come to be a fairly rigid and consequently limited set of ideas. Finally, and not coincidentally, these two parameters are closely aligned with the empirical and theoretical conditions affecting a sociology of the stranger: changing empirical conditions are fundamentally proxemic in nature; while changing theoretical views draw upon establishing membership orientation and the meaning it holds for both the stranger and the host. Together, they form a strong basis upon which to examine the history of the sociology of the stranger.

1.2. "The Stranger" as Stranger

American sociology has never been entirely comfortable with the concept of "the stranger". With its origins in the German idealist tradition, it was imported and given a home at Chicago with Park and Burgess, becoming one of the key tools in the emergence of the pragmatist tradition. In its adoption, "the stranger" has undergone a rather unpleasant assimilation into a different world without much heed paid to the traces (Derrida, 1974) of "home" that by all rights belong to, and are buried within, any stranger.

Whereas the key factors for the German theorists (Simmel, Schutz) who contributed to the sociology of the stranger dealt with the experience of being a stranger, the American approach has consistently reflected that of a disgruntled host. While Simmel and Schutz asked questions such as, How does an actor come to terms with being a stranger?, the pragmatists were concerned about issues such as, What kind of an impact will a stranger have on our community? How are strangers to be received and dealt with? How can we make them more "like us"? For the Germans, analysis dealt with *negotiation:* language, social distance, typification. For the Americans, analysis dealt with *recognition* of the stranger in the context of a disorganized urban ecology.[4] The stranger took on different forms according to his willingness and ability to assimilate, to pass, and thereby to preserve a social order whose homogeneity was being seriously threatened by the massive influx of foreigners.

The treatment received by "the stranger" curiously reflects the essence of the problem that both the Germans and the Americans were trying to deal with: the attribution of characteristics to the other on the basis of minimal information.[5] That is, "the stranger" has suffered the treatment of the one that it was created to explain. As an immigrant from another tradition, "the stranger" has been attributed with certain characteristics that have been convenient in the light of North American social problems. But much of the universal import, on the one hand, and the cultural specificity, on the other, of Simmel's stranger have been lost in the shuffle. "The stranger" has become like Schutz's "man without a history", whose past is open to reconstruction according to present uses of the host group:

> To [the stranger] the cultural pattern of the approached group does not have the authority of a tested system of recipes, and this, if for no other reason, because he does not partake in the vivid historical tradition by which it has been formed. To be sure, from the stranger's point of view, too, the culture of the approached group has its peculiar history, and this history is even accessible to him. But it has never become an integral part of his biography, as did the history of his home group.... Seen from the point of view of the approached group, he is a man without a history. (Schutz, 1944: 502)

Throughout "the stranger's" assimilation to American sociology there has been an uneasy tension. Authors call, on the one hand, for the preservation of the original meaning of Simmel's stranger, which is rather conveniently whittled down to the "potential wanderer". They wish to preserve the "authentic text", however the essence of that text varies with the problem of the day. On the other hand, while disagreeing among themselves about what Simmel had to offer, they criticize each other for trying to take the concept too far, in the creation of various derivative types of the stranger. Because of its origins elsewhere, the concept of "the stranger" is being called upon to do two heroic deeds: to both preserve Simmel and to go beyond him in the context of North American social problems. These are not only antithetical but completely unrealistic in light of the obsolescence of the problems which initially informed American sociology. This was one of the characteristics which Simmel attributed to the stranger: he is often called upon to do the kinds of tasks for which traditional means and resources are unsuited.

Much has happened to change the urban composition of North America since the Chicago for which the concept was originally introduced. At that time, such theorists as Park and Stonequist, followed later by Hughes and Wood, perceived the city as a challenge to traditional homogeneous groupings; an ever-growing collection of immigrants whose rapid accumulation was producing the striking transition of thousands and thousands of "marginal men". This was a social reality for which Simmel's stranger seemed to be a fitting analytic tool. Yet here lay the first difficulty. As I will show in Chapter Two, the world of Simmel's stranger is fundamentally different from that of Park and Stonequist's "marginal man" and its offshoots. Writing in Germany at the turn of the century, Simmel was concerned with the stranger as an oddity in a homogeneous culture.[6] Ethnically, Simmel's stranger tended to be Jewish; professionally, a merchant. His wanderer was worthy of sociological analysis because it problematized the normal, accepted ways. According to Riesman's (1961) typologies of modes of ensuring conformity, Simmel's was a world of tradition-direction.[7] The stranger was a "social problem" because the social type was an institutionalized and legitimate inner-directed actor in a tradition-directed world. It was institutionalized and legitimate because it is the merchant who traditionally acts as a catalyst between groups: trade brings attention to cultural difference and defines group boundaries. Erikson (1966) suggests the importance of boundary-maintenance for group cohesion:

Now people who live together in communities cannot relate to one another in any coherent way or even acquire a sense of their own stature as group members unless they learn something about the boundaries of the territory they occupy in social space, if only because they need to sense what lies beyond the margins of the group before they can appreciate the special quality of the experience which takes place within it. (p. 10)

Although the stranger who comes from outside to enter a homogeneous group will often serve to strengthen boundaries (Barth, 1970; Coser, 1956), the changes in social organization which have occurred in North American society seriously call into question the assumption that the stranger enters a tradition-directed world. This in turn jeopardizes the uncritical use of Simmel's stranger for modern urbanized society.

From this vantage point, it is most appropriate to regard Simmel's stranger as an "importation" which has been used according to purposes for which it was not created. As such, and as it has "melted" into American sociology, it is quite a futile exercise to engage in debates as to its faithfulness to its father. Instead, what I propose to do is threefold: first, to trace how "the stranger" was Americanized; second, to identify the source of current dilemmas over the future of the concept; and third, the project of the remainder of this work, to embark on a new articulation of "the stranger".

1.3. Simmel's Stranger

In a short segment of his *Soziologie* (1968 [fp 1908]), Simmel wrote about *"Der Fremde":* the stranger. His piece, which was first translated for the

American sociological audience by Park and Burgess (1924), introduced the compelling image of the "potential wanderer":

> The stranger will thus not be considered here in the usual sense of the term, as the wanderer who comes today and goes tomorrow, but rather as the man who comes today and stays tomorrow – the potential wanderer, so to speak, who, although he has gone no further, has not quite got over the freedom of coming and going. He is fixed within a certain spatial circle – or within a group whose boundaries are analogous to spatial boundaries – but his position within it is fundamentally affected by the fact that he does not belong in it initially and that he brings qualities into it that are not, and cannot be, indigenous to it. (Simmel, 1971b: 143)

The spatial and membership orientation dimensions are manifest in this typology of the "potential wanderer". The spatial dimension is evident in that the possibility of staying in one place is oriented to the eventuality of leaving it for another. A stranger comes here from away, and may or may not leave. This speaks quite vividly of the world in which Simmel wrote: community was fixed to place. Coming and going were equated with "entering" and "exiting"; to enter an unfamiliar community was to present oneself as a stranger. The tradition-directed attribution of membership, community, "home", to fixed social and geographical coordinates figures centrally in producing Simmel's stranger:

> If wandering, considered as a state of detachment from every given point in space, is the conceptual opposite of attachment to any point, then the sociological form of 'the stranger' presents the synthesis, as it were, of both of these properties. (p. 143)

The second aspect regards membership orientation. Simmel's stranger is not orienting to joining the group, nor does the group encourage him to join. There is a mutual acceptance, particularly of the merchant, as one who chooses to be transient. It is assumed, however, that the stranger does belong, initially at least, somewhere else; that there is a "home" or a point of origin which shapes his history; and that this home is configured in spatial terms.

The combination of proximity and membership orientation, then, is pivotal for Simmel's stranger:

> In the case of the stranger, the union of closeness and remoteness involved in every human relationship is patterned in a way that may be succinctly formulated as follows: the distance within this relation indicates that one who is close by is remote, but his strangeness indicates that one who is remote is near. (p. 143)

Proximity therefore takes both spatial and social forms. The spatial form puts the stranger close to those from whom he is socially distant, and far away from those to whom he feels most close. The social form puts the stranger close to those from whom he is spatially distant, and far from those to whom he is socially close. Simmel identifies *objectivity* as one of the key characteristics of the stranger, and a consequence of both spatial and social proximity.

This objectivity is occasioned not only by detachment and the condition of being an outsider, "but is a distinct structure composed of remoteness and nearness, indifference and involvement" (p. 145). The lens through which the stranger views the strange world is left undeveloped by Simmel, as well as by the later American sociologists. It will be of particular concern in Chapter Three, when the dynamics of nearness and remoteness in the context of observation will be examined.

Simmel's strength was to *make a place* for the stranger on the inside of his world; to show how, given the axes of attachment and detachment, membership may be negotiated on an understanding that one will remain detached.

The stranger is an element of the group itself . . . an element whose membership within the group involves being outside it and confronting it. (p. 144)

That the stranger is a member, albeit a marginal one, is made clear through his remarkable role as "confidant". Because he is not involved enough to affect the outcome of anything he is told, he does not pose a threat; yet he is a compelling listener by virtue of his perceived objective stance. Someone "who's been around" (as strangers are usually perceived to have been), after all, is able to achieve some distance from the immediate situation and see human matters in unclouded perspective. So, as Simmel relates, he may be called upon to adjudicate disputes or to respond to people's problems. For

he is the freer man, practically and theoretically; he examines conditions with less prejudice; he assesses them against standards that are more general and more objective; and his actions are not confined by custom, piety, or precedent. (p. 146)

This ability implies that Simmel's stranger is culturally competent: that he is a member in linguistic terms and is able to communicate in much the same way as Goffman's (1963b) "wise" do, while social variables exclude him from being regarded as one of the "own".

Simmel concludes with the general claim that individuality itself is universally estranging. He contends that it is what humans have in common that makes us familiar; and what we do not have in common that makes us strange. "A trace of strangeness in this sense easily enters even the most intimate relationships" (p. 147). He suggests, therefore, that strangeness is inherently human, anticipating the later work of Schutz.

Simmel's contribution was to place the stranger as a particular kind of member who exists in an autonomous relation to the group. The essential tension of "the stranger", and its theoretical import, lies precisely in the play between nearness and remoteness. What the American theorists left across the Atlantic was this possibility; and their failure to incorporate the paradox of the stranger has been crucial in the development of the concept.

2. Stranger as "Marginal Man"

2.1. Park: Migration and Emancipation

From the beginning, the Americans have treated the stranger as one who has come with the intention of staying, and membership has been the most crucial question. Robert E. Park (1928) was responsible for the introduction of the concept of the "marginal man" to American sociology. According to his "catastrophic theory of progress", Park maintained that cultural advance is the result of "migration and the incidental collisions, conflicts, and fusions of people and cultures which they have occasioned" (p. 882).

For Park, migration is a two-phase process through which "the breakdown of social order is initiated by the impact of an invading population, and completed by the contact and fusion of native with alien peoples" (p. 885). Cultural advance constitutes a type of merger between different groups, resulting in a personality type which he called the "cultural hybrid".

Park associated the empirical condition of high rates of migration with the urban disorganization which he observed, particularly in Chicago. For the Chicago theorists, urbanization resulted from migration and in turn produced a breakdown in traditional forms of social organization and a move toward greater rationalization in social life. Park observed that the social change which accompanies the migratory form of cultural advance produces "emancipated individuals". The emancipated individual he equated with the "cosmopolitan", which he in turn derived from Simmel's stranger. Using the example of the European Jew, Park formulated his initial statement on the marginal man:

There appeared a new type of personality, namely a cultural hybrid, a man living and sharing intimately in the cultural life and traditions of two distinct peoples; never quite willing to break, even if he were permitted to do so, with his past and his traditions, and not quite accepted, because of racial prejudice, in the new society in which he now sought to find a place. He was a man on the margin of two cultures and two societies, which never completely interpenetrated and fused. The emancipated Jew was, and is, historically and typically *the marginal man, the first cosmopolite and citizen of the world. He is, par excellence, the "stranger"*, whom Simmel, himself a Jew, has described with such profound insight and understanding in his *Sociologie* [*sic*]. Most if not all the characteristics of the Jew, certainly his pre-eminence as a trader and his keen intellectual interest, his sophistication, his idealism and lack of historical sense, are the characteristics of the city man, the man who ranges widely, lives preferably in a hotel — in short, the cosmopolite. (pp. 891-892 — emphasis added)

In the introduction to Stonequist's *The Marginal Man* (1937), Park elaborated on his earlier appropriation of Simmel:

The marginal man is a personality type that arises at a time and a place where, out of the conflict of races and cultures, new societies, new peoples and cultures are coming into existence. The fate which condemns him to live, at the same time, in two worlds is the same which compels him to assume, in relation to the worlds in which he lives, the role of a cosmopolitan and a stranger. Inevitably he becomes, relatively to his cultural milieu, the individual with the wider horizon, the keener intelligence, the more detached and rational viewpoint. The marginal man is always relatively the more civilized human being. (pp. xvii-xviii)

Park's concept of the marginal man had a significant impact on current sociology, with many authors (such as Antonovsky [1956], Dickie-Clark [1966], Goldberg [1941], Golovensky [1952], Green [1947], Hughes [1949], Kerckhoff and McCormick [1955], Mann [1948], Rose [1967], Siu [1952], and Stonequist [1937]) attempting to respond to and further develop the idea. It was important in its own right, for it seemed to reflect a widespread social type: the immigrant, the newly-arrived. In criticizing the form that his contribution took, therefore, it should be kept in mind that the simple notion of a "cultural hybrid" had, and still has, substantial merit in an increasingly migratory and cosmopolitan society.

The trouble comes with Park's attempt to use the marginal man *cum* cultural hybrid as the rubric under which to typify a number of versions of marginality: Simmel's stranger; the emancipated Jew; the racial hybrid (*i.e.* visibly marginal); the cosmopolite; the city man; the "man who ranges widely"; and "the individual with the wider horizon". This creates competing images of one who suffers yet is better off; is a wanderer yet has a home. By not locating the marginal man according to any continuum of familiarity/ strangeness, Park presents a confusing and contradictory profile. The use of the emancipated Jew as his *example* of a marginal man is particularly problematic because it results in the extension of generalizations about the Jew to the marginal man. For example, he sketches the Jew as:

a man living and sharing intimately in the cultural life and traditions of two distinct peoples; never quite willing to break, even if he were permitted to do so, with his past and his traditions, and not quite accepted, because of racial prejudice, in the new society in which he now sought to find a place. (p. 892)[8]

This raises more questions than solutions: Does "the man who ranges widely, lives preferably in a hotel" orient to membership in the same way as the emancipated Jew coming to "the new society in which he now sought a place"? Is "the city man" necessarily a "potential wanderer . . . who . . . has not quite got over the freedom of coming and going"? In short, does being a "cultural hybrid" necessarily imply being identifiably a stranger; internalizing the view of the stranger; desiring to establish membership in the new city; and being forever on the move?

Without the attendant issues of proximity and membership orientation, Park's version of the marginal man is meaningless and regressive. The consequence has been, however, to introduce a compelling image which is integral to much of the work which has followed. Yet the image is "marginal" sociologically because it was not initially grounded in the very concepts — familiarity/strangeness — which it was introduced to aid.

Clearly, in his enthusiasm to suggest the wide-ranging applications of the concept of the marginal man, Park was somewhat careless in maintaining a consistent image. Nevertheless, it seems desirable to tolerate these inconsistencies in the interest of retrieving the essence of the concept. For the present purposes, Park's marginal man will be delimited as the following: *A marginal man is one who has left one culture with the intention of becoming a member of a new culture.* Thus defined, the questions of racial origin and preferred living and travel arrangements may or may not be invoked in specific cases, but they are not central to the type, "the marginal man". What is central is a concern with the marginal man as one who has physically moved (spatial proximity) to a new culture (cultural distanciation) with the aim of achieving a place in the community (membership orientation).

In looking back to Simmel, it is clear that there are fundamental differences in formulation. For one, Simmel did not emphasize cultural distance as much as social and spatial distance. Group membership was predicated on shared social indicators and fixed spatial indicators. For Park's marginal man, however, the cultural distance between home and away becomes the most problematic factor in defining the stranger. Simmel's world was not a multiracial one to the extent that one's marginality is visibly ascribed. Park cites Mulattos and Eurasians as racial hybrids. In Simmel's world, the marginal man might be a Jew, but Jews are often able to pass and hence need not be discerned as outsiders on the basis of appearance.

Secondly, Simmel's stranger is not necessarily looking for a home. He is captured by the spatially- and socially-defined nature of tradition-directed membership; however, he does not share it. He shares allegiance to another set of criteria, which provides social distance between him and the host community. For Park, Simmel's invisible social distance is translated into concrete cultural distance which .the marginal man must continually seek to overcome in bidding for membership.

Simmel and Park, it appears, are speaking of two separate social types. In proxemic terms, Simmel's stranger is perfectly clear on the spatial and social dynamics which preclude or deny him membership, while Park's marginal man is faced with two proxemically distant cultures and the task of "groping" for membership. In membership orientation terms, Simmel's stranger is self-contained and not necessarily membership-oriented; while Park's marginal man looks to the new society to provide both a home and an identity, and is therefore membership-oriented.

2.2. Stonequist: Internationalism and Ambivalence

Everett Stonequist begins his book, *The Marginal Man* (1937), with the following definition:

The marginal man as conceived in this study is one who is poised in psychological uncertainty between two (or more) social worlds; reflecting in his soul the discords and harmonies, repulsions and attractions of these worlds, one of which is often 'dominant' over the other within which membership is implicitly if not explicitly based upon birth or ancestry (race or nationality); and where exclusion removes the individual from a system of group relations. (p. 8)

Stonequist claims that the marginal man is a universal type, found in all societies and races, characterized by

a contrast, tension or conflict of social groups divergent in race or possessing distinct cultures in which members of one group are seeking to adjust themselves to the group believed to possess greater prestige and power. The groups are in a relationship of inequality, whether or not this is openly asserted. The individuals of the subordinate or minority group whose social contacts have led them to become partially assimilated and psychologically identified with the dominant group without being fully accepted, are in the marginal situation. They are on the margin of each society, partly in and partly out. (p. 121)

Along the two axes of proxemics and membership orientation, Stonequist's marginal man is spatially proximate to the group in which he longs to be a member. The cultural dimension introduced by Park continues to prohibit membership for it belies foreign origins. The marginal man can not pass.

Stonequist is vague as to the specific nature of the interaction between the marginal person and the host culture. What produces the "tension"? How is it resolved? In orienting toward membership in a "group believed to possess greater prestige and power", to what extent is the *culture* – the language, habits, customs, belief systems – considered superior as well? Stonequist paints the picture of the immigrant who comes to America because money is supposed to grow on trees; of the black who aspires to the white world which he knows to be more just, equitable, and wealthy. How does this initial motivation toward altering a position of inequality account for a subsequent failure to completely assimilate? These questions are of great importance even today as we watch refugee groups such as the Vietnamese, the "Boat People", and Castro's 1981 castaways attempt to come to terms with their new environments. Initial reasons for emigrating to North America as opposed to another place would seem to fade in the face of more pressing concerns, such as employment, language of education, nostalgia for ways and people left behind, adapting to metropolitan life, *etc.* Similarly, activist groups representing women, the disabled, and ethnic minorities have made valiant efforts to "extend" the dominant group to include themselves. Yet one may argue that residual marginality lives on long after the battle appears to be over.

Clearly, when the marginal man is formulated as the newcomer to the dominant society, the processes which continue to prohibit assimilation, and hence motivate an ambivalence toward membership, should be addressed. Stonequist addresses the process of coming to regard oneself as a marginal man in much the same way as Goffman (1963b) later comes to account for the moral career of the stigmatized actor:[9]

The marginal person has at least three significant phases in his personal evolution: (1) a phase when he is not aware that the racial or nationality conflict embraces his own career; (2) a period when he consciously experiences this conflict; and (3) the more permanent adjustments, or lack of adjustments, which he makes or attempts to make to his situation. (Stonequist, pp. 121-122)

What the marginal man learns is to see himself from two viewpoints: that of his group of origin, and that of the group in which he aspires to be a member. When these two standpoints conflict, Stonequist notes that this conflict is likely to produce "a dual personality, a 'double consciousness' " (p. 145). This image of the double consciousness is couched in an early symbolic interactionist frame:

It is as if he were placed simultaneously between two looking-glasses, each presenting a sharply different image of himself. The clash in the images gives rise to a mental conflict as well as to a dual self-consciousness and identification. (pp. 145-146)

There are three notable consequences of such double consciousness: acute self-consciousness; a critical attitude toward the dominant group and its culture; and active imitation of and conformity to the patterns of the group which one aspires to join (pp. 148*ff*). Acute self-consciousness arises from being constantly aware of being in between both groups, and a member of neither:

He becomes a problem to himself and supersensitive about his racial connections. He may wish that he belonged to some other race; and may, by a kind of psychological introjection, despise himself as the dominant race despises him. (p. 148)

A critical attitude, which Simmel attributed to the stranger, is a consequence of the combination of inside knowledge and outside perspective. But, unlike Simmel, Stonequist does not regard this as an "objective" point of view:

There is too much emotional tension underneath to make such an attitude easy of achievement. But he is skillful in noting the contradictions and the 'hypocricies' in the dominant culture. (p. 155)

Finally, Stonequist observes that the marginal man is imitative and conformist. The most important goal is to fit in with the dominant culture, which "sometimes produces social conformity at the expense of inner harmony" (p. 156).[10]

In attempting to come to terms with the struggle of the marginal man, Stonequist asks what the "best" form of adjustment might be to the dual personality and status held. He shows a clear preference for what he calls an "intermediary role". He maintains that where it is possible to be accepted as a member, either through assimilation or passing,

the natural tendency toward assimilation automatically produces a certain degree of adjustment. Indeed, the danger often arises of too rapid assimilation. In the United States many immigrants, and particularly the children of immigrants, have been only too willing to discard their traditional values. Like innumerable well-meaning native exponents of Americanization, they have confused good citizenship with 100 per cent cultural conformity. *Perhaps the finest citizens of foreign origin are those who have been able to preserve the best in their ancestral heritage while reaching out for the best that America could offer.* They have been able to create a balance between continuity and change and so have maintained reasonably stable characters. (p. 206 – emphasis added)

Stonequist notes that the role of the intermediary is often taken by the marginal man, because he is in a position to speak the language of both groups. When clarifying the intermediary role, Stonequist is careful to distinguish Simmel's trader as the one whose intermediacy is limited to business relationships, whereas "the intermediary role of the marginal man involves a cultural relationship" (p. 178). So Stonequist clearly differentiates his marginal man from Simmel's stranger on cultural grounds. In turn, he improves on Park's initial confusion over the marginal man by creating two sub-types: the "international mind" and the *"déraciné* cosmopolitan". The international mind is the productive, creative use of the marginal situation. It is the ideal form of adaptation to

the modern world with its large-scale communication and movement [which] has brought many individuals into wider cultural participation. Trade and commerce, the travels of the student and sometimes of the tourist, are making more individuals multi-cultural. Each acquisition of a foreign language opens the door to a new way of life. The individual who penetrates deeply enough into a foreign culture becomes a richer personality. He readily shifts from one language to another; from one set of habits, attitudes and values to another. Thus he is in a position to look at problems from more than one viewpoint, and to see the essential ethnocentrism of each. This is undoubtedly what is involved in the creation of the 'international mind'. (pp. 178-179)

It may be that Stonequist was trying to shed some light on an otherwise unhappy existence: that the trials suffered by the marginal man were paving the way toward a new world where cultural fluency would be an advantage, a source of identity, rather than the disadvantageous state of being "lost" that his marginal man seems to suffer. In Chapter Two, Stonequist's vision will be pursued with an examination into how the "international mind" has in fact become the new, preferential mode of urban adaptation. It is the *"déraciné* cosmopolitan", however, that Stonequist sees as being the unfortunate version of the marginal man, who

has broken away from his traditional moorings and is culturally adrift. He lives on the surface of life, becomes blasé and easily bored, and restlessly moves about looking for new thrills. He is an unstable personality; whereas the internationalist, as defined above, has consciously grasped the distinctive meaning and values of each of the rounded cultures in which he moves. (p. 179)

The chief distinction between the two types may be seen in light of proximity and membership orientation. The internationalist has a clear sense of belonging — an identity rooted in a "home" — from which he is able to move in and out of other cultures, other worlds, with a critical and intermediary stance. The place of home, and the other worlds, is clearly *not* rooted in geographic and social distance as in Simmel's world, but has as its locus a cultural distance. The internationalist is culturally fluent, communicatively competent.

Along the membership orientation axis, membership is not a principal concern for the internationalist, for he is secure in another space called "home". The internationalist

is able to understand the values in other national cultures because he understands and is basically in harmony with those of his own. Self-understanding promotes the understanding of others. (p. 179)

The absence of membership aspirations helps the internationalist to avoid the status tensions and conflicts inherent in the self-reflective, self-conscious process of achieving membership in the dominant society. Like Simmel's stranger, non-membership orientation *within* a context of spatial proximity confers a special kind of membership (intermediary) that, paradoxically, is often unavailable to the one who "tries too hard" to be accepted. The internationalist as a type therefore conforms to Simmel's stranger on the membership orientation axis, while differing substantially on the basis of proximity.

The *déraciné* cosmopolitan, on the other hand, represents the aimless wanderer whose presence is predicated solely on the indicator of spatial proximity. Whereas Park was unwilling to distinguish between the man of the city and the marginal man, Stonequist is much more sensitive to the interrelationship between origin on the one hand, and destination on the other. Stonequist's marginal man is in between; the difference between the internationalist and the cosmopolitan has to do with his sense of orientation. The cosmopolitan has lost his home, and is not oriented to any new form of membership. He is "culturally adrift". This is a vivid image for it references a sense of being "'blown about", being disengaged, uninvolved, a loner. It is unfortunate that Stonequist did not further elaborate on the cosmopolitan, for the concept will become significant when addressing the question of "home" in Chapter Two. How does this anomalous category fit in to the axes for "placing" the marginal person? If he is only "there" in a physical sense, but completely absent in terms of cultural, social, and membership orientation indicators, then to what extent can these categories be regarded as useful for accounting for marginality?[11] Perhaps one of the reasons that Stonequist was unable to further develop "the cosmopolitan" had to do with the precarious nature of identification. It was comparatively easy to typify the internationalist, for he can at least be accounted for along traditional lines, despite the fact that he may exhibit untraditional adaptations (*i.e.* replacing spatial proximity with cultural fluency; and replacing membership orientation of the "newcomer" variety with non-membership orientation of the "sojourner" [Siu, 1952]). The cosmopolitan, however, can not be accounted for by either proxemics or membership orientation, and is thus an anomalous type. It seems, therefore, that Stonequist's most positive and enduring contribution is that of his internationalist, who is able to shift easily back and forth between groups. In the internationalist, Stonequist presents the first significant challenge to Simmel's stranger.

2.3. Hughes: Status Conflict and Inequality

Park and Stonequist are regarded as the most important authors of the marginal man, and many have followed with attempts to apply the concept to specific social situations. This exercise has not been as fruitful as it might have been had the initial concept been formed on the basis of membership criteria. There are three exceptions, however, which will be examined: Hughes' (1949) attempt to introduce social distance; Siu's (1952) treatise on "the sojourner"; and Rose's (1967) work on the problem of "duality".

In an article which both paid homage to Park's essay and went beyond it, Hughes (1949) suggested that marginality is generalizable to far more than the situation of the cultural hybrid. He noted that the term "marginal man" in American sociology had been solely applied to the "imported" cultural conflicts of the newly arrived, and pointed instead to the need to see the built-in inequalities of American society.

In Trollope's England, marginal social position was almost entirely a matter of class mobility. There was little of ethnic difference in it. In America, marginality is thought of as resulting solely from the mixtures of cultures, races and religions. There may be more of the problem of class mobility in it, however, than Americans have been accustomed to admit. (p. 64)

For Hughes, marginality is a condition brought upon when there is no clearcut answer to the question, "Who am I?", or more accurately, "Who are we?". In taking a conflict approach, he frames marginality in terms of collectivities and collective identities. Status conflict is produced on the level of differences and inequalities between social groupings. Marginality results over conflict in membership between various groups; identity is therefore predicated on membership.

This version of marginality is faithful to Stonequist in the sense that the actor's identity is marginal in relation to that of the dominant group. Hughes points out that the social distance produced by cultural difference may also exist *within* a society whose organization is based on social inequality:

American Negroes, product of migration and of the mixing of races and cultures that they are, are the kind of case to which the term marginal man has been conventionally applied. I have used the case of women to show that the phenomenon is not, in essence, one of racial and cultural mixing. It is one that may occur wherever there is sufficient social change going on to allow the emergence of people who are in a position of confusion of social identity, with its attendant conflicts of loyalty and frustration of personal and group aspirations. (p. 63)

For Hughes, as for others (Antonovsky, 1956; Kerckhoff and McCormick, 1955; Mann, 1948) for whom dominance is seen to produce marginality, the key problem for the marginal man is one of status conflict. Dickie-Clark (1966) notes that

marginal situations can be defined as those hierarchical situations in which there is any inconsistency in the rankings of any of the matters falling within the scope of the hierarchy. (p. 367)

Hughes recognizes, however, that status is closely linked with culture:

It is from the angle of status that I propose to analyze the phenomenon of marginality. Status is a term of society in that it refers specifically to a system of relations between people. But the definition of the status lies in the culture. In fact, one of the essential features of a person's status may be his identification with a culture. (p. 59)

In taking the conflict perspective toward marginality, Hughes introduces a hitherto unexplored vista to the sociology of the stranger. Unlike the social psychologists, he is concerned with neither the viewpoint of the stranger nor that of the host, but rather takes a critical perspective toward little-recognized cases of marginality. By generalizing status conflict to cultural conflict, on the one hand; and by claiming the pervasiveness of status conflict in American society on the other, Hughes provides a basis for the claim that marginality is in fact very widespread among so-called "members". Clearly, then, social proximity is the dominant membership criterion in Hughes' view; and the desire for membership, while pervasive, should not cause the actor to compromise his own identity. That is, marginal men should fight to achieve membership *qua* the social beings that they are — to expand the boundaries of membership to include them rather than to attempt to assimilate into the dominant group.

2.4. Siu: Ethnocentrism and Sojourney

Siu (1952) distinguishes between three types of strangers: the marginal man, the sojourner, and the settler. For Siu, all three are products of the "cultural frontier" ("where two or more cultures are in conflict" [p. 34]). In his article, "The Sojourner", Simmel's concept of the stranger "is applied only in the general context of race and cultural contacts; it has no reference to, for example, a New Yorker who moves to San Francisco" (p. 35).

Whereas the marginal man is characterized by a "bicultural complex", "the essential characteristic of the sojourner is that he clings to the culture of his own ethnic group" (p. 34).

No doubt, in many instances, the sojourner has something in common with the marginal man. It is convenient, therefore, to define the "sojourner" as a stranger who spends many years of his lifetime in a foreign country without being assimilated by it. The sojourner is par excellence an ethnocentrist. This is the case of a large number of immigrants in America and also of Americans who live abroad. (p. 34)

The worlds inhabited by the marginal man and the sojourner prior to their migration to the new society were not characterized by the empirical conditions (urbanization, mobility, and sophisticated global communications) which produce "cosmopolitanism" in modern western society. Immigrants were unlikely to know what they were "in for" when migrating to the United States, and reasons may have been, as Siu claims, largely mercenary, with the overriding interest one of returning "home" once one's job had been done. Siu regards sojourning as a job — a job being a means to another end — making the sojourn less of a choice of a home so much as an inconvenience on the path of one's choice.

The sojourner neither aspires to membership through assimilation, nor is offered it; instead, he is ghettoized with other fellow expatriates, and ethnic communities result. Siu claims that these represent "an effort to create a home away from home" (p. 37). The process of ghettoization follows a general pattern of "accommodation, isolation, and unassimilation" (p. 41). Siu points out that the sojourner is only possible as "a social type of the urban community" (p. 43). It is only in urban centres where the apparently antithetical conditions of being an inside outsider and preserving one's culture of origin through ghettoization can really coexist.

Siu's use of the term "sojourner" responds implicitly to the ambiguities contained in existing treatises on the marginal man concerning membership orientation. Siu was attempting to account for those who, like Simmel's stranger, were not planning to stay, but were not necessarily in a hurry to leave. There is little incentive to become a member when the stranger does not foresee a long-time commitment to the community. So in membership orientation terms, the sojourner differs from the marginal man by not wanting to join in the sense of making the new place his permanent home. In proxemic terms, home is far away and irreplaceable, although the sojourner stays among members of the new group and is confronted daily by reminders of home within the group, and by a situation of cultural difference outside of the group. Along the two axes, Siu has not succeeded in generating a concept significantly different from Simmel's stranger. What he has done, however, is to demonstrate one social type for which the original term still seems applicable. Others, such as gypsies, drifters, migrant workers, travellers, runaways — in general, those who define themselves as temporarily or permanently homeless, might be accounted for under this rubric.[12]

2.5. Rose: Small-town Duality

In another attempt to reformulate the concept of the marginal man, Rose (1967) studied a number of Jews who had moved from an urban setting where they "belonged" to a rural setting where they constituted a minority. Here, Rose introduces the term "duality" as a more positive replacement for "marginality". Finding that rural Jews are accepted into the community as well as being oriented to keeping their own culture, Rose states:

Complete assimilation into the Christian community is not the goal of the American Jew. This means giving up a part of himself, a part that sometimes even he cannot explain. (p. 471) He is more a part of his community than he is apart from it. He is far more assimilated to the Gentile milieu than his urban cousin [the urban Jew]. But, as indicated below, he remains a Jew. (p. 472)

Whereas marginality expresses an unwillingness to be between two worlds — a sense of process, of victimization — duality reflects a positive choice to forge a third way in recognition of the impossibility of either complete assimilation on the one hand, or complete preservation of the old ways on the other. Whereas marginality brings with it a sense that there is resistance — either by the stranger or the host — duality suggests co-operation and mutual acceptance.

It is curious that such a liberal accommodation of difference would be expressed in a rural community, traditionally noted for being more ethnocentrically-oriented than urban areas.[13] This begs the question of what kinds of pressures are created in urban settings which might mitigate against the acceptance of different groups. Rose gives one possible reason for this paradox. He suggests that at least partial assimilation becomes a technique of survival for the stranger who is in a minority:

Once the minority member enters the new 'alien' situation, he finds himself in the position of representing his 'people' to the community at large. As a stranger his ethnic identity becomes particularly salient to the community and to himself. More often than not, consciousness of minority membership increases when one becomes an isolate . . . The minority member who lives in the milieu of the majority has infinitely greater opportunity to adapt himself to the folkways of the dominant group than does one who lives in the middle of the ethnic community. (p. 473)

Unlike the situation of the stranger in the city, the small town of Rose's study replicates in many ways the conditions which created strangeness in Simmel's essay. Because the present interest is with the consequences of urbanization upon the stranger, Rose's concept of duality is only useful in a negative way. It suggests conditions which no longer prevail. Duality is only a possibility when a homogeneous group with a longstanding identity and tradition is confronted by strangeness and that strangeness needs to be negotiated. This is no longer characteristic of large-scale urban community life in North America; consequently, duality is of little use in helping us to come to terms with the modern stranger.

2.6. Limits of the Marginal Man

Although the applications and attempted reformulations of the concept of marginal man seem plentiful, the initial definition as gleaned from Park has yet to be seriously challenged. In asserting that a marginal man is one who has left one culture with the intention of becoming a member of a new culture, I have sketched the marginal man as one who is spatially proximate, culturally distant, and membership oriented.

Underlying the possibility of being marginal to one culture, however, is a residual allegiance to a previous culture. It is the conflict entailed in attempting to deal with a past member of another culture through the traditional viewpoint of the approached culture which makes marginality problematic for the host. That these accounts, written from the perspective of the host, call for an allegiance-free internationalism with a decided interest in assimilation is telling. In the tradition of American sociology, the work on marginal man has largely been directed at problem-solving from the point of view of the dominant society, with complete assimilation – and the eradication, therefore, of the marginal personality – as the goal.

It is also telling that the work reviewed has barely dealt with the actor's motivations. Except for Stonequist's brief encounter with the double consciousness of the marginal man, there has been no interest in why the stranger leaves his home in the first place, nor in how he initially encounters the host culture.[14] This constitutes another thread to be picked up in the literature on the stranger: that of the "newcomer". The chief proponents are Wood and Schutz.

3. Stranger as Newcomer

3.1. Wood: First Encounters

In *The Stranger: A Study in Social Relationships* (1934), Margaret Mary
Wood directed attention to the stranger as newcomer. Although there are
several important moments in Wood's piece, it did not achieve the profound
reputation held by the works of Simmel, Park, Stonequist, and Schutz.
Instead, it has been largely ignored by latter-day sociologists of the stranger.

One reason for this may be that Wood was attempting to universalize the
problem of the stranger, whereas most other theorists have come to the
question of the stranger as a result of contextually specific problems. Wood,
having travelled extensively, sought to account unequivocally for the occasion
of the "first encounter" between the stranger and the new community. To
this end, she devoted much of the book to anthropological accounts of how
primitive societies deal with strangers. Unfortunately, there is no apparent
theoretical link between this interest and her subsequent remarks on western
civilization, particularly the life of the city-dweller, which is of concern to
the present investigation.

Wood defined the stranger as

one who has come into face-to-face contact with the group for the first time. This
concept is broader than that of Simmel . . . For us the stranger may be, as with Simmel,
a potential wanderer, but he may also be a wanderer who comes today and goes tomorrow, or he may come today and remain with us permanently. The condition of being
a stranger is not, for the present study, dependent upon the future duration of the contact, but it is determined by the fact that it is the first face-to-face meeting of individuals
who have not known one another before. (p. 44)

Wood's perspective – typical of American work on the stranger – is to
address the stranger from the standpoint of the group. In defining how the
group responds to the stranger, Wood isolated two factors of importance:
the stranger's purpose, and the probable duration of his stay. These, she
suggested, determine the manner in which the stranger is received. This
enabled her to distinguish between tourists (superficial purpose/temporary
stay leads to tolerance by host) and immigrants (serious purpose/permanent
stay leads to their being left to their own resources) according to their interaction with the host community.[15]

When the stranger's intentions appear to involve the community through
establishing some kind of bond, Wood noted that the first connection to be
made in all societies is "identifying his kinship or friendship with someone
in the community" (p. 208). This generalization is echoed by Pitt-Rivers
(1968): "In contrast to a member of the community whose status is identifiable by reference to its norms and is recognised by everyone, the stranger

is incorporated only through a personal bond with an established member . . ."
(p. 15). Meyer Fortes (1975), in his study of strangeness among the Tallensi,
notes that

Before the "coming of the white man" – say at the turn of the century – as old men
relate, a solitary stranger of another tribe would not have been able to go about freely
in any Tallensi settlement. He would have been seized and enslaved. To be safe, a person
from outside must have either a kinsman or affine or at least a friend to vouch for him,
initially at any rate, in the community he entered. (p. 231)

These observations suggest that the newcomer must paradoxically be recogn-
izable in order that he be given a status – even the status of outsider – in
the group. An apparently commonplace observation, Wood's is the only
case in the early stranger literature in which the possibility of a "language
of membership" was introduced. Apart from Fortes' parallel comments
noted above, however, Wood's pioneering references to a primitive, first-
order language of membership have gone unheeded and undeveloped by
subsequent theorists.[16] Yet her forays into the world of groping for membership, of attempting to establish common ground, are crucial for a well-
balanced sociology of the stranger. Of particular interest is her work on the
city-dweller. In a timeless description of the city, Wood anticipated Lofland
(1973) by forty years:

The city is at once more personal and more impersonal in its relationships than the
country, more lenient and more critical in its judgments of others, more tolerant and
more intolerant in its attitudes toward outsiders. It is not in any one distinctive form of
relationship, therefore, that the source of the unity of city life must be sought, but,
rather, in *the manner in which manifold highly differentiated relationships have become
adjusted to one another.* (Wood, p. 221 – emphasis added)

These relationships are adjusted, Wood implied, according to an underlying
tenor of membership orientation, which takes the form of a desire for recognition:

The individualism of the city dweller . . . is the product of a selective social environment;
it is born of contacts with men rather than with inanimate objects, and it depends for
its fruition upon the recognition of others. . . . The frequency and the variety of the
contacts to which men are subjected in an urban environment make it necessary for
them to respond readily and yet with discrimination. Each different situation requires
a specialized response, and, since much of the success of the city-dweller is dependent
upon his ability to 'get on' with others, he must acquire facility in working with others
and in meeting new people and new situations. In answer to this need various types
of impersonal, secondary relationships have evolved. Such relationships, Simmel has
noted, are based more largely on intellect and less on feelings and emotions than are
country relationships. (pp. 222-223)

More recently, Franck (1980) has noted that the social space of city-
dwellers is clearly divided between public and private worlds: "The world

'in here' is each individual's private world of friends, relatives, acquaintances, and co-workers. The world 'out there' is the public world of strangers, that is, of people who do not know each other personally" (p. 53). She maintains, moreover, that "the distinction between contacts with strangers and contacts with friends is essential for a full understanding of the nature of urban social experience" (p. 53).

Wright (1971) distinguishes between the "urban" man and the "folk" man on the basis of the prevalence of strange and familiar social relationships, respectively. The urban man is one who is educated for strangeness; who learns to see himself and others in terms of categories; who may "spend a great deal of time, even days or months, dealing with no one he knows personally or intimately, all the while receiving the necessary goods and services for survival and comfort" (p. 317).

Wright notes that the urban man exists in two separate realities which conform to the public/private distinction. He is both

the person he is in the enacted category and the whole person he is apart from that. So he is capable of experiencing himself in a double sense, as an *object* which can be manipulated in certain social situations, and as an integrated personality aside from those situations . . . (p. 318)

And, as Wirth (1938) contends,

Being reduced to a stage of virtual impotence as an individual, the urbanite is bound to exert himself by joining with others of similar interest into organized groups to obtain his ends. (p. 22)

For Wood as well, the city-dweller is not content merely with secondary relationships, and therefore engages in an active search for primary relationships, mainly through interest groups.

The stranger who is actively interested in forming new relations presents whatever credentials he possesses which will give him an entrée into one or more of such groups. It may be a union card, or a certificate of membership in a fraternal lodge, in a church, or in some such organization as the Young Men's or Young Women's Christian Association. Or again it may be a letter of introduction to someone or group who may be of assistance to him in making the desired contacts. (p. 233)

Anything that proves membership as "one of us" will serve as an *entrée*. For Wood, the credentials for membership took the form of signs as opposed to symbols. The sign stands in a direct, reflexive relationship to its referent. It is "self-evident" in the sense that it clearly conveys its meaning in a public way. A union card is a sign in that it clearly states membership in a union. A symbol, on the other hand, is not self-evidently related to its referent and thus requires "inside knowledge" in order to establish its meaning reflectively (Harman, 1986).[17]

The city described by Wood is one in which being alone is intolerable;

membership in intimate, primary groups is sought; and available means are public and institutionalized. This is the city in transition; the context of rapid growth which had not yet evolved its own norms of secularized, rationalized social organization. With the combined migration from rural areas and massive influx of foreigners which characterized urbanized North America in the first half of this century, it is understandable that strangeness would be viewed as equal to loneliness and a negative condition to be overcome, with more traditional rules for social organization surfacing and regaining importance in a transitional context. It will become clear, however, that as traditional modes of social organization are replaced, and as the secondary encounters in everyday urban life radically outnumber the primary encounters, Wood's piece is clearly dated. Belongingness takes on new meaning for the modern stranger. Wood's stranger as the lost one will be replaced by the expert navigator; the assumption that urban life is basically undesirable will have to be rethought in terms of more recent historical developments. Even Louis Wirth, Wood's contemporary, saw the inevitability of adaptation to "urbanism as a way of life". For recent authors such as Franck (1980), Lofland (1973), and Wright (1971), who write of strangeness as *the* mode of social interaction in the city, the sense of desperation with which Wood wrote has been replaced by an acceptance that members adapt to urban spaces and are still capable of living fulfilling lives.

Despite her interest in universalizing the experience of the stranger, and her many references to anthropological case studies, Wood studiously ignored the questions of culture, language, and negotiation of membership which were touched on by Stonequist and later picked up by Schutz. Nevertheless, her contribution was to draw attention to what she saw as a desire for membership, and to the creation of an urban social structure which orchestrated membership.

The stranger formulated as a newcomer, whether for a brief or a lengthy time, is concerned with joining. As compared to the marginal man, who is unlikely to overcome his strangeness and is seen by Park and Stonequist as a fixed personality type, the newcomer becomes involved in actively joining in order to overcome the temporary state of a "newcomer" for the permanency of a member. For Wood, the means for such joining were straightforward and available to all. This had to do with the spatial proxemics of the city of 1934, and the undeveloped nature of attention to social and cultural proxemics in her work. Membership credentials were self-evident; there were *places* (fraternity lodge, church, YM/YWCA) where one went to be a member and there were *concrete signs* (union cards, certificates of membership, letters of introduction) expressive of membership.

There was little to be negotiated in Wood's world of strangers. After the basic criteria of spatial proximity ("being there") and membership orientation ("having something in common") were established, one ceased to be a stranger. The city was a large version of the small town, in which fundamentally similar rules of social organization came into play. This account has little relevance today. Major changes in social organization show that the applicability of the small-town model has remained limited to the small town. Modern cities demand a re-education into the language of membership, which Schutz began to suggest. When he wrote of the newcomer from the perspective of the newcomer, the question of negotiation could no longer be ignored.

3.2. Schutz: Reflexive Crisis

For Schutz (1944),

> The term "stranger" shall mean an adult individual of our times and civilization who tries to be permanently accepted or at least tolerated by the group which he approaches. The outstanding example for the social situation under scrutiny is that of the immigrant. ... The applicant for membership in a closed club, the prospective bridegroom who wants to be admitted to the girl's family, the farmer's son who enters college, the city-dweller who settles in a rural environment, the "selectee" who joins the Army, the family of the war worker who moves into a boom town – all are strangers according to the definition just given, although in these cases the typical "crisis" that the immigrant undergoes may assume milder forms or even be entirely absent. (p. 499)

Schutz deliberately excluded three categories of people: individuals who were not orienting to membership (guests, visitors, tourists); children; and members of "different levels of civilization" (p. 494). The exclusion of transients underlined from the beginning the importance of membership orientation for Schutz, and his exclusion of those who are by inference not "culturally competent" introduced the element of cultural proxemics into the question of establishing membership. Although for Schutz spatial proximity remained a key factor in establishing membership (one joins a "place" as much as a group), his account of the plight of the newcomer was enriched by the assumption that membership is not automatically offered and achieved, but is a precarious relationship which must be worked at.

It is to Schutz's credit that he began by outlining "how the cultural pattern of group life presents itself to the common sense of a man who lives his everyday life within the group among his fellow-men" (p. 499). In order to come to terms with the crisis faced by the stranger, the taken-for-granted cultural world and the ease with which interaction is facilitated among members must first be addressed. Although Wood alluded to the group as the context for familiarity, Schutz was able to communicate this crucial concern much more parsimoniously.

> We use the term "cultural pattern of group life" for designating all the peculiar variations, institutions, and systems of orientation and guidance (such as the folkways, mores,

laws, habits, customs, etiquette, fashions) which, in the common opinion of sociologists of our time, characterize – if not constitute – any social group at a given moment in its history. (pp. 499-500)

For Schutz, however, this "pattern" was "not homogeneous; it is (1) incoherent, (2) only partially clear, and (3) not at all free from contradictions" (p. 500). This is because any "pattern" becomes chaotic and random at the level of individual interests, motivations, and relevances. It is only called upon to perform certain tasks, and as such it

takes on for the members of the in-group the appearance of a *sufficient* coherence, clarity, and consistency to give anybody a reasonable chance of understanding and of being understood. . . . It is a knowledge of trustworthy *recipes* for interpreting the social world. . . . Thus it is the function of the cultural pattern to eliminate troublesome inquiries by offering ready-made directions for use, to replace truth hard to attain by comfortable truisms and to substitute the self-explanatory for the questionable. (p. 501)

Schutz regarded group life as being founded on an assumption of basic communicative competence: a set of "of-course" assumptions. Very little is left up to the imagination in the taken-for-granted world. It is only when the free-flowing taken-for-granted world of communicative competence breaks down, that the "of-course" expectations become apparent.[18] Upon encountering a new group the stranger, in not being familiar with that world, both produces a crisis for the group, and is faced with a crisis of negotiation of the language of membership: he is forced to try to discover, through trial and error, how to become inconspicuous and restore the taken-for-granted. Only then will he be on the road to membership.

The stranger, by reason of his personal crisis, does not share the above-mentioned basic assumptions. He becomes essentially the man who has to place in question nearly everything that seems to be unquestionable to the members of the approached group. . . . The stranger, therefore, approaches the other group as a newcomer in the true meaning of the term. At best he may be willing and able to share the present and the future with the approached group in vivid and immediate experience; under all circumstances, however, he remains excluded from such experiences of its past. Seen from the point of view of the approached group, he is a man without a history. (p. 502)

The road to membership entails three transformations for the stranger. The first is to the "would-be member". The stranger moves from one looking from the outside in, to a co-actor in a social situation. The second transformation involves a change from cultural remoteness to the cultural proximity of the new cultural pattern. It can no longer be regarded, in abstract form, from afar, but is encountered as present-to-hand. The third transformation occurs when the stranger realizes that previous assumptions and understandings of the cultural pattern are no longer applicable in his quest for membership. Previous assumptions had been predicated on spatial and cultural distance. The immediacy of "being there" brings the realization that "his ideas of the foreign group, its cultural pattern, and its way of life, do not stand the test of vivid experience and social interaction" (p. 503). Approaching a new group therefore produces a crisis in which

the discovery that things in his new surroundings look quite different from what he expected them to be at home is frequently the first shock to the stranger's confidence in the validity of his habitual "thinking as usual". (p. 503)

At the same time as he realizes that his scheme of interpretations is useless for the new environment, the stranger is also confronted with the fact of being an outsider to the system that *does* work. The stranger lacks status as a member, and "is therefore unable to get a starting-point to take his bearings" (p. 504).[19]

For the first time, the notion of status becomes problematic in the quest for membership. Whereas Stonequist and Hughes regarded the unequal status of the marginal man as an incentive for joining the group, Schutz located status inequality as a *consequence* of the quest for membership. Once one has been forced to abandon one's old ways, one is at the mercy of the dominant group.

Schutz made significant strides in the direction of articulating a language of membership. Whereas Wood began by delimiting the exclusionary role of language, Schutz was interested in the process of negotiating membership through language. "The approaching stranger has to 'translate' its terms into terms of the cultural pattern of his home group, provided that, within the latter, interpretive equivalents exist at all" (P. 504).

Schutz suggested four propositions about the role of language for the stranger: (1) spoken and written language is surrounded by "fringes" which give added emotional and irrational meaning; (2) linguistic terms have many connotations, both formal and informal; (3) every social group evolves its own "private code"; and (4) the whole history of a group is embodied in its language (p. 505). For present purposes, these principles will be named, respectively: (1) the principle of cultural contextualization; (2) the principle of cultural polysemy; (3) the principle of colloquiality; and (4) the principle of historical embodiment.[20]

Schutz recognized through these principles that the stranger may "speak the language" without being able to pass as a member. For Gumperz (1972a), this entails a distinction between linguistic competence and communicative competence.

Whereas linguistic competence covers the speaker's ability to produce grammatically correct sentences, communicative competence describes his ability to select, from the totality of grammatically correct expressions available to him, forms which appropriately reflect the social norms governing behavior in specific encounters. (p. 205)

One may have a "working knowledge" of a language and still remain an outsider. It is only after mastering a language in all four of its lived manifestations that one can become a "native speaker":

In order to command a language freely as a scheme of expression, one must have written love letters in it, one has to know how to pray and curse in it and how to say things with every shade appropriate to the addressee and to the situation. (Schutz, 1944: p. 505)

Every indigenous member of a group is educated into the subtleties of its language through socialization. Socialization, particularly of children, is successful because it is ideally predicated on a *complete acceptance* of the child as a potential other – as a potential member who is "just a child" and therefore "doesn't know better". Unlike children, however, adult newcomers are expected to have an initial communicative competence in membership, which will allow them to function well once the initial "translation period" has been worked out. It is for this reason that Schutz insisted that the category "stranger" was only relevant for "an adult individual of our times and civilization".[21]

There is a translatability about cultural competence which hosts expect of strangers. This expected translatability borders on ethnocentrism. Schutz alluded to this in his comments about the perceived "doubtful loyalty" of the newcomer:

Very frequently the reproach of doubtful loyalty originates in the astonishment of the members of the in-group that the stranger does not accept the total of its cultural pattern as the natural and appropriate way of life and as the best of all possible solutions of any problem. The stranger is called ungrateful, since he refuses to acknowledge that the cultural pattern offered to him grants him shelter and protection. (p. 507)

Strangers are tolerated if it is clear that their mistakes stem from an attempt to change their status from outsider to insider. Toleration is predicated on an initial predisposition of the host toward the stranger as a potential member. It is also, therefore, contingent upon the desire of the stranger for membership.

Where Schutz stopped, however, and where this inquiry must begin, is with the notion that membership competence *can be achieved*. He stated that the categories of strangeness and familiarity are general and essential in the ongoing interpretation of the world. The process of familiarizing ourselves with the strange is our way of increasing our "stock of experiences", and as such it is an ongoing relation to the world. It is based on an assumption that familiarity is possible: that increase in knowledge is possible. Schutz ended his article by drawing a similar conclusion about strangeness/familiarity in social relationships:

What is commonly called the process of social adjustment which the newcomer has to undergo is but a special case of this general principle. The adaptation of the newcomer to the in-group which at first seemed to be strange and unfamiliar to him is a continuous process of inquiry into the cultural pattern of the approached group. If this process of inquiry succeeds, then this pattern and its elements will become to the newcomer a matter of course, an unquestionable way of life, a shelter, and a protection. *But then the stranger is no stranger any more, and his specific problems have been solved.* (p. 507 — emphasis added)

Schutz seemed to lose a bit of the ground gained in his paper with this conclusion. It now appears that, although strangeness and familiarity are fundamental to increasing one's stock of experiences (*i.e.* living), the actor who corresponds to the social type "the stranger", because of having to be oriented toward membership in the approached group, ceases to be a stranger once this membership has been achieved. And it may be achieved. Strangeness is a condition one tries to alter; the stranger is always in a temporarily strange relation to the soon-to-be familiar.

In demonstrating how the coming of the stranger produces a reflexive crisis both for self and other, stranger and host, Schutz has broken new ground. His phenomenology of strangeness awakens the sleeping issues of cultural proxemics and language of membership and gives the concept of "the stranger" the widest relevance and applicability it has yet to attain. Schutz's sensitivity was rooted in his own condition of being a stranger in the United States. Unlike the early American theorists, Schutz took the perspective of the stranger rather than the host. Whereas the Americans viewed newcomers with an attitude which took for granted their desire to assimilate, and consequently viewed marginality as a condition of choice *vis-à-vis* the ideal of assimilation, Schutz recognized, albeit at a preliminary level, the built-in resistance which any system of membership has to fully accepting "outsiders" as "insiders".

The use of a phenomenological approach contributed to the significance of Schutz's piece in that it posited the approach, arrival, crisis, and resolution of crisis as processes involving different sets of perceptions, motivations, and relevances for stranger and host.. It is in the interaction between these different levels of awareness that the problem of the stranger lies. This was weakened in the end, however, in that the problem of one's identity as a stranger was rooted for Schutz ultimately in the perception of the actor. Forgetting the host, he concluded by equating the stranger's perception of the new group as being "matter of course", ending with the dissolution of his identity as a stranger.

This reliance, in the final analysis, on the perceptions of the actor, leads to another significant aspect of Schutz's contribution, which has been ignored in the literature reviews of the stranger: that the stranger is a universal type of actor in modern urban society. Simmel's initial formulation was limited by a culturally-specific definition, and those who focused on the stranger as marginal man wrote from other temporally/culturally-specific perspectives.

Both views were limited because they failed to see the possibility that *one can experience strangeness without there being a clearly-defined host.* Indeed, as mentioned at the outset, one of the central themes in all the literature dealing with the stranger is that the group to which one is strange can be defined, and by implication it is that group which actively defines the stranger.

Schutz, by going to language, to conditions of membership, as opposed to the host group as self-articulated, provided the groundwork for how strangeness can be experienced in a vacuum. It is only by a phenomenology which points to the underlying confluence of perspectives of host and stranger that those perspectives may be surpassed to arrive at what informs them. Clearly, for Schutz at least, it is language which does the work, in a disembodied form, of allowing the stranger to define himself as strange and, ultimately, as familiar. Language articulates difference and similarity in the silence of the stranger's gaze. Language provides a constant barometer for how close one is to achieving membership. The introduction of Schutz's four propositions regarding the role of language for the stranger lay the groundwork for subsequent research on communicative competence in speech communities, by scholars of sociolinguistics. This in turn will provide important theoretical building blocks for a sociology of the modern stranger (Fishman, 1972b).[22]

The importance of typification to the language of membership, although not explicit in recent definitions of the stranger, has been picked up by subsequent theorists of the city. For Lofland, city-dwellers order their relations with strangers on the basis of appearential and spatial dimensions:

Appearential ordering allows you to know a great deal about the stranger you are looking at because you can 'place' him with some degree of accuracy on the basis of his body presentation: clothing, hair style, special markings, and so on. In contrast, spatial ordering allows you to know a great deal about the stranger you are looking at because you know a great deal about 'who' is to be found in the particular location in which you find him. In either instance, you know how to act toward this stranger (acting toward, of course, may involve either interaction or avoidance) because having defined the object, your common sense world provides you with a behavioral repertoire. (p. 27)

Wright (1971) calls this tendency the "urban ground rule":

Accordingly, urban people are quite sensitive to any behavioral cues which allow them to locate an individual categorically, whether that cue is overt behavior or some expressive symbol, such as clothes, property, or even bumper stickers. Indeed, it is virtually impossible to say or do anything in an urban setting without some categorical meaning being attached to it. And since categories tend to be equated with people, perhaps it is in this way that urban men come to consider what they do as being who they are. (pp. 320-321)

Wright's "urban ground rule" and Lofland's forms of ordering are both predicated on a certain kind of membership which is achieved through urbanism as a way of life. They are modes of communicative competence only open to the member who has passed through Schutz's stages of trans-formation. "Would-be membership" entails groping for the clues to the language of membership from the outside. Membership as achieved in the Schutz-Wright-Lofland sense entails communicative competence in a world of strangers.

What these analyses have failed to do is to claim the urban ground rule as the defining characteristic of the modern stranger; and in turn to see the modern stranger as the one who has best adapted to a world in which the clues hold much more information than any explicit signs.

4. Toward the Modern Stranger

One of the weaknesses in past attempts to come to terms with the stranger is a lack of emphasis on the notion of the familiar; a neglect of the conditions of membership and their reflection on strangeness. Strangeness embodies two senses of the familiar: the first is that with which the stranger is familiar occurs because the current social context in which the stranger finds himself is one from which the familiar is *absent* — so the other to which he orients becomes strange.

A second sense in which the familiar may be addressed is that to which the other (host) is familiar. Other exists wtihin a context of familiarity: the community of co-members. The stranger, by his very presence, throws into question the extent of familiarity. By not being a member, by not being familiar, he is strange. Exclusion from one category implies inclusion in the other.

In a recent reassessment of the sociology of the stranger, Donald N. Levine (1979) calls for a new approach. In light of the literature, his aim is to generate a typology organized around the stranger's interest in the host community on the one hand, and the host's response to the stranger on the other.

The complications introduced by suggesting that there may be a difference between the strangeness attributed to an individual by himself and by another are intentional and necessary. Membership entails a purely subjective assess-ment of the familiarity of the situation. This is generated through the welcome expressed to one by other, on the one hand; and the degree to which one feels at home, on the other. This dynamic will be further examined in Chapter Four.

Levine's analysis and critique of the sociology of the stranger take

Simmel's initial formulation as a static model which can not be adapted without significant theoretical loss. He intends, however, to expand on it in response to Wood's definition of the newcomer. Levine formulates six types of the stranger (guest, sojourner, newcomer, intruder, inner enemy, marginal man), each type resulting from a particular combination of the stranger's interest in the host community (visit, residence, or membership) on the one hand, and the host's response to the stranger (compulsive friendliness, compulsive antagonism) on the other. Although Levine appears to wrap up most of his complaints against the history of the sociology of the stranger, there are notable questions remaining. These have to do with empirical changes in social life, and changes in the ways in which sociologists observe and theorize about social life.

Figure 1. Levine's Typology of Stranger Relationships*

Host's Response to Stranger	Stranger's Interest in Host Community		
	Visit	Residence	Membership
Compulsive Friendliness	Guest	Sojourner	Newcomer
Compulsive Antagonism	Intruder	Inner Enemy	Marginal Man

*From Donald N. Levine, "Simmel at a Distance: On the History and Systematics of the Sociology of the Stranger", pp. 21-36 in William Shack and Elliott Skinner (eds.), *Strangers in African Societies.* Berkeley: University of California Press, 1979.

Empirical Changes. How does the typology system of Levine update the applicability of the concept of "the stranger" in light of recent developments in urbanization, mobility, communications, and accompanying social organization? The most pressing question here regards the definition of the host. "Who" is the host? How does it identify itself, identify strangers, and articulate its response? Related to this, of course, is the question of how the stranger is able to communicate his interest in the group. Assuming that stranger and host can find each other, it does not automatically follow that they have concurring definitions of themselves and of each other.

The main problem stemming from Levine's neglect of the communicative element is that it is left up to the sociologist to read both host and stranger. How this is done, and what relevance such categories have to the immediate experiences of the host and stranger, are also not mentioned.

In a world which is so strikingly organized in communicative terms, where one's ability to negotiate within a language of membership is crucial to one's situation as an insider or an outsider, archaic typologies such as Levine's are regressive. What is required is a close study of the relationship between changes in social organization along proxemic lines, and the accompanying introduction of skills at cultural communication. Only then can changes in membership requirements, and hence changes in the category "the stranger", be identified.

Theoretical Changes. How does Levine's typology respond to recent theoretical developments in sociology which have come about largely as a result of the increasingly problematic nature of communication in post-industrial urbanized society? In ignoring the rich potential of Schutz's piece, Levine, again in a fashion typical of American theorists of the stranger, assumes that such categories as stranger's interest and host's response are self-evident once they have been sociologically identified. He calls for a sociology of the stranger in which individuals are typified according to these parameters. There is no need to examine how the stranger/host formulates, articulates, and negotiates such critical factors. There is no acknowledgement of the need to examine communicative competence as problematic — as a condition of strangeness. Strangeness is thus oddly situated within an assumption of sheer communicability. This is particularly perplexing in that Levine claims to be laying the groundwork for a "social psychology" of the stranger, and one would expect such a perspective to view interaction between self and other as problematic at the very least. Levine does not do justice to the important steps taken by Wood and Schutz in identifying the interaction between host and newcomer, and as such neglects an essential element in the history of "the stranger".

Methodologically, Levine's work suffers from the "etic" fallacy through which motivations and subjective experiences of members are ignored in favor of a taxonomic structure imposed by the investigator. For the purposes of the present study, an "emic" approach is preferred. For Fishman (1972b: p. 34), "an *emic* set of speech acts and events must be one that is validated as meaningful via final recourse to the native members of a speech community rather than via appeal to the investigator's ingenuity or intuition alone". This methodological imperative is shared by phenomenology, symbolic interaction, and sociolinguistics.

This book is an attempt to free the stranger from being an outsider. For as long as we relegate to the stranger the condition of speechlessness — of having no voice — then he can only be sociologically significant, as Simmel, Coser, and Erikson have shown, as delimiting that which is beyond, as providing a reminder of the group's boundaries. My intention is to suggest how the stranger has become the most important member in a world in which the quest for membership has become a full-time preoccupation.

It will be argued that, as a consequence of quite radical changes in demographic and lifestyle patterns since Simmel wrote *"Der Fremde",* using a wanderer as a model for the outsider is no longer applicable. It will also be suggested that subsequent attempts to rearticulate the stranger as the marginal man and the newcomer, culminating in Levine's six types, have continued to embody this 19th century world view. In the dominant mode of social organization in western society – the metropolis – the stranger is not the exception but the rule. This is taken for granted by most definitions of the city, as typified by Sennett (1978): "A city is a human settlement in which strangers are likely to meet" (p. 39).

Strangeness is no longer a temporary condition to be overcome, but a way of life. The group, once formulated as homogeneous and self-contained, does not clearly exclude the stranger. Rather, it is the one who is *unfamiliar with the language of strangeness* – the code of behavior predicated on being spatially, socially, *and* culturally proximate but non-membership oriented according to traditional views of what constitutes membership and community – who becomes an anomaly when overtures of membership orientation are made in a "world of strangers".

Whereas Levine observes a differentiation of strangers as a result of modernity, I will propose a new type of stranger which is far more pervasive and hence understudied. The modern stranger is no longer the outsider. Levine's typology fails to recognize perhaps the key cultural trait of today's west: that *marginality has become a condition for membership.* Thus it is not to the visibly and categorically strange that I direct attention, but to Everyperson. It is to the nondifferentiated collective of "members" that the appellation "stranger" now applies. The outsiders identified by Levine serve to draw attention to a much more equivocal question: What is it that characterizes that to which they are strange?

In the following chapters, I will attempt to sketch out a typology of the modern stranger, based on the presupposition that it is the conditions of membership which produce conditions of strangeness. This premise differs from those of Levine, Stonequist, Schutz, and Simmel in that it *contextualizes* strangeness within a setting which mutualizes strangeness, and thus asserts its value in defining membership. For those authors reviewed, the stranger was formulated as an autonomous, self-contained actor who embodied his identity separately from any group to which he might be strange. As I will show in Chapter Two, this premise assumes Riesman's "inner-directed" mode of social organization. The modern stranger is engaged in an ongoing quest for membership *from within:* he is an outsider on the inside, whose autonomy is only possible through a linguistic outward glance.

A second change regards the visibility of the stranger. For previous theorists, the stranger was visibly different through the unmediated unintelligibility of language, foreign customs and dress. It will be contended that today there is a second-order degree of visibility, much like Wright's "urban ground rule", which tests the stranger's competence at joining. Membership is only visible to the trained eye. Passing as a member becomes more difficult when the criteria for membership are demonstrated through a connotative rather than a denotative symbol system. The modern stranger is an articulate semiologist who actively reads the social in an effort to achieve membership. The ongoing nature of the quest for membership in turn continually highlights one's competence at joining.

Competence as a potential member is established through a fluency in the language of membership. It will be contended that the derivative nature of the disclosure of membership produces an ongoing concern with reaffirming membership. This practice of reaffirmation has the unintended consequence of producing a society of strangers who continually look upon each other as barometers of the current state of the language of membership.

Whereas for Simmel and Schutz the stranger was an exception, it will be argued that the modern stranger is the rule. Stonequist chronicled the beginning of this change with his book on marginal man, and many of the American authors since, including Boorstin (1961), Fromm (1947; 1955; 1969), Lasch (1977; 1978), Lifton (1968), MacCannell (1976), Packard (1972), Riesman (1961), Sennett (1978), and Wilson (1977) have provided evidence that the fundamental ground of familiarity has ceased to be the basis for social organization, and that, instead, a new mode of social organization has emerged: that of the modern stranger. In Chapter Two, I will draw upon these and other authors to suggest the type of world in which strangeness has become a prerequisite for membership, beginning with Riesman's thesis of the changing modes of social organization. In Chapter Three, I will turn to the ethnographic literature to suggest how "being in between" can become a way of life. By formulating the "ethnographer as stranger", I will lend an eye to the question of the generation of strangeness in the context of familiarity; that is, by one's very act of observing other one positions him as beyond the familiar. This in turn leads to the central issue of how language posits other as unfamiliar, forcing the modern stranger to "map" in the manner of the trained observer. This chapter is about how the stranger is forced to read the strange in order to get his bearings, and suggests a version of the reading/speaking of membership as producing a transparent yet tangible barrier between self and other.

Chapter Four looks to the search for authenticity in modern society as the key to articulation of membership. It is precisely the perceived inauthenticity of expression, and the desire to go beyond language to the inexpressibly real and fundamental, which produces the transparent barrier separating modern strangers. It is here that I will develop the theoretical grounds for a language of membership; the practice of sustaining strangeness in the guise of familiarity. In Chapter Five, I will sketch out the implications of a sociology of the modern stranger, and point toward directions for further research.

In arriving at a new sociology of the stranger, it will be necessary to depart from the works which have led to the present impasse. Most of the work to be invoked does not in fact reference the stranger as a topic; yet, as a path is traced through Chapters Two and Three, the necessity of a new articulation of the stranger as a particular form of speaker will be made clear.

Notes

1. Alex Inkeles, *What is Sociology?* Englewood Cliffs, N.J.: Prentice-Hall, 1964 p. 12.
2. An "ideal type" is a sociological construct which is used as an heuristic tool in theory building. Weber formulated his "ideal type" as a construct which can never be found in empirical reality. It is a compendium of similar features characterizing unique but generically consistent phenomena, created from a specific sociological point of view. By embodying the "pure" form of cultural phenomena, the ideal type provides for the description and analysis of individual phenomena that correspond to that type.

   The goal of ideal-typical concept-construction is always to make clearly explicit not the class or average character but rather the unique individual character of cultural phenomena. (Weber, 1949: 101)

3. Meyer (1951) recognized that in the city *time* replaces *space* as the predominant dimension in social relations:

   City people consequently conceive of themselves as those who are "ahead of things", the bearers of things to come, more advanced than the outsiders and knowing more than they. The underlying feeling is one of marching with time, and, in its intensity and power to determine the way of life, it equals the feeling of belonging to and being rooted in a place. That is, the city substitutes time for place as the basis for social relationship. (p. 480)

   Although her article is entitled "The Stranger and the City", Meyer does not take the notion of time as the predominant dimension to characterize change in the stranger; rather, her emphasis is on the way that an outsider to the city (*i.e.* one who shares a more traditional sense of grounding in spatial terms) regards members of the city.
   Klapp (1969), although not explicitly contributing to the sociology of the stranger, has noted that with modernity "place" is replaced by "space". This observation is central to the discussion of changing spatial proxemics in Chapter Two.
4. Both recognition *and* negotiation taken together are key processes for the modern stranger, as will be shown in Chapter Four.
5. This problem resurfaced in the work of Howard Becker (1963) and became central to the "labeling perspective" in deviance theory. See Lofland (1969) for an excellent discussion of attribution according to "minimal indicators"; and Hughes (1945) on "master" and "auxiliary" traits.
6. *"Der Fremde"* was first published in his *Soziologie* in 1908.

7. In Chapter Two, Riesman's typologies will be outlined and will form a basis from which to trace changing modes of social organization.

8. Strangeness and Judaism are historically linked. According to Greifer (1945),

   The sense of being a stranger was burned deeply into the Hebrew psyche at the very inception of its group consciousness. The word "Hebrew", which is transliterated from the word "Ivri" means "the man who came from across the river". The very progenitor of the group, Abraham, the traditional father of his people, who was first given the appelation "Ivri", was regarded at the very start of his career as a newcomer, a foreigner and an alien by those among whom he settled. He is described in the Bible as the wandering shepherd Sheik, a stranger in many lands, who had to adjust himself to the culture of his hosts. The manner in which he purchased land for a family burial plot after the death of his wife Sara, is an instance of his attempts to follow the customs of his adopted group. (p. 742)

   In "Some Observations Concerning Marginality", Riesman (1951) notes that the Jew has frequently been used to exemplify marginality. He suggests that

   The position of the Jew as marginal man really develops when he no longer has either his economic function as the court Jew nor his political function as the socialist rebel. Then only his marginality is his function. (p. 119)

   It seems that there are two issues regarding the Jew as stranger/marginal man that must be distinguished. First, it is clear that historically the Jew has been a prime example of a man without a home, caught between different cultures, and consequently the quintessential marginal man. Second, however, is the problem of defining the marginal man *as the Jew*. Although Park was unable to resist the temptation, subsequent changes in factors determining cultural marginality, such as massive social mobility, cosmopolitanism, and the increasing cultural homogeneity of the western world, coupled with the creation of the state of Israel, demand that such an equation not be made. In this study I have clearly avoided making any undue associations between Judaism and marginality, simply because both the questions of Judaism and marginality deserve a much more extensive treatment than that provided by the narrow limits imposed on both by such an equation.

9. The moral career of the stigmatized individual is composed of three phases: (a) socialization into the standpoint of the normal; (b) learning that he possesses a particular stigma; and (c) the "affiliation cycles" in which the individual gradually comes to accept his status as a member of a stigmatized group (Goffman, 1963b: 32-40 *passim*).

10. Nash and Wolfe (1957) conducted a study in which they tested for degrees of creativity in a simulated environment. They were looking to establish what the consequences of different "stranger" relationships would be on creativity. They observed that "taking the role of stranger tends to cause a decline in the number of inventions made by the individual" (p. 403). They maintained, however, that there *is* a "creative marginal man", but that he was not evident in their study because he "is socialized between two cultures, so that he internalizes the value systems of both. He therefore introjects any conflicts that exist between them. It is this introjected conflict that may make him an innovative individual" (p. 405). The present author looks forward to engaging in a more extensive study of creativity and marginality at a later time.

11. Merton's (1968) classic attempt to categorize social modes of adaptation according to one's relation to culturally-prescribed goals and the available means of attaining

them drew a similar blank. He was forced to include the "retreatist" as an anomic mode – rejection of both categories without a suitable replacement.

The literature on homelessness, which will be reviewed in a subsequent work, is strikingly weak in accounting for this large and sociologically invisible group of individuals. The obvious question would seem to be, how is it that an entire category of human beings could appear to be unaccounted for by the sociological axiom that all humans desire acceptability and membership? A partial explanation may be found in subsequent chapters, where it will be argued that changing modes of social organization have produced accompanying means of articulating membership.

12. Clearly there are many "social types" that *do not* orient to membership in the dominant society, and their status as "marginal persons" in terms of the definition gleaned from Park is seriously questioned.

13. See, for example, the distinctions between urban and rural orientations to the stranger in Franck, 1980; Greifer, 1945; Meyer, 1951; Wirth, 1938; Wood, 1934; and Wright, 1971; as well as the literature on modernity, some of which will be reviewed in Chapter Two.

14. With the possible exception of Siu (1952), whose "sojourner" ends up itself to be quite marginal to the marginal man literature.

15. This type of characterization, in which "stranger's interest" and "host's response" are tabulated, is used again by Levine (1979). See Figure 1 (p. 42) for a replication of his table.

16. Chapter Four will explore the question of the "language of membership" in greater depth.

17. The semiological distinction between sign and symbol in the city is clearly made by Sennett (1978), and implied by Lofland (1973), and will become a focal point of Chapter Four.

For the purposes of this essay, a distinction will be made between "reflexivity" and "reflectivity". Reflexivity will be used in the sense of "knee-jerk reaction": the unmediated, habitual response to a stimulus whose meaning is unambiguous. Reflectivity, on the other hand, denotes mediation, the thoughtful interpretation which is produced by a challenge to the taken-for-granted world, as Schutz has suggested.

The distinction between sign and symbol occurs in a parallel fashion to the distinction between reflexivity and reflectivity. A sign does not require interpretation and thus is read reflexively, while the symbol entails the mediation of association and thus is read reflectively.

18. The "reflexive crisis" also emerges in Mannheim's (1940) discussion of the transition from "functional rationalization" to "self-observation and reflection" (p. 57). The implications of the reflexive crisis will be further examined in Chapter Four.

19. The pattern of recognition and negotiation of membership outlined by Stonequist and Goffman (see note 9 above) is repeated here by Schutz.

20. These principles, which are fundamental to the project of sociolinguistics, will be returned to in Chapter Four.

21. In making this claim for the ideal of socialization, I recognize that its realization may be less than typical.

Regarding children, Hymes (1972b) notes that:

We have then to account for the fact that a normal child acquires knowledge of sentences, not only as grammatical, but also as appropriate. He or she acquires competence as to when to speak, when not, and as to what to talk about with whom, when, where, in what manner. In short, a child becomes able to accomplish a repertoire of speech acts, to take part in speech events, and to evaluate their accomplishment by others. (p. 277)

While Hymes seeks to arrive at a theory of the development of communicative competence in children, the current analysis will follow Schutz's deliberate exclusion of children from study. For, while the acquisition of language is a "normal" phase in childhood development and seen as a fundamental component of the process of socialization, children in the process of becoming communicatively competent are never regarded as "strangers"; rather, they constitute a particular type of *member*. Strangers, being restricted to adults, share the common condition of *having been children* and having gained communicative competence in a mother tongue. Their common condition now entails exposure to "other" tongues (Fishman, 1972a).

Another important area to which Hymes pays attention is the problem of "developmental matrices" as contextualizing the learning of language among children:

When a child from one developmental matrix enters a situation in which the communicative expectations are defined in terms of another, misperception and misanalysis may occur at every level. (p. 287)

Here we may say that children *are* strangers. But it cannot be assumed that they react to the strange in a manner similar to that of fully-socialized adults. Hymes, like Bernstein (1972) and Labov (1966), is concerned with the conditions through which differential competence is achieved and through which, by implication, social inequalities are transmitted through exposure to different developmental matrices. While this is clearly an area deserving more detailed investigation, it is beyond the scope of the current project.

22. The work of Fishman, Gumperz, and Hymes will be returned to in this regard in Chapter Four.

Chapter II
The Social Organization of Strangeness:
Toward a Redefinition of Home

Social organization occurs around social relations of strangeness and familiarity. It is the contention of many writers that familiarity as a basis for social organization is being replaced by one of strangeness. This new form of social organization, which relies on embodiment of social types and their decodification, is seen to be one of increasing alienation, in which the "familiar self" is lost in favor of the "translatable stranger". Beginning with the assumption that interaction between self and other is inherently problematic, any examination of the social organization of strangeness must make a claim as to how self is formulated and made evident to other.

From Hegel and Marx we may take the observation that self seeks to objectify itself in the material world. For Hegel, will injects itself into nature through appropriation. Private property, which is the manifestation of self in the world, becomes the basis through which actors recognize each other (1967: p. 38). In his early writing on alienated labor, Marx claimed that species being is actualized through unalienated labor or, in Hegel's terms, through the objectification of self in the external world (1964: p. 128).

That members recognize each other as autonomous selves may be viewed as a consequence of this very process of self-objectification. Through appropriation of the external, *self makes it one's own.* The ability to say "mine", therefore, becomes the ability to say "I exist". Members exist to each other, it follows, through their ability to distinguish between "mine" and "yours"; hence, their ability to distinguish between "what I am" and "what you are".

Such objectification of self in nature takes place through labor: transforming objects in one's own image. Unalienated labor for Marx occurs when this transformation is unimpeded:

It is just in his work upon the objective world that man really proves himself as a *species-being.* This production is his active species-life. By means of it nature appears as *his* work and his reality. The object of labour is, therefore, the *objectification of man's species-life;* for he no longer reproduces himself merely intellectually, as in consciousness, but actively and in a real sense, and he sees his own reflection in a world which he has constructed. (p. 128)

In capitalist society, the meanings attached to property ownership become significant in terms of decoding social class membership. Capital accumulation by members is generally expressed and interpreted through the market value of consumer goods possessed. Because consumer culture is so fundamental to identity in urban society, the insider's knowledge of the "value" of commodities is well known, in fact it becomes a crucial skill in navigating the urban landscape. Value may be either pecuniary or cultural. Pecuniary value is the cost in terms of currency required to purchase the commodity. The pecuniary value of objects owned tends to indicate to others the relative wealth or poverty of the individual. Cultural value, on the other hand, refers to the secondary meanings attached to objects. Advertising is a major source of such meanings. Consumer objects are juxtaposed with "kinds of people" occupying "kinds of lifestyles". The power of the object in generating identity is preyed upon by advertisers, who are able to sell an "image" through the aspirations of members to achieve that particular identity. These objects, which may be utilitarian for certain purposes, take on a secondary role in the play of capitalism. Members learn to see and read each other as they embody the codes created for their consumption by the "captains of consciousness" (Ewen, 1976).

Ewen (1976) notes the early development of advertising and its relation to social identity:

> The social perception was one in which people ameliorated the negative condition of social objectification through consumption − material objectification. The negative condition was portrayed as social failure derived from continual public scrutiny. The positive goal emanated from one's *modern* decision to armor himself against such scrutiny with the accumulated "benefits" of industrial production. (p. 36)

The "armor" of externals, then, develops concomitantly with other social and economic factors which theorists of modernity have identified: industrialization, urbanization, and commodification. What Ewen points out is that through advertising arises the *commodification of the self*:

> Within a society that defined real life in terms of the monotonous insecurities of mass production, advertising attempted to create an alternative organization of life which would serve to channel man's desires for self, for social success, for leisure away from himself and his works, and toward a commoditized acceptance of "civilization". (p. 48)

The interplay of symbols in the world of the urban consumer is of central concern to the current re-examination of the stranger. Inasmuch as we may take with Hegel and Marx that identity is a consequence of one's relation to the external world, so must we also recognize that that identity lacks meaning without a social context through which self is seen by other as a particular "type" (Schutz, 1970). The reading of others in modern urban centers constitutes one setting where selves are put forth to be decoded *through* certain assumptions that they will be correctly interpreted; yet this is also the setting in which most public interaction occurs between strangers. This dilemma constitutes the fundamental contradiction underlying the social organization of strangeness.

The shift to this mode of social organization has been noted by many authors as a product of the process of modernization. In Tönnies' (1955) terms, what is being witnessed is a shift from *Gemeinschaft* to *Gesellschaft* as the basis for social organization. Durkheim (1933) noted a change from "mechanical solidarity" to "organic solidarity" with the increasing division of labor in society; Marx (1964) observed the relationship between industrialization and alienation of the worker from self, other, product, and process; Mannheim (1940) observed a transition from "substantial" rationalization to "functional" rationalization; Riesman (1961) has chronicled the replacement of "tradition-directed" society by "other-directed" society; and Wright (1971) has observed the increasing prevalence of "urban culture" over "folk culture". For Klapp (1969), the defining characteristic of modernity is the shift from "place" to "space" in grounding membership. This, he suggests, is "closely associated with the well-known mobility and 'rootlessness' of Americans" (p. 29), which in turn results in changing "person" into "category".

To transpose categories of "familiarity" and "strangeness" between the two quite different bases for social organization is problematic. The sentimental longing for "home" as it characterized the *gemeinschaftlich* setting is misplaced, for "home" must be redefined within the different socioeconomic structure of modernity (*gesellschaftlich* setting). Indeed, what social organization itself means demands redefinition in light of the shift.

This chapter is written from the perspective that "familiarity" and "strangeness" are the two poles around which the social, and indeed the self, are organized. The underlying mechanism determining strangeness/familiarity is a communicative one. There is a language to membership; it is a language of social types as they are embodied in symbols for which there exist shared cultural meanings. Although the exploration of the semiology of strangeness will be deferred until Chapter Four, through this chapter it should be kept in mind that the creation of familiarity/strangeness is essentially semiological in nature.

The quest for a home is the wider interest in which this chapter has its place. In these pages, I will address some major works which have sought to account for the connection between geographical mobility and home, in the context of modernity. Of these, Riesman's *The Lonely Crowd* (1961) is regarded as seminal. It is with Riesman that I will begin, and with Riesman that I will conclude, that in fact there is room for "home" in the modern world, but that it must be redefined in light of a shift from spatial and social proximity to cultural proximity as providing the ground for a condition of rootedness.

In beginning to think about the social organization of strangeness, it is first important to ask what one could be strange *from*, on the one hand, and what one could be strange *to*, on the other. Strangeness *from* addresses origin:

it asks whether one has "left one's home", or what one considers home to be. Strangeness *to* addresses presence and possibility: if one is a stranger to, then one is faced with a context of familiarity of which one is not a part. Both strangeness from and strangeness to reference community: groupness which is self-conscious and able to differentiate between insiders and outsiders. The social organization of strangeness then begs the question as to what constitutes community, and in turn where the notion of "home" resides within a sense of community. Is home always left behind by the stranger (stranger from), is it oriented to (stranger to), or is it carried by the stranger (both – and neither – stranger from and stranger to) wherever he might go? Further, how has the shift in social organization brought about by modernity produced changing versions of what it is that constitutes a group? How are the axes of proximity and membership orientation implicated in this change, and what effect does this change have on social definitions of home?

1. The Lonely Crowd

Riesman proposes that there are patterns governing the "social character" or "mode of conformity" of a group which are directly linked to the demographic situation of that group. Demography is in turn closely related to economy for any society. He identifies three "stages" of population development: high growth potential; transitional population growth; and incipient population decline. Corresponding to these stages, the modes of social organization are, respectively: tradition-direction; inner-direction; and other-direction.[1] To each mode or "round of life" there corresponds an ideal actor who reflects at the interactive level the fundamental characteristics of the particular form of social organization. The dominant mode limits the scope of individuation and therefore succeeds in ensuring conformity through mirroring itself in the actions of its component parts.

The following is an attempt to present Riesman's categories in such a way as to address in particular the question of changes in the social organization of strangeness, with its subcategories of strange/familiar; inside/outside; and home/away.

1.1. Tradition-direction

The Traveller   *(Chris de Burgh, 1980)*

In from the coast, riding like the wind and racing the moon,
Shadows on the road, dancing and a-weaving like a crazy fool,
A horsemen is coming, death in his heart for a rendezvous,

And where the Traveller goes, nobody know,
Where the Traveller goes, nobody knows;

A candle in the night, fear on every face when he goes inside,
"Maybe he's on the run",
Get back from the bar, a stranger in town is a dangerous sight,
"Maybe he's got a gun",
"Bring a bottle of whisky landlord, I want to talk for awhile,
And where the Traveller goes, a cold wind blows,
Where the Traveller goes, a cold wind blows,

   There is something in his eyes, something in his hands,
   You can almost smell his revenge,
   And whoever he is after, it will be disaster,
   This man is gonna take him to the very end:

Well the landlord he trembled, staring at a face he'd seen somewhere before,
"You laid him in the ground",
Suddenly remembered a killing, yes a murder many years before,
"T'was you that shot him down",
He said to a boy, "Saddle me the black, I'll meet you down below,
With this man I must talk, with the Traveller I'll go,
With this man I must talk, yes with him I must go,

   There is something in his eyes, something in his hands,
   I can almost smell his revenge,
   And it's me that he's after, it will be disaster,
   This man is gonna take me to the very end",
   And they were never seen again . . .

The tradition-directed group is constructed by Riesman as one which organizes itself around traditional cultural beliefs and patterns. It is basically a stable community, most frequently associated with preindustrial society. Necessity and survival are key organizing principles, whereby tradition is the accepted mode of conformity and deviation from the tradition is neither desired nor tolerated. Conformity is ensured through "fitting in" at all costs. The tradition-directed group approximates Tönnies' category of *Gemeinschaft:* a closely-knit community with a set physical location and clearly identifiable boundaries.

In tradition-directed society, home is a definable spatial entity shared by all members. There is a collective identification to *place* which concretizes the ground of home. In turn, "away" becomes that which is not home. In this society, the place of home can not be easily distinguishable from the people of home. A sedentary way of life, in which geographic mobility is rare, leaves little sense of choice about one's home. Rather, the accident of birth in a particular place and community is accepted as determinative of one's home.

From this it ensues that family is an important component of tradition-direction. The familiar is closely bound up with home; the familiar is that with which one identifies. The importance of a family name in this kind of society becomes clear: one is part of a clan first and foremost, even before one is an autonomous individual, a category which tradition-direction virtually precludes.

The strange is opposed to the familiar and home as that which does not belong, which is truly "alien". The infrequency of the occurrence of confrontation with the stranger contributes to make it a source of suspicion and threat (Greifer, 1945). The stranger, it follows, is one without a home, or one who is at least away from home, and because of this is regarded without trust, as someone who has perhaps been banished from home. The townspeople in de Burgh's poem suspect that the stranger is "on the run", and perhaps that "he's got a gun".

The tradition-directed society has clear categories of insider/outsider: the insider is the familiar, the one who is "at home", the one who belongs; the outsider is the stranger, the one who is from "away", the one who does not belong. Because in tradition-directed society every member is known to every other member, the presence of a non-member in one's midst is immediately apparent. The nondiscursiveness and visibility of the stranger makes his strangeness self-evident to all members of the group.

There is little provision for strangeness to occur *within* the boundaries of the community. As Riesman says, even "misfits" are given a place. "Deviance" as a category to include those who are not "normal" is rarely employed within the group. One is normal by virtue of one's membership – it is strangeness which confers deviance.

1.2. Inner-direction

Inner-direction occurs in a context of increasing self-reliance at the individual level. The actor is released somewhat from the talons of tradition to explore alien lands and ideas. The inner-directed age is the age of the self-reflective actor and the opening of frontiers. All that was once alien and threatening becomes new and exciting; the world is open to discovery, and the individual is looking for a new home.

As opposed to the *gemeinschaftlich* character of traditional society, inner-direction leads toward a *gesellschaftlich* mode of social organization, in which the symbiotic community is met with the possibility of expanding boundaries and flexible membership. With this, the individual as a unique and self-directed actor capable of choosing his community of membership begins to emerge. This is a time of frontier mentality; a time in which boundaries dissolve and the whole world becomes a potential home. Home is still regarded in spatial terms, but it becomes something that one must leave in order to find. In tradition-direction the notion of home is never opposed by away; in inner-direction, however, away is that to which one orients, in order to find home again. It is only with inner-direction that the notion of a "home town" can become meaningful. Home town implies the place that one used to call home, which is opposed by the place that one now calls home, that one is a stranger "from".

It is the inner-directed one who is the loner, who can sing:

> *Oh give me a home*
> *Where the buffalo roam*
> *Where the deer and the antelope play,*
> *Where seldom is heard*
> *A discouraging word*
> *And the skies are not cloudy all day.*
> *Home, home on the range.*

In this song there are two themes which are to be found in the inner-directed actor. First, there is a calling out for a home. The inner-directed is without a home, yet orienting to one. Second, there is a sense in which home can represent a symbiosis with nature rather than with people. So in this tradition of the inner-directed we find mythical actors such as Robinson Crusoe, Don Quixote, the Lone Ranger, and Robin Hood.

Inner-direction gives the individual the strength to break away and to use self rather than other as a guide. The world of inner-direction is full of strangers, where the actor is familiar only to himself. Unlike the tradition-directed society in which the similarities between actors far exceed the differences, inner-direction brings increased individuation and with it increasingly less to hold an individual to a community of which he is a member merely by accident. Naming and family heritage, it follows, also go the way of tradition. The individual claims the right to name himself, and to make his own rules. In this context may be understood the pioneering climate of the American "Wild West", for example, which provokes individuals to "take the law into their own hands".

It is a somewhat ironic consequence of the social organization of inner-direction that the less that people have in common, the less it takes for them to become fast friends. The example of travellers in a foreign country comes to mind. Two occidentals meeting in the orient, a strange land, with only their occidentality in common, find remnants of home in each other. Successively more familiar attributes, such as same language, country, dialect, university, home town, neighborhood, school or church of origin may emerge after the initial meeting, serving as even more cause for union.[2]

By and large the inner-directed actor is a loner who looks within himself for familiarity. "Self-reflection" substitutes for community, and he may be satisfied "talking to himself" without necessarily seeking the community of others. The boundaries between insider and outsider are both broadened and narrowed: the insider could now be almost anyone, but in effect is only one – himself. Yet at the same time the outsider becomes a nebulous concept in that almost everyone is an outsider.

1.3. Other-direction

In this mode of social organization, the "other" becomes the source and direction of conformity, as opposed to tradition for tradition-direction, and self for inner-direction. Concern over being accepted by others is paramount; and the standards set by others become the standards one sets for oneself. The actor moves from being an insular island to being everybody's friend.

In this world there is a radical shift away from individuation, back to a compliant conformity somewhat reminiscent of tradition-direction. Yet for Riesman this represents a tremendous loss. Whereas tradition-direction constituted a "genuine" community, and inner-direction the individual's struggle to differentiate from social prescriptions, other-direction appears to be a recapitulation to the womb-like security of other-definitions. An "artificial" community emerges where the social is organized according to a highly complex language of membership.

What does home become in the stage of other-direction? Riesman presents the search for home as the search for the "best neighborhood" (pp. 67-68). Home is still spatially defined, but a good home can be any place as long as the others there are "the best" others (social and cultural proximity). Whereas the inner-directed found a home where he felt good, the other-directed feels good where he can find a home. Away, in turn, refers both to physical absence (spatial proximity) *and* an interactional absence (social and cultural proximity). It is in other-direction that Goffman's (1963a) "away" becomes meaningful as an interactional absenting of self from involvement in the situation (to be likened to daydreaming, for example).

Familiarity in this world is radically more discursive than in the other two modes, and in that it is actively sought, the *reading* of other becomes the primary social activity. Self is embodied in external symbols; symbols which by collective agreement (often subtle and non-verbal) represent certain properties of value in other-orientation. The strange therefore becomes that which can not be read discursively; that which has no place in the language of membership. The strange is that which can not be accounted for through the achieved fluency of the vernacular. The other-directed actor, then, is as rule-governed as is the tradition-directed actor. Although there may be more permutations of acceptability, as, for example, in the case of fashion, the boundaries for insiders and outsiders are nevertheless clearly delimited. Everyone who shares the language of membership is an insider; those who do not share it are outsiders. Being privy to such language accords one instant familiarity with others; but in that it is a language of externals and not internals (Simmel, 1971a), that familiarity breeds strangeness.

Externals, for Simmel, constitute "clothing, social conduct, amusements" which for him were different from internals in that "here no dependence is placed on really vital motives of human action" (p. 289). The superficial nature of externals is implied by Simmel and Riesman, to suggest that the individual's expression is less valid and less "authentic" than that which exists internally, or for Riesman, than that which characterizes the inner-directed actor. Familiarity, in these terms, becomes a superficial familiarity which in orienting self always to other through objectification in the external world appears to negate self. Yet we can not deny that if self cries out to be heard – if expression is desired – the self without a means of being heard is truly a stranger, for it has no language. For Marx (1964), alienation occurs precisely through the failure of the self to be recognized through its objectification in the external world. It would follow that the stranger as formulated within other-direction may be alienated if the primary form of objectification becomes the language of membership.[3]

In a later work, Riesman (1951) elaborates on the dual pull of the other-directed actor. He refers to his concept of "marginal differentiation", introduced in *The Lonely Crowd* as the tendency of members to seek conformity yet retain a certain sense of individuality which distinguishes them from others, to suggest how membership is bearable for the other-directed actor:[4]

Now with the spread of psychological other-direction in the upper middle class, people themselves go in for marginal differentiation of personality. In order to do this they must be sensitive enough to themselves and each other to know how they appear to others. They must keep constantly sensitized concerning the degree to which they are different from others without being too different. This is an anxious, precarious business, to look at it negatively; it is a sensitive and comradely one, to look at it positively, because it keeps people in touch both with themselves and with others. It creates a kind of attitude towards oneself which was absent in the earlier era of inner-direction, when conformity was in some ways perhaps more rigid, and in which people were less aware of these nuances of personality difference.

This awareness, this radar-like sensitivity to how one is navigating in the social world, and this tendency to make that navigation into an end of life as well as a means – these seem to me to be characteristic of the psychological type I have termed other-directed. (1951: 116-117)

Conformity between inner-directed individuals is maintained through close adherence to normatively prescribed externals. But these externals are not "expressive" in the way that they become for the other-directed one. The inner-directed actor clearly distinguishes between "private" and "public" self, or between "internal" and "external". The "internal" is not available for public consumption, while the "external" is quite self-consciously compliant with the conventions of membership. He appears "appropriately dressed" for all occasions; presenting himself with decorum. But it is convention which serves to maintain the private element. Appearance is that beyond which one may not trespass.[5]

Over the other-directed actor, however, formal rules of convention have more limited control. Propriety is negotiable. Although acceptability by other is the primary concern in presentation of self, self nevertheless participates in the mode of expression employed. In other-direction, appearance, or one's display of one's sense of self through the language of membership, is an invitation to "find out more". Cues, which are used by actors to select like-others, exemplify an openness to others which characterizes other-direction, rather than the closedness of inner-direction. There is, therefore, a kind of negotiated order through which informal rules come to govern the codes used to communicate between members.

Fashion as an expression of "openness" is therefore of paramount importance in this relationship. Fashion, however, applies to a whole range of externals beyond clothing. The major shift with other-direction is that externals embody a self which could be "related to". The package deal, so to speak, is what one presents to the stranger. Under the guise of "relating to" there is the adoption of signs which "express". Having read such and such a book, taken this course, traveled to that place, "experienced something", suggest certain qualities within. The symbols that one uses to evidence these "internals" that differentiate actor from other are interesting in and of themselves. This mode of self-expression entails marginal differentiation: individuals distinguish themselves according to trivial differences while maintaining a fundamental commitment to that which makes them similar. "That which makes them similar" becomes the desire for membership; and *both* the similarities and differences must be intelligible through a language of membership (Harman, 1985).

The greater sensitivity to others that Riesman observes in the other-directed becomes a greater sensitivity to symbols. The other-directed is well versed in this more "sophisticated" communications system. Each person in this world becomes a semiologist in that he becomes sensitized to reading others.[6]

1.4. Communicative Normalization

Keeping in mind that Riesman calls his three categories "modes of ensuring conformity", there are two trends emerging in the mode of other-direction. The first is toward what I will call "communicative normalization". Here I refer to *the increasing use of both verbal and non-verbal forms of communication between members as a means of achieving and maintaining mem-*

bership. As Riesman suggests, taking one's cues from others and basing one's self-perceptions on those cues is a mechanism of interaction which is used pervasively in the age of other-direction. Communicative normalization is achieved through the language of membership.

The language of membership of the modern stranger is qualitatively different from that characterizing previous modes of ensuring conformity.[7] With tradition-direction, membership is nondiscursive. By the accident of birth one becomes "one of us" or "one of them". Membership is unproblematic because it is given. The use of symbols serves to reinforce that which goes unquestioned. With inner-direction, where individualism is the rule, communication as a mode of social organization has little import. The solitary figure speaks for himself or remains silent. With other-direction, however, making one's allegiances known is the name of the game; and the game is played through the language of membership. Others are oriented to on the basis of the minimal indicators (Lofland, 1969) of externals.

A consequence of social organization around a discursive symbol system is that as membership is defined, so is normalcy. Communicative normalization occurs, then, as the actor orients his own use of discursive symbols according to the group in which he desires to assume membership. Conformity becomes problematic because others orient among themselves through communicating their membership.

If the first trend of other-direction is communicative normalization, the second becomes one of "discursive strangeness". As individuals orient more to each other as members, their noncompliance with the language of membership also becomes evident. Where a set of symbols is agreed upon as establishing membership, the same or other symbols may also be used to communicate strangeness. Thus deviance as a category becomes quite visible in an age of other-direction. Whereas even the least "fitting" would fit in to tradition-directed groups; and whereas fitting in was not of paramount concern for the inner-directed actor; fitting and misfitting preoccupy the social organization of other-direction.

Communicative normalization has rather serious implications for the social organization of strangeness. The ethic of "relating to" others in other-direction calls for the obsolescence of strangeness; the abundance of familiarity. However, the very pretense of familiarity breeds strangeness. The other-directed mode of conformity yields singles bars, encounter groups, cocktail parties, and "companions wanted" ads. Whereas the ideal of this mode is one of "spontaneous collectivization" (Whyte, 1956), wherein individuals "relate to" each other freely and spontaneously as members, it is in essence one of "false collectivization", wherein individuals do not deeply relate to others as members with anything more in common than their membership. This contention shall underlie the remainder of this book.

With Riesman's third typology, then, belonging is a social ethic; its disobedience constitutes deviance. The loner, the arch individual, the inner-directed one has no place in this mode of conformity. Instead, it is a world in which he who best belongs is exalted. And the one who best belongs is by definition the one who is fluent in the language of membership. Symbols replace what for tradition-direction was self-evident. Through the language of membership a kind of second-order familiarity is engendered. "Understanding" the other occurs only through that which is communicable through symbols. The immediacy of self-disclosure through symbols replaces the "getting to know the other" which prevailed when other, as inner-directed actor, was hard to get to know. Learning of the ways in which other is different, as it characterized inner-direction, is replaced by reading the catalogue of the ways in which he is the same.

But self-disclosure only occurs for those who can read the language of membership. Speech communities emerge on the basis of privatized language. Homosexuals may disclose themselves to other homosexuals through a "queens' vernacular" (Rodgers, 1972) which is not only unintelligible to nonmembers of that "subculture", but may not even be recognized by them as a language.[8]

The epitome of this mode of social organization is seen by the recent phenomenon of "video dating". Through this medium an actor may approach, assess, and accept or reject an other entirely at the level of the language of membership as opposed to any "deeper" exploration or disclosure. The other is a video screen to be read, upon which all of the face-sheet data which are pertinent to membership have been carefully encoded. So, even though presentation of individual self is stressed in other-direction through marginal differentiation, conformity is even more strongly maintained through an ethic of communicative normalization, through which one must know and share the symbols in order to belong.

Riesman states that "the other-directed person is cosmopolitan. For him the border between the familiar and the strange — a border clearly marked in the societies depending on tradition-direction — has broken down" (p. 25). Perhaps this is the case because within a homogeneous society the language of familiarity is pervasive. The strange, which requires decoding, or learning a new code, is rare; for it is the stranger who must learn the prevailing code, not the other way around (Schutz, 1944). The possibility of communication therefore becomes the grounds for the assumption of a relation of familiarity. Any language, therefore, speaks to familiarity by its very inclusion of actor and other as speakers together within a universe of discourse.

If, as Riesman suggests, the other-directed actor is unprepared to deal with the strange, it is because there *is* nothing strange. Although "the other-directed person learns to respond to signals from a far wider circle than is constituted by his parents" (p. 25), this wider circle may be seen as one which replaces the traditional "familiar" as the arena in which membership needs to be established and maintained. The anonymous *Welt* in which it is cultural proximity (rather than spatial or social proximity) which unites members through a language of membership has become the new context for belonging. McLuhan's "global village", brought on in large part through the universalizing of embedded meaning produced *via* mass communications, mass production, and multinational corporations, is suggestive of just such a world in which a universal language of membership seems to prevail. At the Holiday Inn "there are no surprises". McDonald's insists on uniformity of its products, its facilities, and its employees (Boas and Chain, 1976). According to this ideal, the number of french fries in one serving at any McDonald's restaurant in Toronto would be identical to that in Tokyo. Cities replicate each other. The houses, the shops, the entertainment districts, the highways become interchangeable. The map of a city is something that one can "get on to" and then treat as familiar. Joining the "Melitta revolution" means learning the language of cone filter coffee, and then subsequently acting on the basis of that knowledge by treating the practice of Melitta as simply taken for granted.[9] This notion of familiarity, then, defies both spatial and social factors in proxemics and occurs at the level of culture. *Gemeinschaft* and *Gesellschaft* have merged.[10]

The temptation to apply the typology of "tradition-direction" to this global village is strong. Where there is no strangeness, there is only familiarity, and this clearly reflects back to the compliance of the previous mode of social organization. Fromm, as will be shown, takes this perspective. For Fromm, however, the significance of *difference* in other-direction is fundamentally altered — as is the definition of self — from that of tradition-direction. That there could be a global village disallows accident as the determinant of membership, for on such a scale all members are not known. A relation to the unknown — the possibility of finding like-others — and the choice offered by communicative normalization all radically change the context of membership/strangeness from tradition-direction. Key factors in the shift include the obsolescence of spatial and social proximity as a mode for social organization, and the increasing use of communicative normalization at the level of culture, which is eminently discursive.

If home is that which could never be copied and home is the Holiday Inn, there is room beyond Riesman for a stronger sense of what home could be for other-directed society. This search will lead us to a new formulation as well of the stranger, and ultimately to look at community in a new light.

2. Stranger as Automaton and Home as Prison: The Dilemma of Authoritarian Man

It is clear from *The Lonely Crowd* that Riesman had read Fromm, and shared his evolutionary approach to social organization. Fromm identifies the interplay between economy and religion as the mechanism which brought on change between the three states, while Riesman uses the indicator of demography. They both concur on the process, however: that traditional forms of social organization have been supplanted through modernization to bring about a stage of self-reliance (Riesman's inner-directed mode; Fromm's "freedom to") which is succeeded by a stage of other-reliance (Riesman's other-directed mode; Fromm's "freedom from").

Escape from Freedom (1969) is not a sociology, but instead may be grouped with the work of other "humanistic psychologists" such as Bugental (1976), Maslow (1954), and May (1953). Consequently, Fromm's work appears quite naive in its perception of the ability of women and men to define themselves; however, it may nevertheless prove useful for the treatment of the stranger. Fromm identifies two fundamental human social needs: avoiding aloneness; and awareness of self as an individual entity. The two drives compete for prominence at the various stages of social organization.

Social organization begins with what Fromm calls "primary ties". Primary ties both shelter and tie down the pre-individuated person to others, and represent an overwhelming satisfaction of the need to avoid aloneness, without allowing the actor the "freedom" of self-determination. The stage dominated by primary ties is likened to a family environment, and the members of that society to its children. Protected, directed, safe in the shelter of tradition, the individual "self" has yet to emerge.

This image of the family is quite compelling, as it coincides with Riesman's tradition-directed mode of ensuring conformity. Fromm notes that, developmentally speaking, it is a necessary beginning – and one to which more individuated actors tend to desire to return. This point becomes important later when I attempt to redefine "home".

The process of individuation occurs with not a little pain; it is a separation from the security provided by the familiar – a "growing aloneness". The emerging individual parallels Riesman's inner-directed actor. The desire to escape from the confines of primary ties is answered with increasing self-reliance; increasing acceptance of responsibility for one's actions.

Modernity, in resolving the at first liberating trend of individualism, comes to the third stage by creating an alienated modern actor, who "becomes more independent, self-reliant, and critical, and he becomes more isolated, alone, and afraid" (p. 124). For Fromm, the modern actor is not just a stranger to himself but to others as well. This situation is generated by the economic freedom and social and political inequality brought about by capitalism.

Fromm's version of other-direction is embodied in the automaton. "Freedom from" results in a condition where self is determined by other, and has no life of its own. Self is therefore instrumental and alienated in that it feeds on extrinsic responses, which become internalized.

Thus, the self-confidence, the 'feeling of self', is merely an indication of what others think of the person. It is not *he* who is convinced of his value regardless of popularity and his success on the market. If he is sought after, he is somebody; if he is not popular, he is simply nobody. (p. 140)

Of special interest is Fromm's notion of freedom. Whether one is "free from" or "free to" is not such a clearcut matter as he would propose. Although Fromm gives adequate representation to the social forces of coercion which limit "freedom", his recognition of the self's perception of being situated, and of the interaction between self, desire, and situation as influencing perceptions of freedom, is lacking.

"Self" for Fromm can be either real or unreal: under the conditions of "freedom from", the authentic self does not develop; under "freedom to", it takes flight. Again, the obvious problem here is that self is never defined as something that could be "real" by virtue of its existence within a social milieu. Instead, Fromm's notion of freedom demands that the only real self is that which takes no cues at all from the social; that which lacks any social identification, that which is sheer self-reliance. The member, then, does not exist in Fromm's society of "freedom to". "Freedom from", in turn, is a condition in which membership is not only sought but is entirely defining of self. Membership has the connotation in Fromm of compliance rather than choice. The real self would presumably choose not to be a member. Membership and individuality are therefore discrete categories which could never coexist in Fromm's social vision.

Like Riesman, Fromm contends that the effects of other-direction are fundamentally harmful, resulting in alienation. However, the existential dilemma that Fromm identifies − the individual's confrontation with his fundamental "aloneness" − is in many ways an artifact of nostalgia. If the tradition-directed version of home is held up as ideal, then naturally its passage will be regarded as alienating. If the new mode of community is allowed to emerge, however, perhaps members will not be left straddling the ideality and the reality of their existence, but come to see the new mode as necessitating adaptation. What has really happened as a consequence of "modernity" is that through highly sophisticated modes of communication, other-direction is finally possible in a way never before. It is a deeply social mode of community, in which the desire to look to other for reflections of one's self may be met in such a way that "identity" is produced through the interaction of self-definitions and other-definitions. It has taken, in other words, the best from both tradition-direction and inner-direction. If there is no more "home" in the nostalgic sense of the word, members must orient to *finding* a home rather than remembering a home. This search is only possible through participating in a language of membership, which is what characterizes most emphatically the modern age.

This leads to the most problematic aspect of Fromm's work, for he maintains that it is possible to retrieve the "real" self from the alienated or automatized self; that it is possible to transform "freedom from" (alienation) into "freedom to" (be oneself). "Freedom from" is manifested through the authoritarian personality. The individual gives up his right to define self, and becomes "free from" being decisive. The most powerful mechanism of escape is that of "automaton conformity":

> To put it briefly, the individual ceases to be himself; he adopts entirely the kind of personality offered to him by cultural patterns; and he therefore becomes exactly as all others are and as they expect him to be. The discrepancy between 'I' and the world disappears and with it the conscious fear of aloneness and powerlessness. . . . The person who gives up his individual self and becomes an automaton, identical with millions of other automatons around him, need not feel alone and anxious any more. But the price he pays, is high; *it is the loss of his self.* (p. 209)

The question to be put to Fromm at this point is whether, within his vision, there was ever any autonomous self to be lost, on the one hand; and if, on the other hand, the "giving one's self over" is not a necessary step in the learning of the language of membership. That is to say, with the changing mode of community it is essential that members learn the code, and participate in it. This learning and participating must be distinguished from a *becoming* of the code.

The attribution of a false consciousness to actors' sense of individuality is a valid one, which may be made with regard to the hegemonic influence of technology and capitalism over culture, as well as ideologies reflecting free thought and choice. The problem with asserting it as Fromm does, however, resides in the belief in a "real self" that is not socially conditioned. Fromm fails to take the perspective that what emerges as the "social character" of a group is the fundamental socializing power for its members, particularly in an age of other-direction, when community is defined through choice (cultural communicative normalization) rather than by accident (spatial and social proximity). That Fromm calls for an authentic self, yet does not identify what that could be nor how it could be achieved, suggests that he has not come to terms with the cultural contingencies involved in the generation of an other-directed self.

The fact that the contents of our thinking, feeling, willing, are induced from the outside and are not genuine, exists to an extent that gives the impression that these pseudo acts are the rule, while the genuine or indigenous mental acts are the exceptions. (p. 213)

Sociologically speaking, however, they *are* the rule. The age of other-direction is also an age of "socialization", when the rules of the game can not be ignored in favor of "rampant individualism" and "spontaneity" as he calls for.

The world of "freedom to" as Fromm defines it belongs to the age of inner-direction: when the stranger had the freedom to be here today and gone tomorrow; to set his terms for what and where home could be, what and where one's vocation would be; to search for fortune and perhaps find it. In following Riesman, however, the age of other-direction leaves no room for Fromm's version of spontaneity. But this is not to say that there is a loss of self. A change in the mode of social organization demands a concomitant change in mechanisms for self-definition.

The ultimate warning of *Escape from Freedom* is that in escaping, members give themselves over the group and become the breeding ground for movements such as Nazism. Fromm concludes by suggesting that the spontaneous expression of free will is the only way out of the escape from freedom; only through "the realization of his self, by being himself" can one be "free to". This conclusion can not be taken seriously by sociology; however, it is important in view of the mythology that it represents. As long as authors like Fromm continue to preach the need for greater self-definition, the longer the sense of alienation fostered by a feeling of homelessness will prevail. When it is recognized that an "authentic" community is not rooted in tradition-direction; and that an "authentic" self is not possible solely within a context of inner-direction, then perhaps members will be "free to" enjoy the communicative mode available to them through other-direction.

3. The Homeless Mind:
Home as Everywhere and Nowhere

For Berger, Berger and Kellner (1973), the "homeless mind" is a feature of modernity in general. The attitude that others are "anonymous functionaries" (p. 32) — which generates an anomic relation both to others and to one's work — is seen as a concrete result of technology. Anonymous social relations are influenced by one's sense of place, and place becomes treated as inconsequential when the social organization of strangeness makes it a mere contingency rather than an integral dimension which warrants "orientation to". Place becomes part of the apparatus which governs our being, and which through a de-emphasis on spatial proximity in grounding membership therefore breeds detachment and alienation.

A major component of the rational workings of modernization is that "in order for [work] to be performed, the other *must* be anonymized" (p. 32). Similarly, Durkheim (1933) argues that organic solidarity involves anonymizing other such that he *is* what he *does*. Members are defined according to the occupational groups to which they belong. Durkheim maintains, unlike Berger *et al.*, however, that organic solidarity, by producing a more interdependent society, produces society in which members are more likely to find like-others. Berger *et al.* also observe that in order for the social organization of strangeness to be effective, the importance of home or place must be de-emphasized such that one could live anywhere. They state:

> The macro-social implications of this dichotomy in the experience of self is this: there *must* be a private world in which the individual can express those elements of subjective identity which must be denied in the work situation. The alternative to this would be the transformation of individuals into mechanical robots, not only in the external performance of roles but on the subjective level of their own consciousness of self. Such a transformation, the extreme case of alienation, is almost certainly impossible empirically because of deep-seated features in the constitution of man. (p. 35)

For Berger *et al.*, as for Fromm, the distinction between public and private life must be made. Private constitutes "own": that which one possesses, transforms, controls. In a world which is increasingly organized around temporary privacy at best, the assumption that there is always this private dimension to return to is a tenuous one. Yet in the dichotomy between public and private may be discovered a key to the social organization of strangeness. "Private selves" lead to a conscious division between self and other; between "anonymous functionary" and friend/neighbor/substantive individual. Privacy generates a place to go to, and hence a place to be public from. It is a spatial concept, which also has implications for social and cultural proximity. The loss of privacy, in the form of a loss of identity, of home, of sense of "where I belong", in turn results in a loss of the distinction between home and away. It is all away. With nowhere to return to, the present place is only relative to any other place; it has no significance in relation to private self. The social organization of strangeness, then, is constituted of the real lack of privacy. This in turn implies a spatial rootlessness.

If modernity brings homelessness in the sense of sheer publicity (again, paralleling Riesman's "other-direction" and Fromm's "freedom from"), it is then to be asked what constitutes the anonymous self. What is it like to be alone in a world of sheer publicity? In *The Pursuit of Loneliness* (1970), Slater maintains that American society is obsessed with embellishing self with material goods — which serve to *isolate* self from others, behind the mask of things — and suggests that this constitutes a decisive *pursuit* of loneliness. The loneliness comes from the pursuit rather than the objects which are used to portray self, however. As Packard also displays in *A Nation of Strangers* (1972), the very pursuit of privacy leads to the inevitability of its inaccessibility: the further one attempts to distance oneself from others, the more that very pursuit brings attention to oneself.

The kind of society which is organized around the pursuit of privacy is therefore one in which privacy is a scarce commodity, and "commodity fetishism" is pursued in its place. The very pursuit of privacy signifies the temporariness of all that is present-to-hand — in search of something else. The "planned obsolescence" of those objects which are sought after in this light suggests that the good version of privacy, or place, will never be found, for the very activity of seeking suggests a consciousness which is public.

Despite their emphasis on the anonymous self, Berger *et al.* also see the modern self as an autonomous one: the lonely, self-reflective one in search of a home. If anonymity breeds solitude, a social organization which precludes a definition of self in the face of the modern machine breeds the desire to define self. The modern actor is not "given" a satisfactory identity, and therefore must search for it. Berger *et al.* nevertheless view the "homeless mind" as the product of a state of transition in the status of self versus society. They do not give up hope of the possibility of self-determination. In other words, they are claiming a determinism about history in which the "modern" is a mere deviation from the inevitable imposition of order on man.

The risk of "looking for" order is that one will give oneself over to it, as Fromm maintains. However, as Riesman has indicated, a true search entails a certain freedom to define realities. From that perspective it is difficult to transform a society into a closed, monotheologic collectivity where the ontology is shared *and* imposed. The pain of modernity lies not in its vacuity but in the perverse desire for vacuity: the rejection of a determinism such as Berger *et al.* have suggested, which can not be replaced. It is masochism of the identity — a self-imposed mutilation, a nihilism which maintains that it is better to be open and alone than closed and subject to false consciousness. It is an alienating comfort which leads one to believe one has found one's self. The modern actor can not find his self, according to Slater's ethic, because he is looking too hard. The pain of openness is that anything closed appears threatening. For the stranger will never find a home, except the homeless home — which is comforting in its own right.

It is only within the context of a social organization of strangeness that a novel such as Fuentes' *The Hydra Head* (1978) could be written. This is a world where competing versions of reality make it possible for the protagonist to wonder, and to never be entirely sure, whether "I am *really* Felix

Maldonado". It is a world where identity is predicated on recognition; where memories of the past and orientations toward the future are altered and obscured by the uncertainty of the present. There is no comfort in knowing who one was, or who one would have been, when both eventualities are contingent upon an unclear version of what "is". The problem of embodiment of history is clearly faced by Maldonado, who becomes estranged from the language of membership and thus deeply a stranger. Yet it is only by virtue of the exclusion produced by lack of recognition *as* a member that he can even recognize that he has lost his language.[11] The contingency of community or lifeworld or consensus, that Berger *et al.* have pointed out, is made clear.

In fact, phenomenology and hermeneutics, the interpretative disciplines, would have no interest in a world where reality is a given. The contingency of "reality" upon social definition, evident in interpretative theorists from Dilthey on, must have surely corresponded with the onset of the uncertainty of modernity. For phenomenologists such as Schutz and Berger *et al.*, to talk about the manifestations of identity in modernity is to reflect upon their own situations as exiles.[12] In a sense, then, phenomenology has to talk about alienation and identity, because it is only made accessible as a mode of social theorizing within a consciousness which has been secularized, pluralized, and alienated from a given definition of "the way things should be".

4. A Nation of Strangers: Home as Possibility

Whereas Riesman and Fromm cling to the myth of tradition-direction and see little good in the advent of modernity, and Berger *et al.* and Slater recognize a transition but also attribute to it alienation and isolation, Vance Packard is one who has identified the new mode of social organization as one which orients toward establishing community. In *A Nation of Strangers* (1972), he looks at the evolving norm of a highly mobile lifestyle in the United States, and brings into question the present state of the home, the community, and the stranger.

For Packard there is no doubt that this is an age of other-direction; and he suggests that social organization is beginning to accommodate it rather than resist it. Packard maintains that the locus of social organization is shifting from the traditional, place-oriented community to a more interest-oriented sense of community. Through the expanded spheres of influence of the military, the multinational corporations, the diplomatic corps, the mass communications networks, and the development agencies, the likelihood that in one's work one will be transferred, not just within one's own country but anywhere on the globe, is continually growing.[13]

Packard defines an "authentic" community as follows:

An authentic community is a social network of people of various kinds, ranks, and ages who encounter each other on the streets, in the stores, at sports parks, at communal gatherings. A good deal of personal interaction occurs. There are elected leaders or spokesmen whom almost all the people know at least by reputation. Some may not like their community but all recognize it as a special *place* with an ongoing character. It has a central core and well-understood limits. Most members base most of their daily activities in or near the community. And most are interested in cooperating to make it a place they can be proud of. (p. 16 – emphasis added)

This version of "authentic" community is patterned after that of tradition-direction: the accidental, immutable, place-bound community. Packard observes that in modern society the "authentic" community is being replaced by another form of community, the "artificial" one. What is an artificial community, how does it evolve, and how does it speak to the changes in social organization engendered by other-direction?

The first characteristic of the new community is that it transcends the traditional constraints of spatial proximity. The new community evolves in a highly mobile society where one place is easily re-placed by another. It is not so much the place which locates community as the people. Thus the notion of a home town as a place one goes back to is obviated in light of the possibility of finding community *anywhere.* Community therefore becomes portable, and like Hemingway's (1964) moveable feast, can be brought with one instead of being left behind.

The second characteristic of the new community is that it transcends the traditional constraint of social proximity. Whereas once one had to make community with those with whom one was accidentally proximate, now one has the element of *choice.* One does not have to even know one's neighbor; one's best friend may reside thousands of miles away. The new community is deliberate instead of arbitrary. Packard provides evidence to suggest that individuals transcend traditional expectations of community and exercise considerable choice over those with whom they wish to relate. The retiree is a case in point:

I learned in Florida that having a big solid house to retire into is not as important as being among people who respect you, who care about you, who share your concerns, and who have a chance to know you well enough to become an authentic friend. (pp. 97-98)

Packard suggests that the aged are made to feel strangers in the society which is ostensibly their own, and have in a sense to leave it and search for a new framework in which to feel at home. The communities that result are thus intentional rather than accidental. Moving to Florida to join a retirement community, for example, represents action based on deliberate choice. The alternative, which might entail remaining in a living context which one has not "chosen" but which one has passively "slipped in to", would be to follow a more traditional path.

The main element differentiating retirees from other migrants is choice: they are not dependent on place for income or security. Place then takes on a completely different sense. Those who can afford to can literally make their homes wherever they like. This freedom from economic dependency, in addition to feeling that they do not have to worry about their children, is an important factor enabling such uninhibited migration, and is being offered to increasingly diverse sectors of the economy. As our population ages, and as the nature of work and the family change in respond to technological innovation and greater career opportunities for women outside of the home, respectively, it will be interesting to see how the pattern which Packard associated with retirees spreads to other sectors of the population. Presently, his conclusions imply that the "artificial" communities engendered through the massive flow of retirees to Florida embody his version of "authentic community" to a greater extent than the city which has arisen "naturally", but which has become so alienating so as to "disown" its members, especially the elderly.

Marginal groups such as immigrants and gypsies carry their culture with them and reinforce their basis for community through that culture. Immigrants

have always been likely to head directly for the neighborhood or ghetto where many of their native origin live. Here they could ease uprootedness by quickly entering into intimate social relationships (despite a possible poor knowledge of the English language), and find organizations ready to receive and help them. (p. 100)

The mobile home community is one which is consciously oriented to mobility.

There is an aura of mobility and impermanence in mobile home living. Mobile home owners know they can always pick up and move to another location or area in a pinch, which seems to appeal to restless Americans. Their mobile homes also offer such people a chance to make a minimum commitment to both home and community. (p. 123)[14]

In light of this, "alienation" as a problem of modernity needs to be re-examined. It may be that one does not talk to one's neighbors. Perhaps this is a sign of increasing selectivity as opposed to alienation. Attention must be directed at the communicative channels which are open for the establishment of relationships between members of speech communities who are not necessarily related by spatial or social proxemics, but nevertheless have evolved a universe of discourse based on cultural proxemics.

Fishman (1972b) draws the connection between language repertoires and role repertoires. He argues that as social organization shifts from tradition-directed to other-directed, both role repertoires and language repertoires of members become increasingly complex. Traditional societies are characterized by "role compartmentalization", while modern societies are characterized by "role fluidity" (p. 27). The greater the number of roles one is expected to play, the greater the corresponding linguistic repertoires:

How different such compartmentalization is from the fluidity of modern democratic speech communities in which there is such frequent change from one role to another and from one variety to another that individuals are frequently father and pal, or teacher and colleague, simultaneously or in rapid succession! The result of such frequent and easy role shifts is often that the roles themselves become more similar and less distinctive or clearcut. The same occurs in the verbal repertoire as speakers change from one variety (or language) to another with greater frequency and fluidity. (p. 28)

Fishman suggests that the notion of "overarching speech community" be used in recognition of the fact that spatial proximity is no longer necessarily determinative of membership. For example, in the daily round of a government functionary in Brussels,

He *generally* speaks standard French in his office, standard Dutch at his club and a distinctly local variant of Flemish at home. In each instance he identifies himself with a different speech network to which he belongs, wants to belong, and from which he seeks acceptance. All of these networks – and more – are included in his overarching speech community, even though each is more commonly associated with one variety than with another. (1972a: 16)

Fishman also notes that the increasing use of "languages of wider communication", such as English as a second language, serves to both homogenize and differentiate populations. Homogenization occurs as English is being spoken in much of the world, but, he notes, this has also resulted in a mushrooming of the *varieties* of English being spoken (1972b: 89).

One of the latest manifestations of the community of strangers is the escalation of newspaper "Companions Wanted" columns. This phenomenon embodies the chief characteristics of the new overarching speech community. In the best sense, it is the ultimate form of seeking out "like-others". As compared to the "dating game" in traditional society, where one was expected to "marry the boy next door", and where matchmaking, whether deliberate or merely as a consequence of limited or no choice, was the rule, the new community transcends place and familiarity.

The "advertising" approach to relationships has been slow in achieving acceptance, however. This may be attributed to the same mythological umbilical cord which holds back other-directed society in other ways. The advocates of this new approach are met with imputations of "loser" – if one must "resort" to advertising then one must really have problems – and "wearing one's heart on one's sleeve" – opening oneself up for anyone and everyone to read (Austrom and Hanel, 1980). Rarely is it met with a recognition that does not smack of tradition-direction.[15] A more positive response might acknowledge that the one who chooses to advertise is not content with the application of norms of tradition-direction in an other-directed world, and chooses to make use of available communications techno-logy to surmount previous obstacles and search out like-others. In that reading membership is the most crucial organizing mechanism in other-direction, "making oneself an open book" is thus conforming to the new mode of social organization by leaving oneself open to be read. That there is a stigma associated with taking this route suggests that the other-directed character is still not fully developed in our society. If we are in transition, then it is the transitory state of our values that is one of the main problems, as Berger *et al.* make clear.

The self-selective approach to membership in communities is a positive outcome of other-direction. In tradition-direction one had no choice over one's membership; in inner-direction one did not desire membership. In other-direction, where membership has become the prime element of social organization, the proliferation of communities whose membership is based on choice rather than accident is a consequence. Of interest is the relation of place to the new community. Whereas the traditional community tends to be focused on spatial proximity, the breaking off from place as an organ-izing medium occurs for the inner-directed and carries over to other-direction. For the other-directed, it is far more important to belong to a community of like-others (cultural proximity) than to cling to the proverbial "home town". Packard concludes that

... one could argue that many people in the modern world are moving from a traditional *place-bound* society to a society in which they are involved in groups whose members may be widely scattered geographically. (p. 184)

In defense of the new highly mobile community, Packard lists several advantages, including: its "broadening effect"; "a chance to make new friends"; the opportunity to "escape present frustrations or assumed stagna-ting situations"; adding "to the zest of life"; broadening of "an individual's economic opportunities"; creating "a challenge that promotes personal growth"; helping "in preparation for a professional career"; promoting "closer family ties and more equalitarian marriages"; and finally offering "a wider range of choices in picking a spouse, an occupation, or places to live" (p. 174*ff*). This list presents the social organization of strangeness as the panacea for the ills of tradition-directed and inner-directed society. In fact, however, it is just as much a consequence as a cause. In that it has not been entirely accepted yet, however, some of the consequences of attempting to cling nostalgically to the past when confronted with change, are attributed to the change itself. Even Packard is a victim of this, when he expresses reservations as to the benefits of the new community. He holds the ideal of the "authentic" community up against the shadow of the "artificial" community, and suggests that there is a real risk of alienation. Two characteristics contributing to this are loneliness and an "uncertain sense of self" (p. 193). These same characteristics were evident in the work of Fromm and Berger *et al.*

Packard does not address what is clearly one of the least satisfactory aspects of the new community, and one which contributes to the perceived alienation: its lack of history. The actor embodies his own history, and must approach a new experience as a historic being meeting an ahistoric situation, in that all participants in the event are experiencing a "beginning". The phrase, "let me tell you where I'm coming from" has become commonly used in response to encounter group situations, where one must provide a link between one's past and one's *choice* to join this group. Similarly, the resumé, the medical chart, the portfolio, the school record – in general, face-sheet data – all serve to make one's past readable and accessible to a potential like-other.

Being an actor with a biography and confronted with a world of present-oriented, experience-oriented others, where there is a lack of continuity, invites confusion. Self as grounded historically in an authentic community, where familiarity is generated temporally and spatially, is challenged by the immediate demand that familiarity be generated without the conventional time and space associations. Communication in the establishment of community is brief and direct, and may occur in any place. It is the *conflict* between the myth of time- and space-bound community and the reality of the freeing of community from such constraints, that causes a sense of loss, of alienation. So, for Packard,

Man needs a community; he needs continuity. Being a full-fledged card-carrying member of a community is not incompatible – as some assume – with being a free full-fledged individual. It can be, since the community functions through co-operation, consensus and regulations, but it need not be. The community, by encouraging interaction between people, can contribute greatly to the individual's sense of self-respect and can provide opportunities for self-fulfillment. Both contribute to an individual's sense of identity. (p. 257)

For Packard, it is not enough to have a society of "one-layer communities" where people orient to each other *solely* on the basis of interest. Such communities demand the authenticity which only communities *as* communities can offer, and he argues for their creation where the objective of community is part of the planning process. In other words, the kind of communities needed should preserve the delicate balance between choice and accident. This is currently not the case. Choice resists believing the extent of its power; it still feels safest when clinging to the apronstrings of accident. Consequently, we find the paradox of the nation of strangers: that one can be "everyone's friend" in the manner of the other-directed actor. This has led to a real confusion between publicity and privacy, which will be examined in Chapter Four.

There is a sense of excitement in recognizing the translatability of self through the increasing standardization of the language of membership throughout the global village — yet this is tempered by an increasingly specific selectivity about the groups within which one chooses membership. Thus although membership is encoded, the language becomes increasingly more discursive. The member must learn not only the language of the group to which he belongs, but also how to differentiate between that group and others. Communicative competence in a number of language varieties, and the ability to discern through marginal differentiation between speech communities, is a requisite skill. As Hymes (1972b) notes,

As functioning codes, one may find one language, three languages; dialects widely divergent or divergent by a hair; styles almost mutually incomprehensible, or barely detectable as different by the outsider; the objective linguistic differences are secondary and do not tell the story. What must be known is the attitude toward the differences, the functional role assigned to them, the use made of them. (p. 289)

The danger of listening too closely to Packard is that what might otherwise be taken for individualism and self-determination is perceived as alienation, loneliness, and uncertainty of self. It is not necessarily preferable, from the individual's point of view, to have conflict-free society. Reminiscent of tradition-direction, such a condition would suggest limited choices or no choice at all, or worst of all, complacency. It is the ultimate end of Fromm's path of escape from freedom. As long as uncertainty and dissatisfaction exist, actors will continue grappling with their relationship to the language of membership and will not yet acquiesce to other-direction as a preferable mode of social organization.

5. The Migratory Elite: Education for Strangeness

In *The Migratory Elite* (1963), Musgrove confronts the very problems which arise in Packard. For Musgrove, the main question concerns the education of what he calls the "new class" — the migratory elite whose careers revolve around their ability to move frequently and to adapt to alien places and cultures.

In Musgrove's vision, there is no question that mobility is a problem for social organization; one which will not go away. He maintains that institutions will have to meet this problem by changing in response to social organization, rather than remaining static while the world changes around them.

Musgrove suggests that the combination of alienation, urbanization, and excellence generates an achievement-oriented individual who will be prone to move, probably overseas.[16] The member of the migratory elite is adventurous, lacks a sense of place, and has an identity neither with place nor community but with self. Musgrove's actor retains vestiges of inner-direction. His frequent moves and confrontation with different languages of membership, however, make him face the necessity of adaptability, the necessity of other-direction.

Rather than lament the modern age, Musgrove regards it as a vast new opening of the world to the promising youth of England:

The educated man of the second half of the twentieth century must have, in his youth, the opportunity to saturate himself in alien worlds, to liberate himself from his own. His education must not make him the prisoner of his age and culture; he must move with confidence yet sensitivity in worlds to which he is a stranger. (p. 171)

In order to educate for other-direction, however, the role of the school in society must undergo a fundamental change. Musgrove regards the school system in England as one of pandering traditionalism. This attitude only serves to make it more difficult for the mobile ones to adapt to a life of difference. Better to educate them in the mode of social organization (other-direction) which they will be forced to employ once mobile.

The school rather than the parent is the appropriate mediator of a rapidly changing culture; it has the capacity to transcend parochialism and impart universalistic values, attitudes, skills and role dispositions in preparation for life on a wider stage; it prepares the child for effective contact (and competition) with his fellows beyond the confines of his local world. (p. 88)

Musgrove is therefore calling for education for other-directedness. This translates into education to be a "good reader". The successfully socialized other-directed member will be well-versed in learning the codes required for membership; he will be the purely adaptable one, the one who can be at home everywhere, *yet is home nowhere.*

The successfully mobile have not only intelligence but a capacity to give up existing social relationships and to form new but superficial (and more profitable) ones at a higher social level. This gift is useful in their upward climb, but may prove but a poor protection against the stresses that the climb entails. (pp. 116-117)

How does one educate for other-directedness without risking the formation of an "artificial" community as Packard has identified? Berger *et al.* hint that the nation state provides the cultural basis for shared membership by all. This type of hegemony, it seems, is most effectively transmitted through the schools, especially those which conform to a state-run curriculum.

The solution that Musgrove offers is to provide the tools for other-direction within the state institution of the school, while at the same time ensuring the continuity, security, and source of identity provided by the "natural" community of the family. This approach takes elements from both tradition-direction and other-direction: the stability and unqualified acceptance of the family, which mirrors the "home" of the tradition-directed society where by virtue of kinship and habit one is a member, is preserved; however the stultifying constraint of accident is freed. Because the society on the "outside" offers vast opportunities for choice in every dimension of the actor's life, education for other-direction satisfies the desire for "freedom to"; however both dilettantism and alienation are avoided when the generation of identity is grounded in family.

The distinction between private and public is very strong for Musgrove. Whereas the individual's identity in tradition-directed society was virtually all public, in that it was closely bound up with the collective identity of the group; and the individual's identity in inner-directed society was virtually all private, in that there was a keen effort to disassociate with group identity; the two categories become obscured in other-direction, as Slater has shown. As we have seen, the social organization of strangeness creates an actor who is both within and without – a member and a stranger. Before Musgrove, the stranger had been regarded as the alienated member – the one who lost self in favor of other. But now the other-directed actor may be heard as a public relations man – the one who belongs in two worlds: the private, in which he contends with his everyday exigencies; and the public, in which he deals with the rest of the world. Only a clear distinction between the two will prevent the loss of both.

6. The Organization Man: Adaptability as a Way of Life

In Whyte's *The Organization Man* (1956), adaptability becomes a prescription for survival within one's society. Whereas Musgrove saw England as a place to be left in favor of more cosmopolitan pastures, Whyte sketches the contemporary reality of America as one which demands a constant orientation to change, and therefore adjustment, by its members. The central paradox of modernity seems to be that there could be a "public worship of individualism" (p. 5), in which public and private life become indistinguishable, as hinted at by Musgrove.

The "organization man" is caught up in a social organization of strangeness which demands adaptability as a way of life. Typically he is a business man whose survival in the corporation relies on his ability to become a "company man", involving conformity with company rules, standards and policies, and a willingness to travel: in short, "fitting in".

Whyte suggests that there exists a social ethic which resists allowing the individual the freedom of choice, of "spontaneous collectivization", and instead worships the group for the sake of the group, resulting in a "false collectivization" (p. 49). This social ethic opposes the "protestant ethic" which is one of working for self and by self, and is the mode of ensuring conformity which produces the organization man.

The vestiges of tradition-direction are apparent in the other-directedness of this social ethic. The idea of membership as mere accident gives credence to the belief that familiarity can be engendered "artificially" through the creation of groups not on the basis of choice of like-others but rather on the basis of organizational goals and the mandate of "efficient production". Strangers are thrown together in organizations and expected to generate rapport and "company spirit"; a seemingly diverse set of individuals is "rationalized" into a uniform whole, complete with a homogeneous identity and a spirit of consensus.

This misplaced version of community stems from a real fear of individual creativity, which translates itself into an ideal of group production:

> The most misguided attempt at false collectivization is the current attempt to see the group as a creative vehicle. Can it be? People very rarely *think* in groups; they talk together, they exchange information, they adjudicate, they make compromises. But they do not think; they do not create. (p. 51)

This artificial group substitutes group responsibility for individual autonomy. Collective decision-making, under the mandate of democracy, removes from the individual the role of the subject of creation and imposes instead that of the object of creation. The real danger is not that creation will not happen, but that the individual will give himself over to the group such that creation will not be desired. This is the strongest case encountered for the risk of "automaton conformity" expressed by Fromm: the dulling of the spontaneous adventurer that was fostered by inner-direction, and the genesis of the one who orients to the group, any group, to provide direction.

Whyte's successful "organization man" is ironically the one who transcends the organization man. He is the executive who has learned to distance himself from this social ethic. He has given himself over to the group in so far as he functions within the organizational situation of accident; yet at the same time he has resisted the demand that creativity be entirely relegated to the group. In other words, the successful "organization man" is the one who has used the organization for his own ends. For Whyte this results in a condition of loneliness: the proverbial "It's lonely at the top". Because the competing demands of group identification and "leadership" are ever-present for the executive, he is forced to be reflective about the place he takes *vis-à-vis* the group. In this sense he is an aberration:

He knows that he can never fully "belong". The continuity that he seeks in his life is work that satisfies *his* drives, and thus he remains always a potential rebel. In a letter to the author, Richard Tynan describes the situation well: "For the sake of his career the executive must appear to believe in the values of his company, while at the same time he must be able to ignore them when it serves his purpose. What is good for the company is good for the executive – with exceptions. *Perceiving these exceptions is the true executive quality.*" (p. 165)

According to this formulation, the organization must be transcended. The tension between self and system – protestant ethic and social ethic – must be addressed and a choice must be made: in order to survive *as self* within the system, one must break with the model of false collectivization. The tension seems greatest at the point of *becoming* an executive, for it is here that a decision must be made regarding one's loyalty to the group.

Whyte is arguing that in the age of the organization man (other-direction), there is no turning back to the protestant ethic (inner-direction) – nor should there be a desire to – but that members should strive to mediate between the two, in the form of individualism *within* the organization. One must be entirely a part of it before one can get away from it – one is in a sense a product of the organization, but one learns to distinguish between self and system.

This formulation is yet another way of coming to the conclusion which has been emerging from the previous analyses: that in a highly symbol-conscious society, communicative competence is a prerequisite for creative speech. Unalienated autonomy within other-direction suggests that one can be a member both in the accidental (false collectivization) sense as well as in the intentional (spontaneous collectivization) sense.

One of the mechanisms in this process of self-reflection is the transient nature of the organization man. As Whyte points out,

The man who leaves home is not the exception in American society but the key to it. Almost by definition the organization man is a man who left home and, as it was said of the man who went from the Mid-west to Harvard, kept on going. (p. 269)

The community of strangers so produced takes form, as "they assimilate one another, and the fact that they all left home can be more important in bonding them than the kind of home they left is in separating them" (p. 270). The organization becomes their home, their situation of comfort. That which has been left behind is lost forever, Whyte maintains. It is replaced by an abstract uniformity in which an I.B.M. executive could say, "'The training . . . makes our men interchangeable'" (p. 276). Whyte continues:

And is not this the whole drift of our society? We are not interchangeable in the sense of being people without difference, but in the externals of existence we are united by a culture increasingly national. And this is part of the momentum of mobility. The more people move about, the more similar the American environments become, and the more similar they become, the more people move about. (p. 276)

The sense of place for the organization man is implicated in a condition of interchangeability. The "package" communities as well as the people who inhabit them become so similar that to live in one is to live in any; to work with one organization man is to work with any one.

6.1. Adaptability as a Way of Life

The key to the organization man lies in adjustment:

a recurrent cycle of "arrival and departure" – an ability to leave one set of friends and circumstances and affiliate with another, and to repeat this whenever necessary, and repeat it again. (p. 278)

The organization man has no commitment to "home" other than the omnipresent, interchangeable "home" of the company. The most successful one is the adaptable one. The ability to *adjust* is the most valuable attribute within the organization.

Yet the very demand for adjustment speaks to an underlying condition of *maladjustment:* one has to adjust to the fundamental maladjustment of other-direction. Where adjustment requires that one could "fit in" anywhere, it also reveals that there is a constant need to adjust to the fact that the community in which "fitting in" is no problem – the traditional context of familiarity – has ceased to be a presence in the social organization of strangeness. The organization man orients to all situations as strange ones, as demanding a "fitting in". So the organization presents itself as a community in which one is invited to "make oneself at home" – yet the very effort to do so precludes the possibility that one could ever be, spontaneously, "at home".

Whyte does not disparage this adaptability, however; instead, he regards it as a necessity:

The more small [roots], in short, the easier the transplanting. The transients do hunger for deeper roots, but because they have sought so hard they have found something of what they have been looking for. They are beginning to find it in one another. Through a sort of national, floating co-operative, they are developing a *new* kind of roots. The roots are, to be sure, shallow – but like those of the redwood tree, even shallow roots, if there are enough of them, can give a great deal of support. (p. 289)

But the question arises as to what it is that these frail roots cling to: Adjustment to what? The constant, the unchanging element for the organization man, turns out to be the need for adjustment itself. Adjustment becomes a way of life; that which is adjusted to becomes a mere contingency. A life of adaptability is also one of publicity; of belongingness. The web of roots needs to be hopelessly intertwined in order to subsist; the lone shallow root has neither soil nor company; neither nurturance nor community. In this context, Whyte points out, the ones who are successful, *i.e.* in the "executive category", recognize this tension:

Above all, they do not get too close. The transients' defense against rootlessness, as we have noted, is to get involved in meaningful activity; at the same time, however, like the seasoned ship board traveller, the wisest transients don't get too involved. (p. 364)

For Whyte, the real tragedy is not that adaptability has become a way of life, but that it has happened within the context of the organization; within the tyrannical dictates of the group. As he says, it is one thing for a society to feel that "they are all in the same boat". But the real question should be, "Where is the boat going?" (p. 395). The organization man is indeed the victim of a tyranny of the group; and "he is doing it for what he feels are good reasons, but this only makes the tyranny more powerful, not less" (p. 396).

Whyte has shown how a social ethic which preaches adaptability as a way of life obviates the distinctions between private and public, inside and outside, home and away, familiar and strange. It is the realization of the global speech community — one in which the members "talk the same language" (p. 277). The consequence of this unilingual society is silence: in obviating difference the need to speak disappears.

What must be retrieved is a version of adaptability which preserves the possibility of community as something which need not be artificial. To do this it seems wise to return to the question, "Adaptability to what?". It is an unfortunate fact that the authors addressed have created ideal types of social organization which are fundamentally distinct and unnegotiable. It is only with Whyte that the extreme impoverishment of the individual is made compelling; it is also Whyte who provides a ray of hope, through his notion of adaptability. In his usage, adaptability implies choice and desire. It is neither coping nor toleration. Adjustment suggests that that to which one is adjusting is desired; that adjustment itself is desired; and that the individual is free to adjust or not.

Adjustment does not entail the rejection of the accidental community of tradition-direction as a coercive situation of company, in which membership is not desired. There is another version of accidental community. It has been suggested that other-direction leads members to relate to each other anonymously, yet on the basis of shared interests. One assumes that there are "like-others" out there, and it is merely a process of discovering them, often through groups or functions specifically organized for this purpose (*e.g.* professional associations, interest groups, travel groups, hobby groups, encounter groups). It is assumed by Whyte that such "accidental" communities can be generated through choice; but that most "anonymous functionaries" act as though they had no such choice. There is a struggle involved in coming to the position of choice. Within the ideal type of the social organization of other-direction, the hegemony of the "social ethic" of the group as tyrant is pervasive. The executive, in Whyte's vision, is one who has transcended that hegemony; the future migratory elite of Musgrove must achieve a distance from their compliance to other-direction in order to survive; Packard's actor must strive to locate self in a nation of strangers; Berger *et al.*'s homeless mind must find a home; Fromm's automaton must become "free to". There is consensus that "adaptability", the survival of other-direction, requires that "self" not be lost. Does it imply, therefore, a return to inner-direction? Whyte, Musgrove and Packard have shown quite compellingly that survival must be *in terms of* the existing order – which is one of other-direction. To withdraw would be to deny one's participation in social organization, to deny the conditions for community which have emerged.

Perhaps what is needed, as Musgrove suggests, is the collective freedom to explore identity. This means a fundamental loosening of the talons of the group; an easing of the social ethic – such that "self" (whatever that might be) is not lost in the process. Riesman echoes these sentiments in a call for the "autonomous self". Here, the term "adjustment" takes on a different meaning than for Whyte. Riesman suggests that those actors who conform most closely to the social character are the "adjusted". So, Fromm's "automaton" and Whyte's "organization man" both fall into this category.

The "adjusted" are those whom for the most part we have been describing. They are the typical tradition-directed, inner-directed, or other-directed people – those who respond in their character structure to the demands of their society or social class at its particular stage on the curve of population. Such people fit the culture as though they were made for it, as in fact they are. (Riesman, 1961: 241-242)

The term "anomic" refers to the maladjusted, and corresponds to the current use of "alienated". The anomic can not adjust to the character expected of them, and may find other ways of relating to the mode of social organization. Finally, the ones who can transcend rule, Riesman calls "autonomous": "those who on the whole are capable of conforming to the behavioral norms of their society ... but are free to choose whether to conform or not" (p. 242). Riesman's autonomous man embodies the ideal of "adaptability" as it has been put forward above.

Both anomie and autonomy are clearly deviations from the standard

(p. 250), adjustment to the standard being maintained by two mechanisms, which have appeared in other forms above, which Riesman calls "false personalization" and "enforced privatization". Corresponding to Whyte's notion of "false collectivization" is "false personalization" − that which sees accident as a reason for sociability and efficiency in the work place. Riesman also introduces the notion of "enforced privatization" to depict the leisure time which results from an increasingly standardized and bureaucratized conception of work. He sees leisure as a prescribed activity which is defined by one's "place",

consumed in guilty or anxious efforts to act in accordance with definitions of one's location on the American scene, a location which, like a surviving superstition, the individual cannot fully accept or dare fully to reject. (p. 285)

The choices open to the adjusted member are virtually preprogrammed, and both "false personalization" in the work place and "enforced privatization" in leisure are barriers to autonomy. They do not invite the member to question; they do not invite the spontaneous behavior called for by Fromm and Whyte, nor the seeking out of like-others called for by Packard, nor the seeking out of difference called for by Musgrove − all of which are characteristics of the autonomous actor, rare as he may be.

Both false personalization and enforced privatization emerge in the age of other-direction, and it is in this stage that Riesman sees the most difficulty in attaining autonomy; yet at the same time the most potential. He claims that other-direction inherently discourages individualism, as has been shown; however, the potential for autonomy lies in the hope that self might somehow assert itself (although "how" is not made clear) *through* the emphasis on communication brought about in other-direction.

In many ways, autonomy as outlined above is a utopian ideal. Riesman shows the power of the desire to conform in the areas of work and leisure as being enormously pervasive. It is not the purpose of this chapter to propose a manifesto for utopia; rather, I would like to address my remaining comments to the role of *myth* in presenting a strong barrier to autonomy, as it creates both adjustment (through the collective false consciousness that other-direction is good) and anomie (or alienation − through the lament for a home in the style of tradition-direction).

7. Protean Man: Home as Myth

It is human history which converts reality into speech, and it alone rules the life and the death of mythical language. (Barthes, 1976: p. 110)

Lifton (1968) has used the term "protean man" to typify the well-socialized, adaptable member of modern society:

> We know from Greek mythology that Proteus was able to change his shape with relative ease − from wild boar to lion to dragon to fire to flood. But what he did find difficult, and would not do unless seized and chained, was to commit himself to a single form, the form most his own, and carry out his function of prophecy. We can say the same about protean man, but we must keep in mind his possibilities as well as his difficulties. (pp. 16-17)

Protean man is the creature of two historical developments associated with modernity. First is what Lifton calls "historical dislocation", "the break in the sense of connection which men have long felt with the vital and nourishing symbols of their cultural tradition − symbols revolving around family, idea systems, religions, and the life cycle in general" (p. 16). Second is what Lifton designates as the "flooding of imagery" through mass communications networks, which "permit each individual to be touched by everything, but at the same time cause him to be overwhelmed by superficial messages and undigested cultural elements ..." (p. 16).

Lifton suggests that the underlying problem for protean man is change itself. Change, the inevitable tide that sweeps up even the most unwilling member into the flow, is awesome in its speed, direction, and control. We look to change − primarily in the form of technology − as a force above us, that subjugates us, that we participate in only to the extent that as consumers of technology we finance its perpetuation.

Change, as a "mode of transformation", makes actors long for a time and place in which they had "more control". The tendency of protean man is to mythologize the past as an era of choice, and to fantasize about a restoration of traditional ways:

> Involved in all of these patterns is a profound psychic struggle with the idea of change itself. For here too protean man finds himself ambivalent in the extreme. He is profoundly attracted to the idea of making all things, including himself, totally new − to the "mode of transformation". But he is equally drawn to an image of a mythical past of perfect harmony and prescientific wholeness, to the "mode of restoration". Moreover, beneath his transformationism is nostalgia, and beneath his restorationism is his fascinated attraction to contemporary forms and symbols. Constantly balancing these elements midst the extraordinarily rapid change surrounding his own life, the nostalgia is pervasive, and can be one of his most explosive and dangerous emotions. (pp. 25-26)

As much as the nostalgic desire to return to a state of tradition-direction has emerged through the literature, so has the risk of any sense of community, accidental or otherwise, being lost in favor of artificial or false collectivization. In either case, it seems that we have become imprisoned by the cultural definition of home. It is necessary to come to see both strategies as emerging from a mythological relationship to home. Toward this end,

Barthes' article, "Myth today" (1976), a major contribution to semiotic theory, presents myth as a type of speech, and its reading as involving both the "myth reader" and the "myth consumer".[17]

Barthes presents myth as something which merely states — it does not evoke. If it evokes, then it is seen as an instrument and therefore fails as myth. It is only for the one who reads myth as myth (his critical myth reader as opposed to his innocent myth consumer) that myth is allowed to evoke, to show its colors as speaking a "stolen language". It is only the myth reader who may see myth as a necessary replacement of that which is with that which must be evoked.

Riesman, Fromm, Berger *et al.,* Packard, Musgrove and Whyte are all innocent myth consumers in that they do not see their participation in the myth; they do not recognize that their version of an "authentic community" is embodied by their very words rather than an empirical condition. The success of myth is, however, that the words *become* the empirical condition.

"How does [the myth consumer] receive this particular myth *today?"* is the significant question, for it embodies the temporality which grounds myth (p. 129). Myth is necessary when the "is" does not approximate the "ought to be". The way myth is heard *today* asks, therefore, how the present is transformed by myth to become the nonpresent "ought to be" — it asks how today is reassured (although it is only seen as reassuring by the myth reader; the myth consumer sees it as reflecting in the first order) by myth.

Myth reading takes place at both first- and second-order levels (see Figure 2). First-order reading is done from within myth, with little interest in "reading" *per se.* The myth reader, however, imposes a second-order semiological framework, as being evidence that there is a clear break between the "is" and the "ought to be", but not in the mind of the myth consumer. So it is that myth "transforms history into nature" (p. 129), into a first-order, taken for granted fact of life.

Myth is a comfortable place to hide. As Barthes suggests, it is apolitical speech: it denies the ground from which it grows but sees itself as self-perpetuating, as immortal. It could not do otherwise. Myth thrives by masking in the guise of reflecting; and, like the emperor with his new clothes, it sustains itself by never imagining that it could be wrong.

To debunk the myth of home is not necessarily the interest here, for as Barthes has shown, that in itself would entail the generation of a new myth:

It thus appears that it is extremely difficult to vanquish myth from the inside: for the very effort one makes in order to escape its stranglehold becomes in its turn the prey of myth: myth can always, as a last resort, signify the resistance which is brought to bear against it. Truth to tell, the best weapon against myth is perhaps to mythify it in its turn, and to produce an *artificial myth:* and this reconstituted myth will in fact be a mythology. (p. 135)

There are two ways in which the notion of home as myth can be useful. The first addresses the relation of the modern stranger to myth; the second regards the need to see the social implications of the pervasive myth of home.

The stranger is a reader of myths, because he can not consume them. Being an outsider implies illiteracy in the first-order reading of mythologies, for that is the language of membership. Rather, the stranger, like the second-order reader of myths, sees myth as myth because it is that which is in need of explanation yet sees itself to be self-explanatory.

Figure 2. Barthes' Semiological Chain*

Language	1. Signifier	2. Signified	
MYTH	3. Sign I. SIGNIFIER		II. SIGNIFIED
	III. SIGN		

*Source: Barthes (1976: 115)

This is not to say that the stranger does not participate in a different set of myths, or further that those myths will be lost once their origins are left behind. The myth that "America is the land of opportunity" comes to mind. The "truth" held in this belief may motivate the stranger to travel to America in search of fortune; however the fortune is defined not in terms of the "reality" of the American lifestyle (that "reality" being that immigrants often have a harder time than indigenous members and if so are considered by those members to be "misfortunate") but in terms of the "ought to be" produced by the originator of the myth (because the new life is better along the lines of the promised fortune, the immigrant sees himself as "fortunate"). The transformation of the outsider governed by one set of myths generated by "home", into an insider who comes to see the relative hardship of his life through the myth of the new society in which he desires membership, entails a transformation from the innocent myth-consumption of one community's myths to the innocent myth-consumption of another's. Membership in a community entails the unquestioning adoption of the myth-consuming stance. Even the professional myth reader is an innocent consumer of the myth that myth may be read. It is only this knowledge which prevents this analysis from taking the position of myth-debunking; and it is the constant grappling with this knowledge which forces the sociologist to reflect upon his own status as a consumer of the very myths he claims to read. The trained observer as the prototypical stranger — as one caught between myth consumption and myth reading — between publicity and privacy — between tradition-direction and other-direction — will be the focus of Chapter Three.

The social implications of the myth of home involve the hegemonic throwback to tradition-direction within a context of other-direction. Myth states that there is such a thing as home, according to the definitions set out by tradition-direction. The "alienated" ones that we find today, therefore, are those who read "myth today" and find that they are not part of the "ought to be". Home no longer exists as an independent "is" — a fact which is only available, it seems, to the sociologist and the stranger: both, as the readers of myth rather than the consumers of myth, can see the disparity between ideality and reality, caused by the strength of myth to deny that there could never be a distinction between the two.

The alienation noted by the authors cited is a product, therefore, not of modernization so much as of myth. Myth denies the social impact of modernization and blames the individual for not having a home. Alienation occurs when there is a fundamental difference between ideality and reality — through how life is dreamed and how it is lived — and when that difference is masked by artificial attempts to deny it.

In the case of the myth of home, there is no room for the reality of social change (the shift to other-direction) to assert itself in social organization. The myth that home is a place of security and familiarity is so strong that even the demand that social reorganization occur in light of the death of tradition-direction, fails. Myth evokes sentimentality, nostalgia; it resurrects the home of tradition-direction by denying that it could ever be dead. Consequently, however, those who are living out other-direction with the (social) ethic of tradition-direction are deeply dissatisfied: their lives lack meaning. Those who do not have such a home are presented by myth as failing. The stranger, an inevitable product of other-direction and an essential member of the other-directed society, is rejected by tradition-direction as one who could never be a member.

The social organization of strangeness is one which occurs despite myth. Even with myth against one, one must survive. The tragedy is that for as long as myth maintains the sanctity of tradition-direction, members who do not live out that dream, those members becoming more and more numerous, become stranded in between two worlds: the one left behind, and the one just beyond their grasp. Grasping for membership when home is myth entails a perpetual striving for an elusive state that fails to satisfy either tradition-directed or other-directed society.

8. A Redefinition: Home as a Moveable Feast

For the theorists addressed, the central theme has been that loss of self occurs with modernity. Concurrently, a "nation of strangers" emerges where communicative normalization breeds strangeness, to self as well as to other. There is a nostalgic sense of loss with regard to "home", and modern woman and man are regrettably shallow and without community. It has been contended that "home" as reminisced about in this way is a myth. As myth it is firmly embedded in the language of membership; it is a cultural icon which proves to be pervasive in its impact.

The myth that it is possible to go back to the tradition-directed round of life must be dispelled with. There is no turning back: even the choice to "go back to the land" remains first of all a choice. The choice to situate self, however, may also be a myth, in light of Fromm's treatment of freedom. But is this not a basic premise of sociology? That one may feel free to do that which one must do would seem to be a necessity for an unalienated way of being. The mode of social organization, of ensuring conformity, must have at its root the *community* to which conformity is ensured; to work, myth must convince the member that there is no myth. It needs, therefore, to convince that there is no other community which could compete for his membership.

In tradition-directed society, community was fixed both in terms of place and membership. What we now face is a myth which fails to recognize that community may be changing in light of changing modes of social organization. Lamenting the "breakdown of tradition" may in fact be the source of the "alienation" which has been identified. The propagation of the myth that there still *could* be tradition-direction despite the evident changes which social organization has undergone with modernity invites an anomic response to the rules of social organization. Instead, home and community need to be reformulated in light of what we know rather than what we remember. If place and membership cease to be fixed, home may take on a richer sense not tied to tradition. Mythically, home is accidental and determined. One's "home town" is a constant which anchors one's identity. Modernity demands that identity be portable; that you not only wear your heart on your sleeve, but your home in your heart. Now the maxim, "Home is where the heart is", may be heard as distinct from a fixed sense of place. "Where I hang my hat is home" may have been the myth of the inner-directed one; for the other-directed, home becomes a situation of comfort, of community with like-others.

The apparent reluctance among members to accept wholeheartedly the demise of spatial proximity as the primary determinant of community, as expressed in myth, indicates that membership orientation remains a very strong driving force for the modern stranger. He wants to belong, to be a part. But the question is, a part of what? How is he to define a group, or to define himself as a potential member, when traditional signposts of membership, like those which existed for tradition-directed actors, have disappeared? With what eyes is he to see himself as rooted when the soil refuses to yield? The easy security provided by tradition-direction is the kind that does not ask his opinion, that does not free him to feel and to choose. But choice itself, however limited, looks for easy answers. The home that is *chosen*, then, becomes the goal of the modern stranger.

Home as a Moveable Feast. I would like to propose that in a world of other-direction, home is a moveable feast; and the modern stranger is the harvester. Home as a moveable feast speaks to home as that which one brings along, like a suitcase, and sets up where one might. But it is not a living out of a suitcase, which implies temporariness, sojourning, and a home to go back to. Rather it is to say that "home is where the heart is", where "heart" suggests "interest" (as opposed to necessarily "family"). Home is the overarching speech community, to which one brings one's package of interests; one's unique biography. Unlike inner-direction, where home is the accident of the "company compound"; home as a moveable feast suggests that the individual comports the desire for a home, and becomes a willing and active member in a community of like-others, which provides for him a situation of comfort.

Home is a moveable feast because it is inherently translatable. There has never been a society in which the language of membership has been so standardized and self-evident, yet where the room for self to find its own home through discursiveness has been so great. Home can be moveable because the stranger is able to go anywhere – and leave – and become almost instantly a member on the level of general acceptability, although perhaps not on the level of particular interests. The modern stranger need not feel umbilically tied to a "home town" where familiarity prevails, for familiarity is everywhere and nowhere. One is at once a member and a stranger; one is home yet away.

Fromm's plea for a mode of social organization in which one is "free to" be rather than "free from" being now begs a response. If we were ever free to be anything, it is now; if we were ever free from being anything, it is now. Now the stranger wears the guise of the friend, and what appears to be strange evokes familiarity. Home and away can no longer be spoken of as discrete from each other. A new ethos of familiarity in strangeness has emerged.

Notes

1. Riesman's categories are clearly ideal types which may not necessarily be found in any particular case. He is used here because he goes to considerable lengths to develop categories which seem to be representative of much of the literature on modernity. The critical point to be taken is that the society which produces a stranger such as Simmel's had definite rules of exclusion and inclusion that are no longer applicable in urbanized North America. The accuracy of exact details and claims of Riesman's study, which may be debated (especially when applied to non-western societies) is not of concern in the present study.

2. This progression from "general" or objective ideal type to "personal" or subjective ideal type in "coming to know the other" is an important consideration regarding establishment of membership/strangeness, which Schutz (1967) has dealt with extensively.

3. There is a difference between the means utilized for expression (externals) and that which is expressed (internals) which some theorists, such as Ewen and Ewen (1982), tend to neglect. In reflecting upon the ways in which mass culture has come to determine for the actor how he is to identify "authentic experience", it must not necessarily be assumed that the meaning held *for the actor* is any less authentic in the mode of other-direction than in previous modes. In *Channels of Desire*, the Ewens opt for a virtual eclipse of the actor's will in defining authentic experience, in favor of a cultural imperialistic stance which leaves no room for self-definition.

4. The concept of marginal differentiation stems from Veblen's term "invidious distinction", introduced in *The Theory of the Leisure Class* (1953 [fp 1899]). Almost concurrently, in 1904, Simmel identified the two drives of "imitation" and "differentiation" as necessary for the social process of fashion (1971a). Earlier, in the 1890s, Tarde (1969) claimed that the three social processes of invention, imitation, and opposition are necessary counterparts in cultural creation.

5. Simmel, in clearly delimiting "internals" and "externals", suggests that he was writing at a time of inner-direction. His work on fashion and the stranger must be taken with this in mind.

6. Chapter Three addresses this problem, and considers the effect of self-perception as an insider or an outsider on the act of reading.

7. Style in dress, custom and mannerisms is an almost universal tool in differentiating social groupings. This is not an attempt to suggest that such recognition is only possible in modern society. My intent is to use Riesman's types in order to provide a basis for answering the question, "How is it possible for humans to adapt socially to changing conditions of membership?". To this end, the changing nature of "recognition" and "negotiation" in the language of membership will be examined.

8. The term "subculture" is being used with caution, as the definitional implications may not be fully embodied in the present context of a "community of like-others". Self-identification both politically and culturally, which is often associated with subcultures, is not necessarily a component of "communities of like-others" in general.

9. Holiday Inn, McDonald's, and Melitta are registered trade marks.

10. The hegemonic influence of monopoly capital over the lifestyle of individuals is clearly the major factor contributing to the other-directed mode of social organization. The reader is asked to assume that underlying causality and to treat the present undertaking as one which attempts to make sense of the place of the stranger in this new world. Above all I attempt to demonstrate how incredibly

adaptive humans are to material conditions, and how in fact we are able to treat the givenness of something which for most of us, for most of the time, appears beyond our control, as something that we may control and in turn may use as a source of identification. See Appendix A for further comments.

11. I am indebted to H.T. Wilson for this observation.

12. See Schutz, "The Homecomer" (1945).

13. H.T. Wilson has commented that this trend may in fact be reversing itself, as the need for physical mobility is decreasing through rapid sophistication of mass communications and the growing use of computer terminals in the work force. Perhaps there is a link, however, between attitudes necessary for successful adaptation to the physical mobility that was necessitated in the fifties, sixties, and seventies, and the current demand for adaptation to rapidly changing technology which enables instantaneous transmission of images and ideas. In a sense this communication transcends the physical yet requires a similar shift in thinking such that members may disengage from a spatially proxemic world view.

14. Packard notes that trailer groups may spontaneously erupt on the basis of same-brand trailers, often resulting in going off on long trips together.

15. In a study on the use of companions wanted ads in two Toronto newspapers, Austrom and Hanel (1980) found that most of their sample who were using the ads were secretive about it; and of those who told family and friends most were not met with approval for their actions. The authors conclude that there is considerable resistance to the idea of "advertising for love", by those who do it as well as by those who do not.
    They cite some of the myths associated with the use of these ads:

    Examples of popular notions include the following: 1) Most of the ads are placed by prostitutes or triflers; 2) People who place ads must be "losers"; 3) Placing an ad is degrading; 4) It is dangerous for women; 5) The only people who reply to ads are kooks; 6) Men do not receive very many replies; and 7) Women, on the other hand, receive hundreds of replies. (p. 1)

    Their findings suggest that some of these myths are misleading. The underlying motivation for submitting and responding to the ads is loneliness – something which seems to transcend barriers of occupation, income, or other barometers of "success" – implying that those who use the ads are not necessarily "losers" but just see the ads as an appropriate way of meeting others. The majority of those submitting ads did so because it was an easy, convenient and anonymous way to meet prospective companions.

16. That Musgrove is writing in Britain in the early 1960s is significant here: if he were writing in the United States or Canada at that time, mobility would have been restricted primarily within the country, although in the "global village" of the 1980s Musgrove's "probably overseas" becomes more of a reality in many more parts of the western world.

17. In semiotics, the Saussurian distinction between *signifier* and *signified* is essential to understanding representation. "For Saussure (1966), representation involves a relation between a *signifier* (a denotative sensory stimulus) and a *signified* (a meaning denoted by the signifier). Together, sensory stimulus and attendant meaning constitute a 'sign relation' " (Harman, 1986: 149). For further elaboration see Barthes (1976) and Saussure (1966).

Chapter III
On Being in Between: Observation and Marginality

The passage from the status of stranger to that of guest, then to that of friend and, with luck, eventually to that of quasi-kinship of the accredited sojourner, is familiar to anthropologists from their own experience. (Fortes, 1975: 250)

Chapter Two has demonstrated that marginality is increasingly a condition of modern life. To be marginal is, paradoxically, to be in the main stream. Marginality is also a condition which may be produced through coercion, such as in the case of the refugee, the exile, the outcast; or through wilful estrangement, as with the immigrant, the gypsy, the diplomat, the journalist, the traveller, the ethnographer. Of the latter group who choose marginality as a way of life, professional observers are of particular interest. The explorer, the journalist, and the ethnographer have in common an accountability. They are missionaries whose duty it is to leave the familiar, confront the strange, and report back home as to their findings. This chapter deals with the duty of the professional observer: the task of making the strange familiar. In particular, focus will be on the ethnographer, as one who is asked to preserve the autonomy of the strange while at the same time making it apperceptible within the taken-for-granted language of membership of his "home group".

I will propose that the attitude of being "in between" taken by the professional observer may be generalized to the modern stranger as a technique of adjustment to changing conditions of membership. This attitude in turn can be seen to enable the modern stranger to make productive use of his marginality in the effective navigation of membership by way of the language of membership. I will suggest that it is only through adopting the reflective gaze of in between that the stranger may achieve the necessary "insight and possibility of choice" that Riesman calls for in order to have a "rational system of conduct" (1951: 125). Unless the modern stranger is postulated as capable of adapting through the lens of in between, there is a real danger that he will be seen as a compliant victim of technology and modernization; as one who is frozen "with anxiety and nostalgia".

"People watching" entails a particular form of marginality which has been the subject of much discussion in the ethnographical literature.[1] The opening paragraph of Hortense Powdermaker's book, *Stranger and Friend: The Way of an Anthropologist* (1966), is suggestive of the conflicts entailed in the work of the ethnographer:

> To understand a strange society, the anthropologist has traditionally immersed himself in it, learning, as far as possible, to think, see, feel, and sometimes act as a member of its culture and at the same time as a trained anthropologist from another culture. This is the heart of the participant observation method – involvement and detachment. Its practice is both an art and a science. Involvement is necessary to understand the psychological realities of a culture, that is, its meanings for the indigenous members. Detachment is necessary to construct the abstract reality: a network of social relations including the rules and how they function – not necessarily real to the people studied. (p. 9)

Such is the dilemma faced when coming to "understand a strange society": the observer, a product and envoy of one society, undertakes to make sense of a strange society and bring it home – to translate one world, an alien world, into a familiar one.

The professional observer always comes to the thing to be known as an outsider; for him, being faced with difference inevitably brings up questions of membership. The very promise of *coming to know* is limited by the prospect of *coming to be*. This tension, which will be figured in *spatial* and *temporal* terms, suspends the observer *in between* the poles of home and away. But, unlike the static sense of "suspension" implied by, for instance, the term "post" (in a diplomatic or military sense), the observer is suspended more as if on a trapeze, such that at every moment he is aware of swinging between both the parameters of home and away. Such suspension, which allows the observer to be drawn first to one way of seeing, then to another – swinging back and forth and at some point coming to rest at a comfortable mediation – deserves our attention. This is the form of strangeness which I will call "in between". The observer who stands in between wills away, perhaps forever, the kind of unquestionable membership characterized by trustworthy recipes defining the taken-for-granted world; for in distancing himself from both the familiar and the strange, the observer becomes marginal to both – an outsider.

1. In Between

In the last chapter, home was formulated as a situation of comfort, in a world in which actors are forced to seek it out, and to carry it with them. Home as a moveable feast is suggestive of a multidimensional world of sociability: of a grounding in a language of membership, upon which a tradition of individualism and freedom of association have generated a variety of speech communities in which membership may be achieved. The member of such a society was formulated as one who was in effect a stranger everywhere and at home everywhere; who could find comfort if he worked at it. Take away the underlying structure of commonality — the society of successfully socialized like-others — however, and the universal grounding of home also disappears.

Unlike the modern stranger, for whom strangeness is a product of cultural proximity (possibly mixed with spatial and social distanciation), the one who travels to a foreign culture is faced with sheer difference on the cultural level as well. Language, social practice, social beliefs that are the preserve of the taken-for-granted world at home suddenly loom problematic. Bourdieu (1977) points to the scope of the assault upon the senses:

Every successfully socialized agent thus possesses, in their incorporated state, the instruments of an ordering of the world, a system of classifying schemes which organizes all practices ... [of] the *socially informed body,* with its tastes and distastes, its compulsions and repulsions, with, in a word, all its *senses,* that is to say, not only the traditional five senses — which never escape the structuring action of social determinisms — but also the sense of necessity and the sense of duty, the sense of direction and the sense of reality, the sense of balance and the sense of beauty, common sense and the sense of the sacred, tactical sense and the sense of responsibility, business sense and the sense of propriety, the sense of humour and the sense of absurdity, moral sense and the sense of practicality, and so on. (pp. 123-124)

The professional observer, whose stay in a strange culture is limited by the limitless condition of "having seen enough", is not expected to find comfort in the new place. It is through the lens of home that he is to view, in the microscopic capacity lent by his proximity to social practices, the everyday structuring of the foreign world. And when he reports back, he is to know it as well as "any ethnographer could" who had done his job well. In other words, the ethnographer is expected to maintain an instrumental, interchangeable relation to the society under study, and to never let the professional lens slip down his nose. The license to self-sufficiency and complete adaptability which is the preserve of the wanderer, the hobo, the gypsy, is not extended to the one whose task it is to be ever conscious of the tensions produced by home and away. So for the observer there is a new metaphor: that of "in between".

The concept of in between is definitive of the stranger, and gives added richness to the tension felt by the observer between home and away. In between demands that the dimensions of time and space be seen as *positioning* the stranger, and concomitantly as *variable.* The distance — both spatial and temporal — in between home and away is always changing. It remains to be explored whether this changeability makes one any more or less of a stranger, or whether strangeness itself consists in being in between.

Home is mythologized as that space in which there is complete comfort, total acceptance, unquestioned membership. It may be configured in spatial, social and/or cultural terms, although for the modern stranger cultural proximity is most readily applicable. Away is that space which one may or may not be able to see when looking out from behind a window: unfamiliar territory which lies "beyond". Where familiar and unfamiliar meet, there is a space in between. The laneway, the airport, the border: these empty spaces are gathering places, places for waiting, watching, arriving, taking leave. In between holds out the possibility of many openings, many windows, but it lacks the comforts of home, of the given. In between promises difference; it is a state of expectancy, of discovery, of confrontation; when in between one is always confronting one's own difference. The condition of familiarity is gone; commitment to hearing a new set of existential conditions prevails. "Anything can happen" in between; predictability and communicability are lost; in between is a bizarre world that lacks the dimensions of a world: without rules, without language, without members, without history.

In leaving home, the explorer hungers for the sensation of the discovery of place, the naming of place: while in between he is never indifferent to his surroundings. In between one is still "somewhere": the place of no name becoming a landmark in memory. As a landmark, this place comes to be different from that place. The landmark is configured through the tangible forces of nature, which demand that human life adapt to a particular *environ*, and the human work which has gone into transforming that nature to human ends. The landmark is a place with no name that gains a name; in finding his bearings the one who is in between carves out a trail by making landmarks, by rendering the previously insignificant significant.

The milieu which is felt by this stranger is a subjectively perceived world which touches every sense; which makes its mark upon memory as having a particular character. It lives out its difference, its particularity, for to become a place with a name (*i.e.* to remain in memory, to find a spot in the ongoing *durée* of the traveller) it presents itself as incomplete − as a world to be entered into, experienced, and taken when one leaves. It is nameless; its horizons are undefined until through "having been there" they crystallize in the memory of the traveller.

The place of the imagination ("Egypt") becomes *my* Egypt when the stares from black eyes, the heavy spicy scent of the market, mingled with jasmine perfume and excrement-muddied gutters, can be evoked; the Great Pyramid of Giza is transformed from a wonder of the ancient world of textbook lore to the haunting magnetic force whose claustrophobic interiors evoked a magical transformation of the sandswept infinity beyond to a dark and silent tomb within that time had not touched. The oldest-building-on-earth, the Steppe Pyramid at Sakarra, becomes a silent place ringing with the ancient songs of wind through hollow graves; a land of hiding places and solitude; a safe place for poetry and meditation; a place to which I return again and again *because I know it exists:* I have created it. As author, I authorize its existence, I command it to surface, and I live it again.

One is only "in between" in the moment between arrival and departure. Arrival defines the place; departure defines one's having been there. The in between is in the making it one's own; to know it exists is to create it. The "having been there" is both a necessity and a superfluity. Defoe is Robinson Crusoe; he was certainly on his island, for it became his sanctuary in the milling streets of London (Defoe, 1975: 264-265). Baudelaire too had been to such a place, for how else could he say:

Multitude, solitude: identical terms, and interchangeable by the active and fertile poet. The man who is unable to people his solitude is equally unable to be alone in a bustling crowd. (1947, p. 20)

The traveller, as both the recipient of place and the creator of place, is always interfering. Travel interferes both with the place at which one arrives, stays, and leaves, and with one's itinerary, with one's diary, with one's biography − for in taking it with one, one must make a place for it in one's baggage. The new, displaced weight influences where one can, and will, go to next. Having "done" Egypt, one can now move on; but the direction of that movement is influenced by the transformation incurred in the coming-to-know of Egypt. Being in between is to be open to redirection. It is not to be indifferent to the place that one now inhabits, so much as to make that place a part of one, to absorb it as one gives to it one's presence, to take from it the sensations which in turn are the fabric of which one fashions it. But "it" in turn becomes possessed; Egypt will always be "my Egypt", and will color the next place I go.

Where, in all this, lies home? Home becomes the repository of all places; the situation of comfort which does not purport to be an "in between" nor an end; it may be returned to, but more importantly it may be portable. It is a world of familiarity − populated by the milieu of the present-to-hand as well as that of the beyond − it is the place from which one may relive other places, and from which one may imagine another "in between". Home is never in between because it holds out no surprises. It presents no possibility for moving on, such as open doors and departing planes, but instead it is always waiting to be returned to. Home is so familiar that it stays the same; it anchors everything new. Because it is the same, home evokes imaginations of difference. It is from home that "the grass is always greener", it is from home that one goes "away". But it is always to home that one returns.

The path in between home and away becomes circular: the paradox of away is that it is always seen from afar; once one arrives, having approached it from in between, one is no longer a stranger there: one has come home. But it is never seen as "home" from afar; as a potential home, perhaps, but never as something familiar. The traveller knows when he has found a home because he finds himself living through eyes which have seen other places; fashioning a world which takes the best of those memories, and makes them timeless, placeless, such a part of himself that those which were once in between have found a home themselves.

1.1. Mapping

Being in between is a condition that we seek to overcome. Strangeness begs to become familiarity; the unknown cries out to be reformed into the known. Coming to know, or emerging from in between, is a gradual process. It involves time (between "now" and "then" we gain familiarity) and space (between "here" and "there" we journey — further away from home and attaining closer proximity to our destination). The destination is a situation of comfort; of making the away home. This transformation takes place through the activity of mapping, of naming, of accounting for, and thus of appropriation. The one who conquers the strange owns it.

Mapping is an everyday activity invoked with the confrontation with the strange. It is a sense-making device. Its correspondence to "reality" is irre- levant in that it becomes reality; the comfort achieved through "getting one's bearings" is a real, lived comfort; to know "where one is" according to one's map is to know where one is in relation to the familiar. Mapping, then, transforms the strange to the familiar and that is all; as a sense-making device one's map can never be wrong. To map is to possess, and hence to create. Mapping reifies as does ownership; it claims completion, resolution, famil- iarity, once one has mapped, one no longer has a need for the map; it has become obsolete. It has become part of one's repertoire; a story that one can pass on when "asked directions".

Several of the activities and interests of ethnography may be organized under the rubric of cartography, including seeing everything as important at first until categories are established (paralleled in Glaser and Strauss [1967] by the notion of "theoretical saturation"), taking notes, attempting to delimit and construct the language of membership, attempting to obtain both insiders' and outsiders' views (worm's eye and bird's eye views, res- pectively), and finally the finished product of encoding a version of the problem/group for others that follow to use as their guide, in the form of a "report". Having been planted in a strange culture and suddenly finding herself without bearings in a completely unfamiliar world, Bowen (1954) tells of her sense of loss. The unanswerable questions of where to begin, and what is important here, caused her to begin with what was before her, noting every detail observed as a "social fact" to be reorganized, discarded, or rein-terpreted later once her map had achieved "validity". Powdermaker suggests that the "process" of mapping renders initial efforts obsolete:

> Malinowski had also told us to note down everything we saw and heard, since in the beginning it is not possible to know what may or may not be significant. I faithfully tried to carry out this injunction but, of course, all observation is selective. Later I found that some of the first impressions were keen and important, while others were incorrect or insignificant. (p. 61)

The anthropological stance taken by Bowen and Powdermaker (as well as by Benedict, 1934; Mead, 1928; and others) is one in which one's "first impression" is of a world which exists totally independently of oneself, the observer. The task becomes one of unlocking that world to which there is no obvious key, and of translating it into familiar terms. It is to render that world readable, and hence replicable.

But maps are merely ways of seeing whose grammar is shared by cart-ographers and orienteers — not necessarily by the hills, oceans, cities and peoples they serve to reify. So the interest in mapping, however keenly it demands to be regarded as "objective", however rigidly it claims to abide by reconstituted rules of representation, presents to the orienteer (not to mention the cartographer) a *fait accompli,* a Cook's tour, complete with sightseeing packages and restaurant guide. To the orienteer, a map in hand defines a place as existing and worth travelling to. In Greene's *A Journey Without Maps* (1980), the protagonist has maps in hand yet no self-evident correspondence between the journey and the maps; a desire to walk through Sierra Leone, where Sierra Leone is just a name, a possibility, a place to go and "find out" about Africa.

> It would have been easier if I had been able to obtain maps. But the Republic is almost entirely covered by forest, and has never been properly mapped, mapped that is to say even to the rather rough extent of the French colonies which lie on two sides of it. I could find only two large-scale maps for sale. One issued by the British General Staff, quite openly confesses ignorance; there is a large white space covering the greater part of the Republic, with a few dotted lines indicating the conjectural course of rivers (incorrectly, I usually found) and a fringe of names along the boundary. These names have been curiously chosen: most of them are quite unknown to anyone in the Republic; they must have belonged to obscure villages now abandoned. The other map is issued by the United States War Department. There is a dashing quality about it; it shows a vigorous imagination. Where the English map is content to leave a blank space, the American in large letters fills it with the word "Cannibals". It has no use for dotted lines and confessions of ignorance; it is so inaccurate that it would be useless, perhaps even dangerous, to follow it, though there is something Elizabethan in its imagination. "Dense Forest"; "Cannibals"; rivers which don't exist, at any rate anywhere near where they are put; one expects to find Eldorado, two-headed men and fabulous beasts represented in little pictures in the Gola Forest. (p. 45-46)

Later, Greene relates:

> I only mentioned these plans which came to nothing, these routes which were not
> followed, because they may give some idea of the vagueness of my ideas when I landed
> at Freetown. I had never been out of Europe before; I was a complete amateur at travel
> in Africa. I intended to walk across the Republic, but I had no idea of what route to
> follow or the conditions we would meet. Looking at the unreliable map I had thought
> vaguely that we would go up to the Sierre Leone railway terminus at Pendembu, then
> go across the frontier the nearest way and strike diagonally down to the capital. There
> seemed to be a lot of rivers to cross, but I supposed there would be bridges of some kind;
> there was the forest, of course, but that was everywhere. One apparently reliable book
> I had read on Sierra Leone mentioned a number of prospectors who had crossed the
> border into what was supposed to be an uninhabited part of the forest looking for gold
> and had never returned; but that was a little lower down (the Republic was on the bulge
> of Africa's coast-line, and I could never properly remember the points of the compass).
> (pp. 47-48)

Despite Greene's awareness of the "inaccuracy" of the maps he had in hand,
all reference to the place he was to go to was *vis-à-vis* those maps. "Go up
to", "go across", "strike diagonally down", "a little lower down": map talk
that suggests that what is "known", although wrong, is preferable to the
complete sense of loss of the unknown, speaks beautifully to the absurd
lengths to which faith in maps for getting one's bearings may lead. Also in
this excerpt the forest is ubiquitous and therefore of no import for mapping.
It is precisely because something is "everywhere" that it is not specified
on a map. It is only the *boundaries* between everywhere and somewhere
that are mapworthy. What maps do is to chart out differences in the midst
of sameness; to mark the spaces "in between".

The interest of the cartographer is to approach the uncharted and master
it; to make it real, known, and tangible. In doing so, the successful mapmaker
obliterates the need for maps: once a place has been defined, complete with
landmarks, then it is no longer unknown, no longer the subject of mapmaking. The observer steps forward as the envoy of the culture in which he
claims membership; to confront the strange with the five senses of the group,
and to report back with the facts, with the map which unequivocally positions the unfamiliar *vis-à-vis* the familiar. Whether tentative, as in the case
of the British General Staff map, or pompous, as with the United States
War Department map, they are nonetheless maps. What the grand theorist
has in common with the grounded theorist is that they are cartographers,
and envisage themselves as producing maps which not only can be read but
that members will want to read.

The mapping of the observer occurs at three levels. The first-order map
is like a diary, or a travelogue, in which the traveller/explorer tells what he
saw, without any real interest in convincing or making it believable. Here
we find the accounts of Marco Polo, T.E. Lawrence, and Grey Owl (1935),

for example. The second-order map is that of the mercenary: the journalist or the conquistador whose mission is one of reaffirming; of continuing the known world without encountering resistance. Here we find Antonio de Berrio (Naipaul, 1969), Kipling (Raskin, 1971), and Charles Krause (1978). The third-order map is that which the ethnographer is entrusted with charting: to it belongs a culturally relativist lens, which demands that the *truth* be conveyed — but that it also convince.

First-Order Mapping: The Explorer/Traveller. For the explorer, keeping a record of what he saw is in direct confrontation with the collective wisdom of his culture. The explorer is out to contradict and expand the limits of the "known world". The traveller, who may venture in the completely self-interested desire to "find out", becomes the possessor of a rare gem, "having been there", and hence knows. The personalized creation becomes public property, conventional wisdom; the author, the authority. Travelogue becomes a textbook; traveller, teacher. The readers of the diary or travelogue are consumers of images; they have neither "been there" nor created them, but come to the stories vicariously.

The traveller does not live vicariously. He comes to all as for the first time, and lives it, and is subsequently *lived through* by those at home. Hence travel accounts, slide shows, maps, geography books, replace "being there" for their consumers. The world created by the traveller is in turn re-created in the imaginations of those at home; until, in its familiarity, it becomes a part of home, a part of the mythology of the culture. The far away is possessed through the eyes of the discoverer, who, in coming home, claims (or re-claims) it for home.

Marco Polo was interested in remapping the Orient according to *what he saw (i.e.* the "truth"); in recounting another society of which Europeans "knew" nothing, for their only "knowledge" was grounded in the mystification by the Church of all things unfamiliar as evil/pagan. Grey Owl becomes the absurd epitomization of this traveller. As one whose first "knowledge" of Canada and its "Red Indians" was a vicarious one, drawn from the popular wisdom of the late 19th century British lore, he was to become author of a new version of that world; he was to become a living part of that world, and to create it in such a way as to be re-creatable in the England of the 1930s. As Dickson (1973) relates his story, Grey-Owl (*alias* Archie Belaney) ventured with the dream of "finding out" what it meant to be an Indian. Once he had appropriated "Indian" to the point of *becoming* Indian, Grey Owl set out to produce accounts for the English public of life as an Indian. According to Dickson, the question "Will they buy it?", haunted Grey Owl's struggle to make what was real to him, his world, come to life in another world. This is the same question put by Raskin to Kipling's fiction:

the most important element of any account of difference is that it be convincing — that it bring the reader to it. Real or unreal vanish as questions — the task of the translator is to create a real world that the reader will live vicariously. Thus, *Robinson Crusoe* is a travelogue, in the same way that *The Travels of Marco Polo* can be read as fiction.

For all intents and purposes, "what really happened" did not: the first-order account is given over, as it were, to be read as it might. The comfort which medieval Italy found in relegating *The Travels of Marco Polo* to a vivid imagination; the ease with which Archie Belaney *became* Grey Owl and came to represent the "Red Indian" to British audiences; the lively debate since 17th century England as to whether *Robinson Crusoe* was fact or fiction, attest to this.

Second-Order Mapping: The Journalist/Conquistador. Unlike explorers and travellers, who head for the unknown out of their own sense of adventure, journalists and imperialists are basically functionaries. Their job is to confirm that things are as we would like them to be; to report back on a world that is just as our domestic ideology defines it.

Journalists are assigned objects for observation; are sent as envoys for one form of publication to return with "a story". Knowing what constitutes a story defines the good journalist: he will always know where to look and what details to recount. A good story is in a sense a pregiven reality. The interest of a newspaper or other medium of "news" is in making a compelling presentation such that members will attend to *that* particular station/paper as opposed to another. The medium has therefore to anticipate what its readers would want to read, and look for a story there. The interest in finding out is secondary to the interest in affirming: the newsworthy world has already been mapped; the journalist would be wise to stick to the vision of the world that it is his job to re-create through "stories" rather than attempt to generate new maps.

It is interesting to note that journalists also go by the appellation "correspondents". To "correspond" may be read as either a transitive or an intransitive verb. Given the interest in observing in the first place, both senses of the verb are required and coexist in the "good" journalist; the one who produces "good stories". To correspond in the intransitive sense is to conform with, to ally with. It is to fit in to a pregiven world without question, without rocking the boat. The good journalist exists to affirm the expectations of his readers and therefore must correspond *with* those expectations. To correspond in the transitive sense is to produce letters directed to another; to conduct a conversation through a medium, conventionally the written word, although that has now expanded to include the electronic communications media: to record, to write down, something that is to be read to/by another. It is a communicative situation of production and consumption. In the first sense of correspondence, production is geared toward the probability of unquestioning consumption. The concern with "whether they'll buy it" is a chronic one; in *The Guyana Massacre* reporter Charles Krause recounts his concern about whether anyone "back home" would believe the Jonestown mass suicide: it was just too bizarre, too far-fetched, too strange and unexpected. As with the atrocities of Viet Nam and the Watergate affair, Jonestown shook up the conventional wisdom of the world beyond the familiar boundaries of home, and for that reason was on the verge of not being newsworthy at all, of being a "bad story".

The observer *qua* journalist is thus bound to misrepresent. Krause, as a good journalist, knew that there was no point in reporting that which could not be heard. The authenticity of the text resides in its intelligibility; in its finding a place in the existing and indelible world of its reception. Good news is that which doesn't cause trouble to our everyday vision of the world; the eleven o'clock news should lull us to sleep, not provide a rude awakening.

The imperialism of the particular mapping of journalists is mirrored by conquistadors who allow their project to reify itself in whatever they find. As Naipaul tells, the search for El Dorado, a place of mythology, took many lives and possessed many ambitious men before it eventually died down. The claim by the Spaniard, Domingo de Vera, that he had found El Dorado, and the truth which was attributed to fiction – the earnestness with which the "map" was followed, are reflected in the following passages:

El Dorado, which had begun as a search for gold, was becoming something more. It was becoming a New World romance, a dream of Shangri-la, a complete, unviolated world. Such a world had existed and the Spaniards had violated it. Now, with a sense of loss that quickened their imagination, the Spaniards wished to have the adventure again. (p. 31)

The legend of El Dorado, narrative within narrative, witness within witness, had become like the finest fiction, indistinguishable from truth. (p. 38)

The conquistador always finds what he is looking for: Columbus "found" India, just as Vera "found" El Dorado.

What the first and second forms of mapping have in common is their imperialism. Both explorers and journalists are out to appropriate the unknown; to find comfort in the strange by taming the foreign, enslaving the threatening, giving form to the formless, making the unknown self-evident. From the ancient human interest in tales from afar, to the popularity of travelogues, to Grey Owl's unprecedented rise to freakish fame in Britain, to *National Geographic* magazine, the desire to appropriate difference, strangeness, exoticism has been a definitive characteristic of human society. Said's *Orientalism* (1978) calls for a redefinition of what it means to explore, to find out about, that which could have been called the "unknown". He suggests that the unknown is constructed so as to compel members of the known world to want to confirm its condition of being known; which is to say that whatever the unknown turns out to be after its "discovery" was known all along. The approach taken by Said may be fruitfully applied to other versions of imperialistic mapping: from the development of western North America and the accompanying genocide of its indigenous inhabitants (which, to follow the metaphor of Columbus, is really an extension of Orientalism rather than another case of it), to the creation of "outer space".

The recent film, *E.T.,* exemplifies such a mythologization of the unknown. *E.T.* reminds us that our real fear is not a nuclear holocaust nor the identifiable "powers that be" on earth. Because we know them, we believe we can control them. It is the unknown conquistadors from the sky that fill our imaginations, of which we have to somehow provide an account. Extraterrestrial beings are configured as similar enough to evoke empathy from humans, yet different enough to not share our version of home and thus pose a threat to it. E.T. is friendly (but shy), cute (but not beautiful), wise (but not dogmatic), healing (but not pushy), and fundamentally sensitive to human morality — yet home and family are to be found *elsewhere* ("E.T. phone home"). This mythological creature confirms the goodness of our own structure of sentimentality by showing that more "advanced", "powerful", "intelligent" beings have not lost the sense of belongingness, community (*ergo:* the future, which promises to make us a race more advanced, powerful, and intelligent, yet which also threatens to make us more "otherdirected", will not compromise the tradition-directed values that we hold so dear). The second reassuring message is that when they come, it will be to learn and then to leave — they will not be latter-day conquistadors come to make us *their* own. Their home is elsewhere; they are like first-order mappers who want to find out and then go away again.

Dorothy found that Oz, for all its fantastic renderings of the unimaginable into the tangible, lacked the comforts of home; *The Wizard of Oz* reminded us that there is no place like home, and whatever lies at the end of the rainbow is better off left alone, or at least wondered at from afar. *E.T.* presents a new promise: there is comfort at the end of the rainbow. Somewhere there is a land of light and power, of good old human sentiments of family and home, truth and honesty. We have nothing to fear. When the time comes to leave, when the space odyssey really begins, there will be a home, a safe place to go, and all our troubles will be healed. By thus configuring extraterrestrial beings, by reassuring ourselves that the last vestige of the unknown — outer space — is a kind world, we appropriate it mythologically. The appropriation of the strange into an extension of the world over which our familiarity exercises control, then, is the essence of mapping; where there is no Orient, one will be created.

One of the most current examples of Orientalism regards the desire to "appropriate" the problem of the computer age and its resultant impact on social life. Bittner (1983), in a compelling piece on "Technique and the Conduct of Life", suggests that the tendency toward seeing computers as increasingly intelligible may be a result of the increasingly technical structuring of human intelligence rather than the increasing humanization of the computer:

Because so much of what is available to *us* as knowledge is ensconced in bodies of knowledge that subsist without knowing subjects, because knowledge exists in standardized terms and can be fragmented into pieces without drawing blood, therefore the computer's artificial intelligence increasingly appears to resemble our own real intelligence. (p. 259)

Orientalism is the imagined confluence between us and them; and this confluence is mirrored in our efforts to personify the machines which we employ in our relations to the world. To conquer machines is to make them "like us" and of little threat; yet, as Bittner points out, the process that enables such fiction is a co-optation of human intelligence by the machine.

The dilemma faced by the modern stranger as he finds himself thrown into an other-directed world in which spatial proximity has been replaced by cultural proximity finds a solution in the ideology of second-order mapping. He may rest assured that the mythological values of home and community have not vanished when they predominate in a world which goes far beyond Riesman's third mode of social organization in its distance from tradition-direction. And even at home, where the unknown is embodied pervasively by *technè* – and paradoxically, for *technè* should be that which humans perfect in order to maintain control over nature, the fear of the control that *technè* itself has over our world results in the fiction of mapping which produces "user friendly" computers.

Imaginative Geography.

It is perfectly possible to argue that some distinctive objects are made by the mind, and that these objects, while appearing to exist objectively, have only a fictional reality. A group of people living on a few acres of land will set up boundaries between their land and its immediate surroundings and the territory beyond, which they call 'the land of the barbarians'. In other words, this universal practice of designation in one's mind a familiar space which is 'ours' and an unfamiliar space beyond 'ours' which is 'theirs' is a way of making geographical distinctions that *can be* entirely arbitrary. I use the word 'arbitrary' here because imaginative geography of the 'our land – barbarian land' variety does not require that the barbarians acknowledge the distinction. It is enough for 'us' to set up these boundaries in our own minds; 'they' become 'they' accordingly, and both their territory and their mentality are designated as different from 'ours'. To a certain extent modern and primitive societies seem thus to derive a sense of their identities negatively. A fifth-century Athenian was very likely to feel himself to be nonbarbarian as much as he positively felt himself to be Athenian. The geographic boundaries accompany the social, ethnic, and cultural ones in expected ways. Yet often the sense in which someone feels himself to be not-foreign is based on a very unrigorous idea of what is 'out there', beyond one's own territory. All kinds of suppositions, associations, and fictions appear to crowd the unfamiliar space outside one's own. (Said, p. 54)

Said's concept of imaginative geography underpins the entire work, and collects the mapping work done by explorers and conquistadors. It alludes to the practice of creating boundaries, delimiting space as "familiar" and "strange"; "ours" and "theirs"; "known" and "unknown". As it implies, the "geography" is fabricated – but as it comes to ground practice it also becomes real. Borders are the physical manifestations of imaginative geography: the intentional creation of a space "in between" which sets one world off from another.

Orientalism is a form of discourse which emerges in order to preserve, justify, and strengthen the spatial configurations of imaginative geography. The workings of Orientalism are hegemonic, but in a way such that the discourse takes on its own hegemony over the imaginative geography. Orientalism convinces both "us" and "them" of its validity; in this way, like Barthes' mythology, it "reproduces itself" (Barthes, 1976). Orientalism suffers, as does any objectivist way of seeing, from the tendency to adopt an "etic" perspective toward the strange. Both first- and second-order mapping, through their imperialism, are only rendered possible by virtue of their ongoing blindness to the "emic" possibility.

Said's interest is ultimately in destroying Orientalism. He follows Barthes by suggesting that the way to render myth impotent is to deny its definitive role. In the case of Orientalism, Said argues that in revealing it *as* discourse; in unveiling its produced and self re-producing nature; in objectifying the discourse (Foucault, 1972), it will be brought to its knees.

This begs the question, however: brought to its knees before whom? What speaker will engage in what discourse to confront Orientalism? If it is the case, as Said claims, that Orientalism produces itself, and produces a way of seeing Orient and Occident that implicates every speaker of each – that is, that Orientalism speaks for us, or that we speak through Orientalism, then where does Said place himself *vis-à-vis* this discourse? Is he the only one who can see it, and if so, why? From what discourse does *he* speak, that he can stand outside of it? In objectifying Orientalism, he treats it as a thing which he has discovered, mapped out. The leap that needs to be identified, however, is that of coming-to-see-Orientalism *as* a form of Orientalism itself; of confronting a discourse, of which one is supposed to be a native speaker; and of attempting to deconstruct it and thereby leave it powerless.

Said's identification of Orientalism as a *product of* imaginative geography; as an objectification of a way of seeing that he as an observer sees as such, exemplifies the work of third-order mapping. Third-order mapping is the task of the ethnographer: to mediate between a way of seeing in which imaginative geography creates and destroys the strange (the "etic"), on the one hand, and the potential familiarity of the strange, producible through "being there" (the "emic"), on the other.

For Bourdieu (1977), the limits of "disinterested observation" are "phenomenological social science" on the one hand, and "objectivist social science" on the other. The third-order account is reflective work which is bounded by the risks of "going native" on the one hand (akin to the first-order map, and paralleled by Bourdieu's "phenomenological social science"), and "armchair theorizing" on the other (akin to the second-order map, paralleled by Bourdieu's "objectivist social science"). The "disinterested" stance of the ethnographer is interested in only one thing: in letting the subject of observation find its way into imaginative geography on its own; to be open to the strange practices insinuating themselves upon the familiar, without co-opting the familiar. It is a kind of reverse imperialism; a form of "instant writing" in which the map is left to take on its own form.

Third-order mapping transcends the landmarking work of first- and second-order mapping because it identifies cultural bases for establishing familiarity and strangeness. In Chapter One, it was shown that strangeness and familiarity are not as discrete as theorists of the stranger would have us believe. So, in suggesting that the conditions of membership produce conditions of strangeness, I argued in Chapter Two that conditions of membership have shifted from tradition-directed (spatial proximity) to other-directed (cultural proximity) through modernization in urban North American society.

Third-order mapping, once the sole preserve of the professionally trained observer, is adopted as a mode of navigating everyday life by the modern stranger. It responds to the problematic nature of establishing familiarity and strangeness on the grounds of trustworthy recipes, and relies upon recognition and negotiation in the placing of self in defining the culture approached.

To arrive at the necessity of third-order mapping as the adaptive technique of the modern stranger, it is warranted to show how being in between serves the professional observer. In Chapter Four, I will argue for the identity between the modern stranger and the professional observer in managing self in the language of membership. Now, however, in inquiring into how it is possible for observation to produce such a third-order, reflective account at all, the work of Bourdieu demands closer attention.

2. Observation and Marginality

2.1. Habitus

> *habitus: condition, habit, bearing; of*
> *dress, style; of places, lie of the*
> *land; abstr. nature, character,*
> *disposition, attitude.* [2]

So far in discussing first- and second-order mapping, strangeness and familiarity have been treated as self-evident events, as they were for tradition- and inner-direction in Chapter Two. Problems raised by mapping, imperialism, and imaginative geography call for a closer look at how the strange and familiar are formulated by the observer, and how "in between", as a function of both, positions the observer as in between not only home and away, but the parametric temptations offered by first- and second-order modes of mapping. In order to recognize what the unknown could be, the *known* must first be formulated. The known is informed by a collective definition, which is historically reproduced and sustained, frequently referred to as "culture". Pierre Bourdieu (1977) has introduced the term "habitus" to give culture a richer sense of that which is lived, "inhabited". Habitus is

understood as a system of lasting, transposable dispositions which, integrating past experiences, functions at every moment as a matrix of *perceptions, appreciations, and actions* and makes possible the achievement of infinitely diversified tasks . . . (pp. 82-83)

The "dispositions" of habitus are acquired through membership. Sociologists use the term "socialization" in reference to the learning of dispositions; the "fully-socialized member" is the one who has an unquestioning acceptance of the dispositions of other fully-socialized members. The "deviant" on the inside or the "stranger" on the outside is the one who brings into question the taken-for-granted; who forces the member to confront a different set of dispositions by embodying other than the taken-for-granted. Bourdieu's habitus lends to shared practice a tangibility, a dimensionality, which culture has typically eluded. Habitus can almost be seen, touched, smelled, tasted, and heard from without; for these reasons, it is appropriate here as the context for and object of observation.

The concept of habitus makes it possible to find a place for every social actor within the context of embedded necessity. For Bourdieu, action is contingent upon the historically laid out options for action; choice is delimited by the dialectic between structure and the means available for "structuring structure". Action is, therefore, always a restructuring. Like ants whose work it is to constantly rebuild their structure of habitation, humans in society engage in a perpetual rearticulation of their own habitus.

Habitus can only be seen from the outside. It is the invisible dome that covers the *Lebenswelt* of a people; that invades every crevice of their lives, that colors the sky and perfumes the air. Habitus is in us and through us; it is a life-force that we only miss when we leave its protective ubiquity. From without, habitus is opaque and plastic; it can be seen as a vague, shapeless mass from afar; it can be approached; and through changing proximity it becomes more or less familiar. From within, habitus is transparent and concrete; because it is the essence of familiarity, it goes unnoticed as long as things remain the same. The introduction of the stranger brings habitus into sudden focus, both from within and without: from without, because the stranger has come to confront it; from within, because the presence of the unknown (*i.e.* the stranger) brings trouble to the taken-for-granted and demands to be made sense of. Observation consists of the confrontation of the habitus of the observer with that of the observed, and the evolution of "first impressions" in the coming to know of their difference.

The confrontation between habitus' produced by the coming of the stranger is like Schutz's reflexive crisis. It forces the member to rethink what has heretofore been taken for granted. Mannheim (1940) suggests that such confrontation produces "reflection and self-observation":

Normally man's attention is directed not towards himself but towards things. . . . He usually does not observe how he himself functions. He lives in immediate acts of experience; he is absorbed in them without ordinarily comprehending them. He reflects, and sees himself for the first time when he fails to carry through some projected action and, as a result of this failure, is thrown, so to speak, back upon himself. "Reflection", "self-observation", "taking account of one's own situation" assume, in such moments, the functions of self-reorganization. (p. 57)

The absorption into the everyday routine of habit, of the taken-for-granted world, is the *reflexive* mode. Mannheim's association of this mode with an unawareness of how one "functions" suggests that functional rationality takes place as a reflexive relation to self, other, and the environment. The *reflective* mode is introduced when that taken-for-granted world fails to satisfy reflexive functioning; when the individual is forced to reassess that which he has not had prior cause to think about because it has *always worked*.

The distinction between reflexivity, which is unmediated, habitual action; and reflectivity, which is mediated, thoughtful, interpretative action, is critical for the question of observation and being in between. Both are forms of social action; the former, typical of everyday life in habitus in which habitus remains invisible; the latter, the consequence of the reflexive crisis in which habitus is challenged by that which is outside of its scheme of interpretation and consequently challenges it, in the process clearly defining its limits and its boundaries.

It is with the reflexive crisis that imaginative geography gives texture to strangeness; it configures the habitus of difference. It always applies to that which is beyond, not that which is at home. To be at home is to be indifferent to one's surroundings; it is only when the milieu calls for mapping, when one is forced to structure an unfamiliar habitus, that imaginative geography is invoked.

Invited by the anthropologist's questioning to effect a reflexive and quasi-theoretical return on to his own practice, the best-informed informant produces a discourse which *compounds two opposing systems of lacunae.* Insofar as it is a *discourse of familiarity,* it leaves unsaid all that goes without saying: the informant's remarks . . . take for granted the presuppositions taken for granted by the historical agents – are inevitably subject to the censorship inherent in their habitus, a system of schemes of perception and thought which cannot give what it does give to be thought and perceived without *ipso facto* producing an unthinkable and unnameable. Insofar as it is an *outsider-oriented discourse* it tends to exclude all direct reference to particular cases (that is, virtually all information directly attached to *proper names* evoking and summarizing a whole system of previous information). Because the native is that much less inclined to slip into the language of familiarity to the extent that his questioner strikes him as unfamiliar with the universe of reference implied by his discourse . . . it is understandable that anthropologists should so often forget the distance between learned reconstruction of the native world and the native experience of that world, an experience which finds expression only in the silences, ellipses, and lacunae of the language of familiarity. (Bourdieu, p. 18)

The stranger who asks questions like, "What are your customs?", or "Why do you do this?", forces the member into a reflective position which the free-flowing regularity of habitus prevents; and as Bourdieu points out, forces the member to account for practices which have no accountability within the structure of the habitus. Because habitus *is,* it never asks why, for it does not know otherwise. The language of familiarity presumes habitus, and therefore ignores it. But because native speakers live their lives through habitus, conduct their speech in the language of familiarity, when questioned about that which is taken-for-granted they are often unable to articulate it in the language of the ethnographer. The "of course" is far more likely to animate their talk, for it contains the admonition that things could be otherwise. "Of course" one would never marry a "so and so", constitutes the "structure" of kinship to the native speaker who has been confronted by the unthinkable, and can only come to terms with it by rendering it unthinkable once more (through negating it, the "of course not").

The explanation agents may provide for their own practice, thanks to a quasi theoretical reflection on their practice, conceals, even from their own eyes, the true nature of their practical mastery, i.e. that it is *learned ignorance (docta ignorantia),* a mode of practical knowledge not comprising knowledge of its own principles. If follows that this learned ignorance can only give rise to the misleading discourse of a speaker himself misled, ignorant both of the objective truth about his practical mastery (which is that it is

ignorant of its own truth) and of the true principle of the knowledge his practical
mastery contains. (p. 19)

The learned ignorance which Bourdieu attributes to the native speaker begs
the question: Where must the ethnographer stand in order to perceive this
ignorance and see through it to the "truth"? Keeping in mind that the ethnographer is also a native speaker in his own habitus, coming to a strange
habitus would have the dual effect of causing him to reflect upon his own
taken-for-granted world, as well as bringing to light the inability of native
speakers to uncover the "true structure" of their habitus. The confrontation
between the two habitus', therefore, produces a reflexive crisis for *both* the
observer and the observed.

The question with which Bourdieu begins: How can one come to "understand" a society from the outside?, he answers in the somewhat oblique
manner of fashioning a "theory of practice" through his own practice of
fieldwork in Kabylia. The meaning of actions is contained in their doing.
He suggests that the significance which social practice may hold for the
ethnographer is not at all clear to the actors engaged in that practice; and
furthermore that the distortions entailed in attempting to employ objectivist
social science structures to "restructure" habitus, whether through "participation" (taking the role of the native speaker), or through "disinterested
observation" (armchair theorizing), both fail to accomplish the interest in
"finding out": the former because the native speaker, in being so embedded
himself in the practice of habitus, distorts through viewing the microscopic
necessity of actions without an eye to the whole; and the latter because it
attempts to restructure habitus through the disconnected eyes of the outsider
with no sense of the connectedness between action and habitus. Both of
these modes are imperialistic — the first from within, the second from
without — and parallel the first- and second-order forms of mapping introduced above. The attempt to take the role of the native speaker parallels first-
order mapping in that it is a native interest in "finding out the *truth*" without
the reflective savvy of the one who "knows" that habitus of origin can not be
completely elided in favor of "going native". Armchair theorizing parallels
second-order mapping because it avoids any confrontation with the habitus
of difference that might jeopardize the foregone conclusion that characterizes
that version of "observation". Both avoid the reflexive crisis to the extent
that the first- and second-order mapper *cum* observer does not entertain the
possibility that the strange habitus could in any way conflict with his
expectations.

As against these two forms of mapping, Bourdieu is arguing for the position of marginality as offering the clearest, least distorted picture of things.
From this vantage point one can reach out and touch the actors: they appear
real; one is close enough to peek "behind the scenes"; yet it is also possible

to sit back and watch passively, taking in "the whole picture".

Bourdieu's observer has to have flirted with membership, and remained chaste; neither content as the voyeur who gazes on from a distance with binoculars, nor aggressive enough to jump into bed with a native; the ideal observer himself becomes disembodied, ephemeral. He is there but not really; you can pass your hand through him but still see his shadow.

Bourdieu does not address the question of the ideal observer other than in a negative sense. And although he superficially rejects the imperialism of conventional mapping practices, what seems to underlie his language is a kind of colonial version of the supremacy of European civilization. Primitive habitus is the problem to be dealt with: it has insinuated itself on the ethnographer by its *being there* – and must be done away with. But how? He is discouraged from going native because that will only blind him. He is discouraged from trying to reconstruct a culture with his own preexisting objectivist questions and categories. Habitus invades both ways of seeing: the former, because getting in "too deeply" entails forgetting one's reason for being there; the latter, because the habitus of objectivist social science pre-empts any fair reception of the habitus under study.

Bourdieu's circuitous route returns to the familiar dilemma of observation: how to be within and without; how to make sense of difference both in its own terms and then to have difference inform our own terms. He claims to reject the phenomenological *epoché* (p. 233) because of its insistence on the "moment-to-hand" as containing all that needs to be known; Bourdieu demands to see every action as embedded in historical necessity. Yet how is that to be done? Surely the action, if read as a text *within* a discourse (in Foucault's sense, 1972), can be seen to contain in it its essence. Somewhere between the phenomenological interest in discovering the immediate intentionality embodied in any objectification, and Bourdieu's interest in showing that such supposedly value-free observation in fact devalues the object by removing it from the historic-economic context of habitus, is the observer's interest in *being there*. There is a sense in which Bourdieu demands that the observer have a "calling" – when habitus calls, his objectivism flies out the window. Observer responds "in kind" – understanding is no longer a question of intentionality nor application, but one of "being there". To be there is to know.

What is it that the ethnographer can hope to find out by "being there"? If the interest were in learning how a group makes sense of their world, then the interventionist approach (the "emic"), with an interest in subjecting the observer to habitus and therefore learning what it means to be a native speaker, would be warranted. If the interest were in making sense of difference from the comfort of one's own habitus, then the objectivist approach (the "etic") would continue to produce satisfactory results by demanding that the foreign habitus conform to the expectations held out to it by conventional social science. Bourdieu is calling for neither of these, yet strangely in his own *practice* he incorporates both. He is calling for a stance which has as its only presupposition that practice is *functional for the continued restructuring of habitus.* That is to say, he has adopted a lens through which to interpret the actions of a strange society: everything that people do is grounded in historical necessity. This lens thus directs his attentions and colors his observations. It is yet another bias. What purpose does this practice serve? It is neither adequate nor professionally responsible to merely report on practices; it is expected that the professional observer will have something to say regarding the teleology of any action. Ethnographers by their very vocation are thus engaged in their own structuring of a habitus. What Bourdieu is calling for, as against this, must therefore be seen as a denial of the cultural relativist lens of ethnography rather than of the interest in structuring *per se;* and deeply, as another version of appropriation.

2.2. Going Native

I am not sure what constitutes going native. It depends on the conception of the word "native". Have the Americans and Britons who settle in the Pays Basque or on the Riviera and wear the local berets and the fishermen's trousers gone native? Have the same type of people who occupy palazzos in Venice and eat spaghetti and drink Chianti and murder the Italian language gone native? Had the Agha Khan when he wore a morning coat and a grey top hat at Epsom and Longchamps gone native? Neither he nor the "Venetians" nor the "Nicoise" nor the "Biarrots" were living or dressing or eating as they did in their own homes. They were observing the customs of the natives of England or Italy or France. If what they did constitutes going native, then I most certainly was guilty.

I wore the Arab dress because it was the most suitable for desert life. I ate the Arab food because it was all I could get, and also because I liked it. I practiced the Moslem faith and did not drink wine or eat pork because otherwise I would have seemed an outsider, a kind of disguised tourist, watching my Arab companions but not being one of them. But I did not bring my turban or my Arab customs with me to Europe, like the Anglo-Saxons who cannot be separated from their berets, and continue to talk bad French in London and New York. I did not bring them back, any more than the Agha Khan took his grey top hat and his race horses to India. (Bodley, 1944: viii-ix)

The introduction of habitus as that opaque dome which structures and separates societies, and the accompanying dilemma over which side of the dome the ethnographer should take in order to map out habitus, raises questions for ethnographical procedure. The most pressing concern is that over "going native": becoming absorbed into the habitus of strangeness to the point of becoming a native speaker, and losing the ethnographical lens through which one should be able to map out without being "sucked in".

Ethnographers relate ambivalently to the notion of going native. On the one hand, it is seen as desirable, for it suggests attaining the hallowed position of an "insider". On the other hand, it suggests another threat to objectivity, in that once one has gone native one has ceased to be an ethnographer. Powdermaker recounts a brief and frightening flirtation with such a feeling at a "dance" in Lesu:

I was unable to pay much attention, consumed with self-consciousness, I imagined my family and friends sitting in the background and muttering in disapproving tone, "Hortense, dancing with the savages." How could I get up before all these people of the Stone Age and dance with them? I prayed for an earthquake – the island was volcanic. But the earth was still, and all too soon it was our turn to dance. I wondered if I would not collapse on my way to the open clearing which served as the stage. But there I was in my proper place in the circle; the drums began; I danced. Something happened. I forgot myself and was one with the dancers. Under the full moon and for the brief time of the dance, I ceased to be an anthropologist from a modern society. I danced. When it was over I realized that, for this short period, I had been emotionally part of the tribe. Then out came my notebook. (p. 112)

As Bodley suggests, going native in the worst sense consists in sheer intentionality which is not balanced by a willingness to discover wherein difference lies. In the best sense, it is a giving over of oneself to habitus; a way of dealing with necessity through the means of least resistance. So, Bodley did not don "native" dress upon arriving in the Sahara – he thought it presumptuous, incongruous, and therefore sensed the inauthentic relationship he would have with the clothing. It would represent a contrived attempt to fit in; something that a tourist might do. Instead, he waited until it became apparent through necessity and expediency – upon which his acceptability relied – that he dress in the most appropriate manner for the environment. Only then could it become the most "natural" thing in the world.

2.3. Note-taking

The ethnographer employs the technique of note-taking in order to map out the strange habitus. Note-taking has the effect of making visible the dome around habitus; of constantly reminding both the observer and the observed that he is suspended between two worlds. For the observer, the notebook acts as a tangible barrier to going native. As long as notes are taken, he is forced to "translate" the new habitus into the habitus of origin. He is forced, in a sense, to see the strange – not *in light of* home (first- and second-order mapping) – but by virtue of the demand that he consciously *bracket* home.

Bracketing, as Husserl has shown, entails first a fluency in that which one brackets. One can only attempt to distance oneself from one's bias once one is familiar with that bias. In the case of the ethnographer, in between can only be sustained through the reminder – the tangible barrier of the notebook – that one acts as an envoy, that one is, under the mandate of one's calling, obliged to take in all from the perspective of eventual translation. The point is that habitus of origin only gains texture once it has been set beside a new habitus. It is only the production of boundaries *through* opposition, *through* being in between, that enables observation at all; and that enables the ethnographer to see that there is anything there to be observed.

Powdermaker relates her first experience with mortuary rites in Lesu, at which the back-and-forth, or insider/outsider, dilemma of the ethnographer is underscored:

I took my notebook out of a pocket and was about to begin to write. But suddenly I said to myself, "How can you take notes in the midst of human sorrow? Have you no feeling for the mourners?" I had a quick vision of a stranger with a notebook walking into the living room of my Baltimore home at the time of a death. The notebook went back into my pocket. But I continued, "Are you not an anthropologist? This may be the only mortuary rite you will witness. Think of what you will miss, if you do not record it. A knowledge of these rites is absolutely essential." The notebook came out of my pocket. Before I could begin writing, the dialogue with myself began all over again and continued as the notebook went in and out of my pocket. This uncomfortable ambivalence was finally resolved. I took the notebook out and wrote what was happening. (p. 85)

That Powdermaker never took the position of an insider during this interlocution is clear. Her concern was preeminently with presentation of self *cum* anthropologist. The notebook out or the notebook in represented her dilemma over appropriate behavior as an anthropologist, to people of whose interpretation of such presentation she was not entirely sure, as opposed to an effort to be seen as a member. If she had been an "insider", a member familiar with the *rites de passage* of the Lesu, then there would have been no ambiguity. But then, there also would have been no notebook.

As such, the concern with appearances was predicated on the only version of the mortuary rite with which she was familiar — that of her "own" native group. Unlike the well-socialized member, however, Powdermaker was not secure in her role at Lesu; she was not met by any response that validated her actions (*i.e.* notebook in, notebook out) in any way that was meaningful to her; and therefore was not "interacting" at all. As she soon discovered, her behavior had been so insignificant to the occasion to go unnoticed; her confusion had been totally of her own making:

I had already explained that I would write down everything because my memory was not good enough to recall it all accurately when I went home. The Lesu people understood this, and since they did not have writing, they had none of my associations with it. Moreover, in this particular situation, the widow's wailing was purely ritual. She had two husbands; the dead one had been old and she much preferred the younger one. (p. 85)

Judging from her accounts, it seems that for Powdermaker the ubiquitous notebook was a constant reminder of her ethnographic mission. At times when she put the notebook aside, as in the experience related above, the ethnographic distance became difficult to maintain. It was as if to "observe" in a way that preserved her as an outsider, and at the same time protected her against becoming "too involved", she needed to be engaged in the side involvement (Goffman, 1963a) of note-taking. Like simultaneous translation, note-taking encodes one "reality" into another; and demands that the note-taker retain a marginal position to both worlds. As with the task of the translator (Benjamin, 1969), the task of the ethnographic note-taker demands that he have an eye to two worlds simultaneously.[3]

For Goffman,

A side involvement is an activity that an individual can carry on in an abstracted fashion without threatening or confusing simultaneous maintenance of a main involvement. (p. 43)

Note-taking for the ethnographer is an appropriate side involvement. The photographic journalist engages in the side involvement of taking photographs to represent "what happened" — the "being there" which points to this photograph being taken rather than that one, however, is the main involvement: the camera translates the experience, focuses it, and accentuates what the observer has deemed important. Similarly, the ethnographer utilizes note-taking as a tool for *positioning* strange practices in the *structuring* of habitus which is his calling. It is perfectly consistent with the observer's job of appropriating; the last thing it could do would be to interfere with observation. Rather, it serves to constantly remind of the need to note, to map, to structure. Note-taking thus keeps a distance between the ethnographer and the habitus under study.

But what the passage from Powdermaker suggests is that when in between it is only with enormous reflective discipline that one comes to wonder what it is that one is observing. What makes a thing of any interest for observation? What gives a thing the status of "datum"?

Note-taking is a form of constant transcription performed through the ethnographic lens, which seeks to make sense of the strange in terms of the familiar. To "go native", or even to orient to doing so, would be to suggest that note-taking is neither necessary nor possible; would be to lay down the ethnographic lens with the notebook, and see only through the eyes of the would-be member; to lower the barrier of the notebook and leave oneself free of the demand to transcribe. Powdermaker's confusion at the mortuary rite arose from her concern over the propriety of a side involvement. In her native habitus, note-taking at a funeral would be deemed inappropriate. However, in her "role" as ethnographer in Lesu, the notebook was viewed almost as a personal appendage by those whom she was studying;

and positively as a form of recognition that what was being experienced was worthy of a place in her restructuring of their world. The notebook signified signification. Putting down the notebook, in turn, suggested "mere conversation" or idle passing of time. For the Lesu, Powdermaker had been introduced as one who was there to learn and report back. Lapses in her role as observer were viewed as unacceptable. In her efforts to see death in Lesu as intelligible through western eyes, she temporarily forgot that the vantage point through which she was allowed to see this in the first place was as a note-taker. It became apparent on several occasions in Bowen's account, as well as in Powdermaker's, that if she neglected to record someone's story in her notebook, she was perceived as being disinterested in the story, or as regarding it as unimportant. In short, then, her identity *to the Lesu* as a visitor, and to herself as an observer, hovered around the ubiquity of the notebook.

Note-taking is therefore a tool enabling the observer to maintain a reflective stance; to step back from the immediacy of experiencing habitus and to reinforce his mandate of "finding out". The main involvement for the note-taker is one of translating the event as experienced into significance; in "collecting souvenirs" of the occasion in the form of jottings, which will reproduce the immediately lived presence through the medium of "in between". Only when in between, as aided by note-taking, can the observer relate to the different habitus as something which may become known; as a form of speech which he may one day share. It is toward the eventuality of membership in a universe of discourse belonging to this different habitus that he orients his note-taking, for the speech is only valuable when it may be translated somehow into his habitus of origin. For an ethnographer must not only go into the field, but come out of it. It is with an eye to the eventual transformation of the field experience that observation is carried out. As Powdermaker reports, the ethnographer is constantly engaged in reminding himself of how his report will be read. The notebook serves to illuminate the invisible barrier which is "in between": as long as it is carried and entered into, the translation of one speech community into another is mediated by the constant reminder that this is in fact an exercise in translation. Once the notebook is set aside, the strange habitus once again becomes invisible and engulfs the ethnographer. A native speaker is no longer seen as such, but rather becomes the other to which the ethnographer orients as one who is subject to the same exigencies of living. The notebook thus serves to sustain the trapeze of in between.

Wax (1971) recommends that the ethnographer spend more time processing his observations once out of the field, than actually spent in the field; which is to say that the work of seeing one's life in the field as embodied action, as practice which was under the shadow of the condition of being in between which informed the entire context of observation as well as the subject of observation, is difficult and thus only possible when one is again in the world in which one's report is to be read — when one has stepped back in time and space and retained images in memory of the place in between.

For Powdermaker,

I needed frivolity and time to become detached from it. Detachment did come after a few months. Then I was ready to think and write about the Melanesians. (p. 125)

Memory, however, is an unworthy ally in the effort to render the strange intelligible. Memory fixes in between in its own world, and lives on: it is impossible to become "detached" from memory. Note-taking, on the other hand, articulates the "being there" in the language of the habitus of origin, subjecting it to scrutiny and further reinterpretation brought on in the light of "going home".

3. Through the Looking Glass

The concern with mapping should address not which map is the most accurate/least biased, but rather which bias one prefers: that of the insider, the outsider, or the one in between. The dilemma of the ethnographer, in hovering between note-taking and going native; in deliberating over which world to translate into which; and in recognizing the difficulty if not impossibility of living up to the expectations for such translation, stems from the difficulty of admitting that ethnography is its own bias; that marginality presents its own problems of interpretation, the least concern of which should be the "correctness" or objectivity of observation. The posture taken by the ethnographer precludes going native, just as it precludes armchair theorizing. By going into the field, one suggests commitment to "being there"; by sustaining a constant transcription of one world to the next, one suggests one's resistance to the "coming to be" which overshadows every attempt to "come to know". The marginal position of "in between" is not one that is chosen: it comes along with the job.

At a recent seminar on the sociology of deviance, the question of how one comes to "see" deviants was raised.[4] One colleague related an incident in which he was approached by a female in a hotel lobby at a meeting of sociologists, and asked, "D'ya have the time, big boy?". Taking her to be a fellow sociologist, he looked at his watch. Since that day, so the story goes, all he sees in hotel lobbies are prostitutes. He lamented that this incident cost him his innocence, his common-sense lens for viewing hotel lobbies. It is just such a constant changing of lens which occurs with the confrontation with the strange. When a thing challenges the typical way of seeing, the member rises to it as a thing to be figured out, demanding reflection, which has the net result of altering the configuration of our world. That is to say, the common-sense way of seeing can never be lost. The reflexive crisis necessitates amendments to habitus rather than total replacement. To suggest that habitus could be "wrong" is to say that it should be "right"; it is to reify the everyday lens as the "authentic", "correct" lens through which the well-socialized member sees. It is precisely due to the well-socialized nature of members that they rise to greet the strange; that, indeed, they take anything to be familiar or strange at all. But given a basic set of categories which are employed for recognition, they are forever undergoing transformation, becoming more precise, more discriminatory. However refined sensitivity to difference becomes, it nevertheless remains predicated on the fundamental way of seeing which has been inculcated — which defines the group in which one is a member and for which such a thing becomes strange.

Authenticity relies on the currency of practices to ground itself. The authentic is that which emerges as familiar and necessary; that achieves conventionality through shared practice. For Bodley, there can be no such thing as "going native". To do what the surroundings demand; to find "one's place" in a milieu which one in part creates and in part receives, is both a form of intentionality and a form of survival. It cannot help but be a response — and an imposition. In ethnography, both the observer and the observed step into the nether land of in between, in which practice is neither authentic nor inauthentic in any absolute terms; its authenticity exists solely on the basis of the currency of the practice and its part in the ongoing building of habitus. Confronted by difference which can not be accounted for by past practices, the new demands to be dealt with on its own terms — as it presents itself. In between, the stranger has no past, present, or future.

If pressed, Bourdieu might allow that "going native" is both necessary and impossible, and as such leaves the ethnographer hovering in between. Habitus, in making the "structuring structures" of the life-world taken-for-granted, has a place for the observer who insists on the objectivist doxa that one can "come to know" a different culture. Habitus is generous: it allows itself to be manipulated, destructured and restructured through imposed objectivist categories which find only what they are looking for; habitus takes on the form the cartographer gives it, for it is unable to speak for itself.

To approach difference under Bourdieu's schema would appear to demand a marginality not unlike that outlined by Stonequist. For Bourdieu, inside entails being subject to habitus and having the eyes, ears and voice of the native speaker. Outside entails being subject to a different habitus, of which the outsider is a native speaker, and from which the "strange" habitus in question appears as such. The insider is characterized by "not knowing what he doesn't know", moreover by "not knowing *that* he doesn't know"; a blissful ignorance of the taken-for-granted which sees difference as "only" problematic. The outsider is merely an insider dispossessed; the one who has lost his *naiveté* through opening up to that which has no accountability in the language of familiarity. The confrontation between inside and outside is what illuminates the problem of needing to come to know; and this in turn is only possible by first stepping outside of one's habitus and looking through the utmost clarity of no man's land, of a habitus-free lens, and then bringing the strange back home. The structures of the habitus under study evolve their own forms, independently of the lens of the habitus-bound individual. The "true" form emerges only for the one who watches impassively, without a stake in the outcome of the metamorphosis, who stands in between while the boundaries which form habitus' take shape before his eyes.

In between resembles a tunnel, glassed in by the past habitus and the new habitus. The observer steps into the tunnel by virtue of taking on the new habitus as a world to be mapped; of picking up his notebook and beginning to define the limits of habitus by writing what he sees. To one side are images of the way things were, still vivid in the memory of one who was until recently bound by that habitus. To the other side are strange forms which present themselves as the stuff of first impressions. The glass permits the observer to see all that can be seen, but it holds him back from being part of the picture. As the observer walks further away from the entrance to the tunnel, he looks over his shoulder less and less. The image of the past habitus fades into shadows; the fluid images of the new habitus acquire a solidity through increasing familiarity.

It is from such a point of view that Bourdieu fashions his observer: the one who is both a part and apart; who is simultaneously trying to learn how to be a native speaker of one habitus, while trying not to forget how he has spoken in the past. The tunnel of in between retains some order: it is going somewhere. From the sidelines the observer gains a sort of familiarity with the world on the other side of the glass; a familiarity through which first impressions evolve into meaningful typologies.

Unlike the first-order cartographer who passes from one habitus to the other in the interest of going native, and hence spends very little time in the tunnel; and unlike the second-order cartographer who bypasses the tunnel completely, attempting instead to tease out the images from behind the double layer of glass invoked by looking outward from the habitus of familiarity, the trained observer travels the tunnel to the end, which brings him back to the beginning. The glass is transparent only by virtue of its solidity: it can be shattered only by the wilful neglect of the ethnographer, in putting the notebook aside. As long as the glass remains intact, he may approach the strange, press his nose against the glass, and gaze at a place he will never call his home. In between, he will always look ahead; but in doing so he only looks behind.

4. The Trained Observer as the Modern Stranger

I have tried to show how mapping, in its third-order form as adopted by the trained observer, separates the observer from the observed by the transparent wall of in between. I now would like to venture a claim implicit in H.T. Wilson's *The American Ideology* (1977), namely, that the trained observer *is* the modern stranger, and the modern stranger, it follows, conducts his life through the third-order lens of the trained observer. By sketching out the parameters of what he calls the "American ideology", Wilson shows how the presuppositions of the scientific enterprise provide an ontological basis for membership in North American society. The mapmaking activity of the observer who is in between parallels the sense-making activity of the modern stranger for whom the parameters of difference are pregiven by a scientific world view.

Wilson characterizes the American ideology as constituted of: (1) an anti-reflexive/anti-theoretic bias; (2) a desire for "accumulating knowledge"; (3) a false commitment to objectivity; (4) a "trial-and-error" approach to legitimizing social and political processes; and (5) a universalizing, eminently exportable view of the "open" society in terms of supremacy, longevity and permanence. These attributes, he argues, by clearly delimiting the horizon of the scientist, provide an ideology which implicitly grounds membership in the wider society.

The principal activity of the trained observer is one "aimed at uncovering and realizing the truth" (p. 18). The mandate of science is to *uncover* that which is not self-evident. This in turn is typified as "a continuing oversight which *impedes* the individual from what really are his proper tasks" (p. 90).

It is precisely the need for a continuing oversight which produces hegemonic systems of rationalization such as the American ideology, and which makes them appear to be authentic in grounding the existence of their own members. For a continuing oversight *is* habitus; it is overlooked precisely because it underlies the "groupness" of the community. For the trained observer to observe *within* habitus, a certain amount must be assumed. This is the cultural basis for communication.

The "loyalty" of the trained observer is therefore loyalty to unquestioning membership, to habitus. It continues as an oversight as long as habitus does

122   *On Being in Between*

not see itself reflected in the difference of another habitus. It is such a loyalty that enables the American ideology to embody the principle of both legitimizing and universalizing its social and political order *through* the enterprise of the trained observer.

The crisis facing the modern stranger is one of the failure of tradition to provide authority. I suggested in Chapter Two that much of the blame for the sense of anomie and homelessness in the modern stranger may be placed upon the enormous gaps between myths and reality; and the failure of past formulas to provide foolproof maps or trustworthy recipes for the navigation of modern society. It is precisely this distance – between the past reliance on denotative language and the increasing demand for connotative decoding skills – that has forced the modern stranger to wrest from the preserve of science the reflective stance toward everyday life. This constitutes the imediacy and the urgency with which the "search for authenticity" is perceived.

If the modern stranger confronts everyday life with the eyes of the trained observer, and if that observation itself has become part of habitus – a continuing oversight – then the stance of the modern stranger could be formulated as a "false" one. In order to retrieve the "authenticity" of the continuing oversight of the modern stranger, it must be asked what an "authentic" experience may look like in an other-directed world, and what strategies the modern stranger has developed in order to sustain the continuing oversight. This is the project of Chapter Four.

Notes

1. See, for example, Bowen, 1954; Bruyn, 1966; Cressey, 1983; Daniels, 1967; Fortes, 1975; Nash, 1963; Powdermaker, 1966; Shack and Skinner, 1979; Shaffir, Stebbins and Turowetz, 1980; Wax, 1971; *et al.*
2. Cassel's Latin Dictionary (Concise Edition). London: Cassell Ltd., 1979, 103.
3. For Walter Benjamin, as for members of the Frankfurt School who exiled themselves to the United States during or after the second world war, marginality was a condition of everyday life; for Benjamin, because of his marginality as a Jew; for Adorno, Horkheimer, and others, because of their marginality as German Jews in America. Benjamin's writings reflect his continual crisis of identity; his choices to study Kafka, Baudelaire, and the cabala sketch a man who exhibited the "fragmented identity" that Dreitzel (1981) writes about. I would place Benjamin and the others with Sartre, Camus and Kafka as those whose biographical marginality informed their literary calling; yet who have not contributed to the literature on the "sociological" concept of the stranger and hence have not been treated in the current study.
4. C.S.A.A. Annual Meetings, Ottawa, Canada, June 1982.

Chapter IV
The Language of Membership

One does not know where a man comes
from until he has spoken.
J.-J. Rousseau, 1966: 5.

If it is speech which denotes origin, then it is also speech which places the
stranger *vis-à-vis* the group. Speech must be contextual in order to reveal:
it must first be heard through the use of shared symbols before the difference
that it serves to express may emerge. It is, as Schutz has hinted, the chief
barrier and eventual catalyst for the navigation of membership. But the
"speaking" is a more subtle confession than Rousseau might admit. For the
modern stranger, speaking has itself become problematic. The tension
between public and private — between what one reveals and what one hides
— has never been a greater issue for language, and has never played such a
significant part in the attribution of membership. Rousseau's speaker, in
revealing origin through opening his mouth, could utilize silence as the
preserve of the private yet was open to public scrutiny at his first word.
Confusion regarding origin was fed by appearance, and put to rest as soon
as the stranger used words to provide an account of himself. In tradition-
directed society, the denotative function of language limited reading to first-
order referentiality.

For the modern stranger, language has come to consist of more than
referential speech. The discursiveness of embodied expression encompasses
every dimension of the actor's relation to *Welt* — material, gestural, sartorial
— with these dimensions coming to surpass verbal speech in import. Language
takes on a connotative role, and reading meaning becomes an exercise in
contextualized discursiveness.

In this chapter, the preeminence of a reflective, second-order language
of membership, in which reflexive, first-order referentiality is replaced by
culturally-embedded meaning, will be argued. To this end I will adapt
Barthes' (1976) first- and second-order "semiological chain" (see Figure 2,
p. 87). This secondary form of communication will be presented as the
modern stranger's mode of relating self to *Welt* — as a communicative mode
of being-in-the-world — which consolidates the unique demands placed upon
self and other, member and outsider, in modern urbanized society.

That this second-order mode of communication has come to be the
dominant mode of discourse in the world of the modern stranger demands

that the use of "language" to denote it be more than metaphorical. People who "speak" in the first-order sense do so outside of the realm of member-shipping in the world of the modern stranger. First-order speaking, a language of familiarity which belongs in a context in which the individual's words *really matter,* is a basis for exclusion in the world of the modern stranger. Successful membershipping in this world entails a fluency in second-order communication in which it is what is left unsaid by first-order speech, that is what can only be heard through a fluency in the second-order language of membership, that has become the message.

The first-order language of referentiality corresponds to the kind of talk to be found in Wright's (1971) "folk culture":

> If the urban world is a meeting place of strangers, the personal [folk] world is a meeting place of familiar people. . . . Being familiar with another requires that we consider him as a *unique* person, for the better we know someone the more obvious it is how he differs from all others we know, even people who may be like him in many respects. (p. 326)

Conversation emerges from an interest in the other as someone whose answer to one's question *really matters.* It really matters because discourse occurs at a level of "complete reciprocity" (Habermas, 1979) as to the mutuality of interest and concern between both partners in a discourse. Moreover, the first-order speech is dialogic in the sense that in order for communicative competence to be achieved, both parties agree as to the context of the discourse.

The competency required for the second-order language of membership also demands a complete reciprocity, yet the mutuality of concern is qualita-tively different from that at the first-order level. It is self-consciously interested in *avoiding* the other as one who might be different; as one who might be engaged in dialogue.

> What is relevant are the standardized activities which get the stranger what he wants or needs – his meals, downtown on time, an education, his necktie or whatever. Any number of people could perform the activities associated with any given category; they do not depend upon particular people, nor upon intimate knowledge of the other with whom the category deals. . . . Now, when we deal with other people as categories, it means that we too must act in terms of a category: we become customer, passenger, student and so forth as a counterpart to the first. (Wright, 1971: p. 318)

Second-order speech rebounds not in an unmediated way off of other (as in the case of first-order speech), but against the invisible glass of habitus – of embedded meaning. As long as all parties engage in complete reciprocity as strangers ("urban" culture) rather than as familiar others ("folk" culture), then the glass of habitus remains invisible. It is only when one party in the discourse does not reciprocate within the second-order frame that the embedded meanings emerge as problematic. That is to say, interpretation only becomes necessary when, as Schleiermacher (1959) has shown, there is a possibility of *misunderstanding*. Misunderstanding arises, not from messages which are equivocal in themselves, but from the incomplete reciprocity of the parties involved in the discourse. Misunderstanding within the habitus of the modern stranger is most likely to occur when a second-order message may be mistaken for a first-order message; when an "impersonal" form of speech is mistaken for a "personal" one. It is here that one's lack of fluency in the language of membership becomes as evident to the other as Schutz's stranger's lack of fluency in the first-order language of membership. The one who mistakes the second-order message for a first-order message is excluded, just as the one who mistakes the first-order referential message for a second-order connotation is excluded.

One of the most telling currencies in this regard is the phrase, "Have a nice day". The first-order (folk) speaker hears this closing remark as a personal expression of warmth and interest in his well-being. In a folk context in which such a hearing is met reciprocally, there is an unimpeded discourse in which the other might respond, "Thank you very much. I hope you have a nice day, too" (perhaps followed by, depending on the degree of intimacy, further details about what he plans to do and why or why not it may be a "nice day").

For the second-order speaker, however, the phrase "Have a nice day" has become a ritual closing which is made without the expectation of a response. The ubiquity of the phrase in urban culture — on T-shirts, cash register tapes, bill boards, in jingles, and by sales clerks — suggests its subsumption into the realm of everyday "common courtesies". Yet these courtesies are neither addressed at any particular individual nor invested with any particular interest in another's welfare. In short, it does not matter whether the other has a nice day so much as that it is said. That it is said carries embedded meanings that the accomplished actor complies with within the context of the second-order language of membership. Its commonplaceness provokes reflection only upon its absence. The store clerk who does not conclude a consumer transaction with the phrase is admonished, not for his lack of interest in the other (a first-order cause for admonition), but rather for his failure to do his job. "Common courtesy" is engaged in the interests of customer relations rather than interpersonal concern.

The exclusionary effect of these forms of speech becomes evident when complete reciprocity does not occur. In the case where "Have a nice day" is spoken with first-order intentions, the one who does not respond in a manner appropriate to the contextual expectations shows his true strangeness. The attribution of "superficiality" made by "folk" types toward "urban" types stems from such incomplete reciprocity. Such was the case with the initial example of the man in the subway.

Similarly, the case in which second-order intention is met by a first-order response elicits incomplete reciprocity, forcing the barrier of habitus to become opaque. Take the case, in the context of urban customer relations, of the cashier who closes with "Have a nice day" and immediately turns to the next customer, not expecting a response. The "appropriate" behavior for the other in the second-order language of membership involves taking one's purchases and leaving. The customer who says, "Thank you very much. I hope you have a nice day, too" (*etc.*) responds from a first-order version of common courtesy. This actor displays a lack of fluency in the second-order language of membership and consequently interrupts the smooth-flowing rhythm of the customer relationship. The "common courtesy" of customer relations exists to maintain a pace of transactions aimed at maximizing the profit of the company while ensuring that the customer returns. Common courtesy in a folk context of consumer relations serves exactly the same purpose (ensuring that the customer returns and therefore maximizing profit), yet within an ethos of personal interest. Each is appropriate to its own context; and when complete reciprocity is managed, then familiarity and compliance with the expected behavior leads to forms of familiarity at the respective levels of interaction. The "real" stranger in both situations is the one who inserts an inappropriate response, based on an inaccurate reading of the language of membership, showing himself to have "misunderstood" the nature of discourse expected.

The language of membership in the world of modern strangers is therefore one of second-order embedded meaning in which the social organization of strangeness is sustained through a compliance with the "urban" rather than the "folk" ethic. Further, whereas the first-order mode of folk culture entails dialogue at the level of complete reciprocity, reciprocity in the urban context of second-order speech is predicated on a collective involvement in other-direction to the extent that the individual actor, compliant and perfectly interchangeable with any other, has no need of dialogue and has ultimately ceased to matter.

Such an assertion raises questions as to the nature of communicative competence, authentic experience, and the distinction between private and public realms for the modern stranger. In this chapter, I will excurse into three areas of concern in order to arrive at the language of membership. First, I will look to the search for "authentic experience", which has been identified as the most salient concern of modern existence, and which will be reformulated for the modern stranger. Then I will address the question of "reflectivity" as it speaks to the embedded action necessary for the discovery of that authenticity. Finally, with the search for authenticity articulated as the essential ingredient of discursive strangeness, it will be suggested that this is only possible within a world in which traditional distinctions between publicity and privacy have been blurred, and in which fluency in the secondary "publicity of privacy" has become the primary condition for membership.

The pressing against the glass of in between stands as a metaphor for the tensions experienced by the modern stranger. Like the trained observer, the modern stranger is in between incompatible contexts. Tradition-direction, which serves in its absence to mythologize accidental community, is confronted by other-direction, which provides the two options identified by Riesman: either "anxiety and nostalgia" or "insight and choice" (1951: p. 125). The modern stranger is in between because such insight and choice may only be arrived at through a conscious decision to make the most of the world in which he finds himself. And although being in between always entails a certain looking over one's shoulder, it can only be that of the one whose feet are firmly planted in a forward direction. The modern stranger is an inside actor with an outward glance.

For the inside actor with an outward glance, expression and communicability are terms predicated on the assumption that what is to be said is oriented to a speech community composed of like-others. As shown in Chapter Two, a speech community as present-to-hand in terms of spatial proximity can no longer be assumed. It is not self-evident according to the kinds of referential signs imputed by Wood. How does one know how to act, when the rules are far from self-evident? How does the potential member arrive at a perception of the criteria of membership and come to display that knowledge? How does the modern stranger know not to respond to "Have a nice day"?

With modernity has come the need on behalf of the modern stranger to *recognize* community with potential others and *negotiate* membership on the basis of minimal indicators of commonality. Recognition entails a form of reading at the second-order level, while negotiation entails a form of action requiring the individual to engage in a series of what Cohen has called "exploratory gestures" Exploratory gestures are the "tentative and ambiguous" steps taken by actors in an effort to establish a relationship to the conditions of membership in the group. In the following excerpt, Cohen refers to the individual's attempts toward innovation within the context of a subculture:[1]

But how does one *know* whether a gesture toward innovation will strike a responsive and sympathetic chord in others or whether it will elicit hostility, ridicule and punishment?...

The paradox is resolved when the innovation is broached in such a manner as to elicit from others reactions suggesting their receptivity, and when, at the same time, the innovation occurs by increments so small, tentative and ambiguous as to permit the actor to retreat, if the signs be unfavorable, without having been identified with an unpopular position. Perhaps all social actions have . . . this quality of being *exploratory gestures* . . . (Cohen, 1955: 60)

Fishman recognizes the key role played by such "exploratory gestures" or, as he suggests, "fumbling around", in recognition and negotiation of "incongruent social situations". His example of a "lovers' quarrel" is particularly telling:

Because of incongruent behavior toward each other lovers may interpret each other as employer and employee and the date situation is reinterpreted as a dispassionate work situation. Because of the incongruent time, secretary and boss may view the work situation as more akin to a date than is their usual custom. Because of the incongruent place priest and parishioner may pretend not to recognize each other, or to treat each other as "old pals". In short, after a bit of "fumbling around" in which various and varying tentative redefinitions may be tried out, a new congruent situation is interpreted as existing and *its* behavioral and sociolinguistic requirements are implemented (1972b: 41)

The necessity of making sense out of incongruent situations is underscored by Fishman's observation that:

seemingly incongruent situations frequently occur and are rendered understandable and acceptable. . . . Interlocutors reinterpret incongruences in order to salvage some semblance of the congruency in terms of which they understand and function within their social order. Were this not the case then no seemingly congruent domains could arise and be maintained out of the incongruences of daily life. (1972b: 49)

The contention of this chapter will be that it is the recognition and negotiation of membership in speech communities, through reading and exploratory gestures, which is the true language of membership, for it is only in the space "in between" communicability (habitus) and silence (strangeness) that language is needed and invoked. Language as such could not wish to be complete nor unambiguous (as Habermas calls for in the form of "nondistorted communication", 1971), for once it achieved that state it would no longer be needed. Indeed, this also implies that the achievement of consensus is an ongoing process of negotiation, and that it requires a keen awareness of the connotative element of the language of membership. Finally, it implies that the distance between familiar and strange habitus' is one which must be traversed from behind the glass. The portability of the glass bubble — the growing opacity and expressive function of the various proximities to which the modern stranger orients — renders obsolete prior attempts by Schutz and Habermas to integrate language and membership. The second-order language of membership of the modern stranger supersedes verbal language and must form the basis of any further theorizing on the relationships between language, membership, and the modern stranger.

1. The Search for Authentic Experience: The Publicity of Privacy

Observers of modernity (Bell, 1976; Boorstin, 1961; Dreitzel, 1977, 1981, 1983; Fromm, 1947, 1955, 1969; Hall, 1973, 1977; Klapp, 1969; Lasch, 1977, 1978; Lifton, 1968; Riesman, 1961; Schnall, 1981; Sennett, 1978; Slater, 1970; Trilling, 1972; Wilson, 1977; Wright, 1971; *et al.*) have noted that changing modes of social organization have produced greater atomization, less guidance in the way of strict "formulas" for living, and result for the individual in a void which I have formulated as "looking for a home". This search for home is most often referred to as a search for "authentic experience" – a truthful recognition of one's being-in-the-world which fills the void and confirms one's sense of oneself as a unique individual with a self-regulated path. For Klapp,

Some modern social systems deprive people of psychological "payoffs", the lack of which, expressed by terms such as alienation, meaninglessness, identity problem, motivates a mass groping for activities and symbols with which to restore or find new identity. People grope because they do not really know what is wrong, especially when there is physical prosperity yet a sense of being cheated. (1969: vii)

Klapp's "seeker" is formulated as "a person who is more or less actively, whether or not consciously, searching for a new self; his mobility and mass-mindedness reflect this preoccupation" (p. xi).

Whereas Klapp regards the "seeker" as the prototypical modern man at the level of individual experience, for MacCannell (1976) the principal issue concerning modernity is that of the cultural quest for personal authenticity. MacCannell develops a social type, "the tourist", to illustrate the mode of adaptation required by modernity.

MacCannell's tourist is like Klapp's seeker of authenticity in that he is bored with the self-evidence of home; however this specific type is based on the phenomenal increase in travel as a means for the search. The tourist goes abroad to "discover" the new. It is the "foreign" which becomes authentic to the tourist – the familiar by being commonplace ceases to be original. As the tourist consumes more and more of what was once foreign, by travelling and bringing back souvenirs, or by shopping at import stores and watching travel films, the world of commodities and experiences becomes a "global village" where spatial proximity is transcended by cultural proximity in the form of "foreign experience". The hunger for authenticity persists, with less and less external to the self which can satisfy it. There is a

belief that somewhere, only not right here, not right now, perhaps just over there someplace, in another country, in another life-style, in another social class, perhaps, there is *genuine* society. (p. 155)

The quest for "genuine society" as defining modernity suggests a fundamental dishonesty which it seeks to replace. If "authentic" means genuine,
real, and true, then by implication "inauthentic" modern life is ingenuine,
unreal, and false. The continuing oversight which animates the actor's everyday relation to the world constitutes a blatant denial of that being-in-the-
world. In semiological terms (Saussure, 1966), inauthenticity implies the
signifier taking on an identity of its own which belies its origins in expressing
the original referent. The signifier becomes its own signified; meaning is
found in unmediated appearance. Appearance no longer gives clues to a
hidden reality but exists only in terms of itself. As contextual, it holds
meaning only for the moment. The modern stranger is engaged in a continuous process of reading that meaning and laying claim to membership in
the community for which it is meaningful. This results in looking to that
which is *not* self-evident in order to discover authentic experience. Authenticity resides more in the experience of challenging the trustworthy recipes
than in any objective state. Authenticity ironically is sought in conditions
which are strange to everyday life.

Everyday life and its grinding familiarity stand in opposition to the many versions of
the 'high life' in the modern world. Everyday life threatens the solidarity of modernity
by atomizing individuals and families into isolated local groupings which are not func-
tionally or ideologically interrelated. *But everyday life is composed of souvenirs of life
elsewhere.* In this way, modernity and the modern consciousness infiltrate everyday
existence and, at the same time, subordinate it to life elsewhere. *The dialectics of
authenticity insure the alienation of modern man even within his domestic contexts.*
The more the individual sinks into everyday life, the more he is reminded of reality and
authenticity elsewhere. This structure is, I think, the source of the social fiction that
the individual's personal experience is the center of this our most depersonalized historical epoch. (MacCannell: 159-160 – emphases added)

The "souvenir" stands as a symbol of one's "life elsewhere". In the "grinding
familiarity" of everyday life the modern stranger reaches out for ways to
assert his autonomy *in a language that will be heard by others.* That is to say,
the experience or souvenir must be shared in a context of other-direction;
it must contribute somehow to one's self-sculpture as a particular "category"
on the urban panorama, in order for its value in the pursuit of "genuine
society" to be felt by both actor and other.

As hinted at, MacCannell's tourist bears a striking resemblance to the
modern stranger. But MacCannell, by trivializing everyday life in the Goff-
manesque world of sheer presence; by decontextualizing the search for
authentic experience; and by toying with terms such as "dialectics of authenticity" while in his own work exemplifying a denial of dialectics through
invoking a synchronic structuralist frame, has reified the tourist – an
apparently unintended outcome.

Theoretically, MacCannell contributes little beyond drawing parallels between the "idea" of semiology and the "idea" of tourism. Tourists encode and decode. But why? He adopts Goffman's "front" and "back" regions, and when combined with the semiotic application of "sight-marker" concludes that tourists are really searching for authentic experience. By literally grounding that search in the tour which takes one away, he neglects, however, the ways in which the search for authenticity has become a 52-week-of-the-year preoccupation at home as well. There remains unaddressed the question of why one would seek authenticity in the first place; and finally, the question of how one comes to *identify* an authentic experience is yet to be answered. MacCannell concedes that

A close examination of the act of sightseeing does reveal the individual making his own sight-marker linkages and constructing (or reconstructing) his own part of the modern world. (p. 136)

However, this concession seems to be an end in itself. What needs to be established before the tourist becomes anything more significant than a "category" is to ask what the processes are through which one comes to construct one's "own part of the modern world", and why.

To be salvaged from MacCannell's work is the sense of the modern actor as unfulfilled; as seeking fulfillment. And although the tourist is one actor who seeks authenticity, it is neither the tour nor the travel which gives evidence as to why nor how a "dialectic of authenticity" takes place. Instead, it is basic social processes which make unfulfillment an issue to begin with.

What needs to be asked is whether "the tourist" finds familiarity at home, or must he always be away? Does authenticity reside in *being elsewhere* – and hence is it only possible when one has a place to return to? If so, then the tourist may exemplify certain aspects of the modern stranger only. It needs to be examined how it is possible for home to *become* away; for strangeness to produce the very conditions which make the search for authenticity a form of making it familiar.

Dreitzel (1977) has observed that the crisis in identity occurs with the split between public and private realms, and its consequent creation of public and private selves. This split is characteristic of "industrial culture", which he defines as "the continuous production and consumption of cultural symbols, values, norms, and life styles at all levels of sophistication and educational differentiations" (p. 84), thus putting his finger on the major determining factor of consumer culture:

The cultural consumer is no longer confronted only with the end product, but is made a participant observer of the production process of cultural symbols. The fact that cultural symbols and interpretations are no longer simply given by tradition or either taken for granted or, at most, reinterpreted, but industrially produced and marketed is in itself almost a guarantee for their lack of legitimizing power. (p. 93)

It is experience, then, that confers authenticity. Yet this experience runs the risk of disconnectedness from any creative relation to the world. As Boorstin (1961) has shown, meaningful experience is something that society teaches its members to recognize and appreciate, and therefore takes away from them the power, will, and ability to recognize and define authentic experience. The lack of inner-directedness permitted in the search for authenticity has resulted in a full-fledged culture industry which has produced "formulas" for achieving authentic experience. As Ewen and Ewen (1982) have shown, modes and objects of consumption have come to embody meaning, imputing a pregiven character to the consumer. It may be argued that the thirst for external definitions of authenticity and means for expressing it through "externals" has been taken so far as to constitute a real poverty of self-actualization in the Maslovian sense. Whereby the cultural ideal in North America is clearly one of "pulling one's own strings", the conformist push to be recognized as a certain *kind* of self-actualizing member has resulted in a language of membership in which the shared cultural meanings are embodied in externals. The material appurtenances that one chooses in order to "express" one's authentic self, produce a readable copy with which other is presented. In turn, each other reproduces his image of himself through the expressive tool of externals.

This objectification of self and other may be considered an aesthetic mode at first glance. An entire society and its economy are geared toward the production and dissemination of meaning-endowed goods, which in turn confer identity upon their owners. The self-sculpture which has become a full-time preoccupation of the modern stranger is predicated on a deep desire to externalize that which can not be seen – to publicize what by nature of its location ("internal" – thoughts, feelings, experiences, political beliefs) would otherwise remain private. *It is only through the shift from a verbal to a nonverbal mode of expressing self that the modern stranger is enabled to sustain a sense of his own "authentic self".* For, as Willener (1976: 121) has pointed out, the authentic self sought is the "whole" self, "a fragmented individual being merely a sub-man".

It is the artificial creation of categorical "sub-men" through the autonomous spheres of public and private lives that produces the crisis and the search for an authentic, "whole" self. There is a paradoxical push for self-disclosure through the public realm – which is frustrated by what is perceived as the "artificial compartmentalization" of self in public life. The evolution of voluntary interest groups as "taste communities" (Gans, 1975), which may be perceived as expressive and a means toward self-actualization, Dreitzel regards as limiting the possibilities for articulating and discovering one's "whole self". Because of increasing compartmentalization into speech communities of seemingly infinite language varieties, members disclose only parts of their "personal identities" which are relevant and not discrediting in a particular context. They are forced to be only "partial selves" in an increasingly complex world in which the "authentic" or "whole" self has no audience. Because of the constraints placed upon self-disclosure in particular contexts, there is a heavy weight of restriction placed upon the "whole" self — as if there is no place where one can completely "be oneself" without some degree of role conflict. What the society has artfully engaged in producing is a consumer industry which promises to "sell self" — to provide the key to authenticity through material culture which in turn provides the means for self-disclosure.

Consumer culture promises the key to the reintegration of the compartmentalized self through "images" (Boorstin, 1961; Ewen, 1976). Images are produced and sustained through the member's use of culturally-shared symbols to say more about one's "other selves" than the context allows. It is here, therefore, that the second-order, connotative form which characterizes the language of membership takes on importance in the quest for authenticity. By commodifying other, and taking their cues as to what passes for authentic expression from the ways in which other presents himself, actors orient toward the greater refinement of the connotative role of externals. The "image" comes to reference that which may only be *imagined* — that which is beyond appearance, beyond context, which speaks of the "whole", authentic self.

The responsibility for evolving the connotative function of the language of membership may have been taken on by the mass media and the mass culture and fashion industries, but it is only sustained by the fact that the modern stranger is a willing participant in the generation of meaning. He wants a way to express more than the "natural" self-evidence provided by body. If the means exist by which he may say, "I am more than what you see" by invoking a symbol system which claims, "I am what you see" where what you see is connotative of internals, then these means will be devoured as bringing him closer to the discovery and articulation of his "authentic self". For ultimately that authentic self will only exist insofar as it achieves recognition by others — and the route to that recognition can only be through the least equivocal communication. The irony lies, therefore, in the *embedded equivocality* of the language of membership, and the necessity of that equivocality, and its attendant deconstruction, to give meaning to the sociability of expression.

The commodification of the other, however, is not an aesthetic in the sense that it produces admiration and wonder at other's beauty. Instead, the other as a work of art is predicated on the actor's taking the role of the artist, or author, of other. So, to return to the reflective mode as the truth-finding mode (Wilson, 1977), the modern stranger as observer is constantly engaged in authorizing other's claim to authenticity through the chary distribution of acknowledgement of his entitlement to an aesthetic. The irony is that this second-order realm of communication is so divorced from what authenticity (home) is supposed (mythologically) to be like that there is an *anaesthetic,* numbing effect which results. The search becomes a ritualized following of fashion dictates in order to sustain the surface appearance of membership. Reflectivity, as it comes to ground membership for the modern stranger, articulates the quest for authenticity and in so doing becomes, paradoxically, the only form of authentic behavior.

Arendt (1958) comes to a similar conclusion in her discussion of the "consumer society". She notes that labor, which she defines as the activity necessary in order to perpetuate life, has been redefined as the activity which makes one *socially* accepted in one's relation to the world. Once restricted to the "private" realm, labor has through the increasing commodification of the world become "publicized".

The ideals of *homo faber,* the fabricator of the world, which are permanence, stability, and durability, have been sacrificed to abundance, the ideal of the *animal laborans.* We live in a laborers' society because only laboring, with its inherent fertility, is likely to bring about abundance; and we have changed work into laboring, broken it up into its minute particles until it has lent itself to division where the common denominator of the simplest performance is reached in order to eliminate from the path of human labor power – which is part of nature and perhaps even the most powerful of all natural forces – the obstacle of the "unnatural" and purely worldly stability of the human artifice. (p. 126)

There is a parallel between Arendt's *animal laborans* and the modern stranger. The mandate of abundance is paralleled in a mandate of expression. The desire to produce and use up – to "experience" every "thing" reflects an insatiability which is also evidenced in the increasing scarcity of silence. The push to create the new and then destroy it, in the process producing an ideology of the *necessity* of experiencing novelty in order to experience authentic life, characterizes the consumer society as the seemingly insatiable desire to express, to pour out, to publicize, produces an uncontained echo which reverberates in all ears and compels a response.

Where the two proclivities merge is in the language of membership. Membership is conditional upon a demonstrated capacity to consume endlessly, and a demonstrated competence at using the means of consumption as a mode of expression. Communicative competence is grounded in a labor relation to the world of things. As Arendt implies, labor is translated into consumption. The work of being a member is articulated through an unending stream of expression of one's membership. Authentic experience is that which is sanctioned by the preexisting pressure to make authentic experience itself a form of labor: activity necessary for survival. Survival is grounded in second-order consumption — that is, the feeding of self-image *(homo faber)* at the expense of the species-being instinct to consume food in order to survive (Marx's original *animal laborans*).

The rather uncomfortable truth of the matter is that the triumph the modern world has achieved over necessity is due to the emancipation of labor, that is, to the fact that the *animal laborans* was permitted to occupy the public realm; and yet, as long as the *animal laborans* remains in possession of it, there can be no true public realm, but only private activities displayed in the open. The outcome is what is euphemistically called mass culture, and its deep-rooted trouble is a universal unhappiness, due on one side to the troubled balance between laboring and consumption and, on the other, to the persistent demands of the *animal laborans* to obtain a happiness which can be achieved only where life's processes of exhaustion and regeneration, of pain and release from pain, strike a perfect balance. (p. 134)

By saying that the emancipation of labor through publicity is the dominant change characterizing modernity, Arendt has put her finger on the plight of the modern stranger. Survival is only to be achieved in the public realm. The consumption which goes to feed public existence consists in sheer expression. To empty oneself and replenish oneself with the new through second-order expression constitutes, ironically, the pursuit of authentic experience.

As Arendt remarks,

This worldlessness of the *animal laborans*, to be sure, is entirely different from the active flight from the publicity of the world which we found inherent in the activity of 'good works'. The *animal laborans* does not flee the world but is ejected from it in so far as he is imprisoned in the privacy of his own body, caught in the fulfillment of needs in which nobody can share and which nobody can fully communicate. (pp. 118-119)

Not even Kant could solve the perplexity or enlighten the blindness of *homo faber* with respect to the problem of meaning without turning to the paradoxical "end in itself", and this perplexity lies in the fact that while only fabrication with its instrumentality is capable of building a world, this same world becomes as worthless as the employed material, a mere means for further ends, if the standards which governed its coming into being are permitted to rule it after its establishment. (p. 156)

For the modern stranger, it is precisely the perpetual search for meaning, for authenticity, which becomes an authentic way of being. The consumption and subsequent production of commodities is paralleled by the consumption and subsequent reproduction of self and other that occur through the reflective mode of the language of membership. It is only by objectifying other that one may feed off the other: by making other problematic, more than self-evident, a work of art to be created, aesthetically enjoyed and then replaced, the modern stranger preserves the driving force that is *homo faber*.

That the modern stranger increasingly commodifies other speaks not to the limit of appearance and objectification in being a means to an alienating end. Rather, it speaks to the desperation with which he clings to the creative impulse to find meaning in the means – to validate the estrangement of modern existence as an authentic being-in-the-world.

2. Reflexivity and Reflectivity: The Image of Self in the Broken Mirror

The shift toward the expression of self through participation in the cultural production of images which comes with an other-directed society is grounded in the use of reflectivity in the pursuit of authenticity. Reflectivity entails a "continuing oversight" of looking to what one is not – a potential self as mirrored in other – rather than to what one is now. However, because of the circularity of any mode of interpretation, it is also clear that there is a strong interdependence between one's image of self and of other; and that this is made manifest by the use of and reading of externals in the expression of self.

Cooley's (1964 [fp 1902]) concept of the "looking-glass self" was the first discussion on the reflective function of symbolic interaction to appear in the American sociological literature.[2] For Cooley, however, the mirror reflection provided by the other was an unmediated one. Cooley employed the analogy of the audience as a potter and the individual as a piece of clay in making his point that the response of other has a direct impact on one's self-perception. Human response at the level of the looking-glass self offers a nondiscursive, unmistakable reflection because for Cooley the embedded meaning of a language of membership was yet to be problematic. He wrote in a tradition-directed setting where there was only *one* looking-glass, which reflected the exact meaning intended.[3]

In a recent attempt to point to changes in western society, Dreitzel (1981) observes that

> The symbolic structures of this society are like a broken mirror: man sees himself reflected in his many identity-fragments yet he does not recognize himself as whole. (p.220)

In this sentence, Dreitzel provides the most poignant statement of the condition of the modern stranger yet to be articulated. The crisis of modern identity is framed as a crisis of control. The mirror, once intact and faithful to an undistorted image, can no longer offer a singular reflection. Shattered by the strain placed upon it to reflect back the "whole self", the broken mirror now yields to the many compartmentalized selves presented by the modern stranger.

The changes in the function of the looking-glass self are paralleled by the shift from first- to second-order language of membership; from the *reflexivity* of folk culture to the *reflectivity* of urban culture. *Reflexivity* is beyond control and pre-interpretative. As a function of the looking-glass, it applies in Cooley's tradition-directed world where there is a one-to-one relation between the sign and the referent. *Reflectivity*, on the other hand, implies mediation: the mirror reflects and sheds light upon a pregiven situation, changing it for the actor. It entails the intervention of the actor and the use of an interpretative lens.

The distinction is one predicated on the degree of self-evidence of life-situations encountered by the actor, and the extent to which pregiven formulae suitably account for them. Reflexive actions occur in a taken-for-granted world where the language of membership is a *denotative* one, as Schutz has taught. This is the world of folk culture in which the first-order language of membership is sufficient as a basis for exclusion.

The metaphor of the broken mirror is entirely appropriate for the second-order language of membership confronting the modern stranger. It suggests the transformation which has taken place from the passive, denotative reflexion of everyday life to the active, connotative reflection of modern city life. In a reflexive linguistic setting, the stranger is self-evident by his flagrant failure to fit in. No reading is required on the part of the host — membership, contingent on tradition and long practice, is continually reachieved in the "of course" fashion. The mirror provided for/by host and other is clear and unambiguous. It requires no interpretation. It divides actors reflexively into "in-group" and "out-group" and thus provides inviolable boundaries which in turn must be transcended before membership may be achieved. For Schutz and Mannheim, it was only with the struggle to transcend those reflexive boundaries, the pregiven recipes, with the work to become fluent in the first-order language of membership, that the *reflective* attitude was invoked by the stranger/host. He was forced to read, actively, at every point the effect that his efforts at joining/excluding had on the other. The reflection in turn served as a marker for where the stranger had to do more work in order to achieve membership; and for where the host had to rethink grounds for exclusion as membership competence became more closely approximated. The reflexive crisis produced by the confrontation between habitus', then, produced a need for reflection, for it threw into question the taken-for-granted world.

The shift that has been observed in modes of social organization has resulted in an accompanying shift in linguistic setting to one in which any other is neither a pregiven member and hence taken-for-granted, nor a pregiven outsider and hence defended against and excluded. Instead, the other is a potential member who must be screened according to the discursive non-self-evidence of his presence and presentation of self. Membership continues to be perpetually reachieved; however, the achievement takes the form of an active reading which not only defines other, but defines self in the "identity fragments" reflected off of the other.

For the modern stranger, the management of membership which Schutz identified for the outsider has become part of the everyday groping which grounds his own place in the group, while the anomalies to traditional recipes which once engendered a reflective response from the stranger/host have become so commonplace as to constitute grounds for reflexion. The transition in modes of social organization has produced public settings in which the recognition of potential others and the negotiation of membership have become an ongoing activity for the modern stranger. There is no certainty to be achieved; no end to fragment-gazing; no ultimate reconstruction of the broken mirror. Instead, the new taken-for-granted mode of membershipping is precisely the navigation of strangeness which at one time would have produced a reflexive crisis. Today, that very confrontation with the uncertain and constantly changing reflections of self off of other has become part of the normative order that Riesman calls other-direction. The reading of other, once problematic and requiring reflection, has become habitual, taken-for-granted, reflexive. To repeat Riesman's remarks,

This awareness, this radar-like sensitivity to how one is navigating in the social world, and this tendency to make that navigation into an end of life as well as a means — these seem to me to be characteristic of the psychological type I have termed other-directed. (1951: 117)

If the principal activity for the modern stranger is one of authenticating self, this is achieved through the reflectivity of the broken mirror. The broken mirror sheds flashes of light from every angle. It feeds back a world which gives one a place, and informs one as to that place.

The attempt to mend the broken glass; to establish an identity which combines the techniques of information-control at the actor's disposal in orchestrating his "social identity" (Goffman, 1963b) and the self-perception of adequacy and control is an outward-looking rather than an inward-looking glance. Self-reflection, as classically formulated, has taken a turn from its metaphoric usage to a literal one: the mirror of Mead's (1934) "I" is no longer provided by the "me"; instead, the "fragments" which catch the light and reflect back images are the others who are also looking for a crystal ball.

The broken mirror has made unquestionable that which was once questionable: made an object of "reflexion" that which was once "reflected upon". Dreitzel's play with these terms is made even more interesting with the use of the mirror metaphor. The presence of a clear, unquestionable image through the reflexivity produced by the mirror is complicated when the mirror breaks, and the fragments, bouncing images somewhat contradictorily off of one another in their confusion, produce a need for a self-reflectivity in an effort to organize competing images and arrive at an "authentic", "whole" self. The tension of modernity lies in the impossibility of ever constructing a unified whole once the smooth certain surface has been shattered; yet, as Dreitzel implies, the emancipation promised by the possibility of many images of self may be a cause for optimism.

3. The Language of Membership

I have suggested that the search for authenticity through the fragments of the broken mirror constitutes a shift from a reflexive life to a reflective life. Reflectivity is made necessary by the ambiguous distinction between public and private realms that Arendt has described. If it is so that the "authentic" experience which was once the preserve of the private realm has become publicized, and if the public experience of authenticity has become crucial in defining authentic experience for the individual, then the way in which authenticity is articulated is of importance to understanding the modern stranger.

Schutz's four propositions regarding the linguistic production of and exclusion of strangers are: (i) the principle of cultural contextualization: spoken and written language is surrounded by "fringes" which give added emotional and rational meaning; (2) the principle of cultural polysemy: linguistic terms have many connotations, both formal and informal; (3) the principle of colloquiality: every social group evolves its own "private code"; and (4) the principle of historical embodiment: the whole history of a group is embodied in its language. In suggesting a language of membership for the modern stranger, the task will be to show how the four characteristics of language which served to exclude the outsider in Schutz's world translate to equip the modern stranger with the tools to navigate embedded meaning; how the embedded reading of membership *precedes* the locutionary act and takes place at the level of the illocutionary act; and how it is only by taking the perspective of "in between" that the modern stranger can proceed from reading to interaction – from recognition to speech.

3.1. The Semiological Chain

Barthes' (1976) distinction between first- and second-order semiological systems inspired the current usage of first- and second-order language of membership. He says that

myth is a peculiar system, in that it is constructed from a semiological chain which existed before it: it *is a second-order semiological system*. That which is a sign (namely the associative total of a concept and an image) in the first system, becomes a mere signifier in the second. We must here recall that the materials of mythical speech (the language itself, photography, painting, posters, rituals, objects, etc.), however different at the start, are reduced to a pure signifying function as soon as they are caught by myth. Myth sees in them only the same raw material; their unity is that they all come down to the status of a mere language. Whether it deals with alphabetical or pictorial writing, myth wants to see in them only a sum of signs, a global sign, the final term of a first semiological chain. (p.114)

So,

in myth there are two semiological systems, one of which is staggered in relation to the other: a linguistic system, the language (or the modes of representation which are assimilated to it), which I shall call the *language-object*, because it is the language which myth gets hold of in order to build its own system; and myth itself, which I shall call *metalanguage*, because it is a second language, *in which* one speaks about the first. (p. 115)

Now, there are crucial differences prohibiting the direct application of Barthes' schema to the modern stranger. First, whereas Barthes fashions Everyperson as an *object* of mythology, I have sketched him as a *subject* in the language of membership. For Barthes, the key actor is the semiologist; the clear-sighted myth reader who is able to distinguish between first- and second-order mythological speech. For the innocent myth-consumer, who is in effect consumed *by* myth, there is no "inside action", no claim to skillful learning of a code. The myth consumer is "done to", acted upon by myth. There is no room for negotiation.

I have taken the view that the modern stranger is a willing participant in the ongoing reconstruction of the inside view of meaning; and that this reconstruction is only possible through the continuing oversight of the "outward glance". The modern stranger, like the myth reader, has access by virtue of his membership to the code which defines him as a member; but it is only in the continuing silent language of potential conversation that his fluency is maintained. In aligning the myth reader with the modern stranger I will first suggest structural parallels which speak to the origin of the second-order language of membership in Barthes' second-order semiological system, after which I will turn to the fundamental differences for which the semiological model is unable to account.

Structural Parallels. The key parallel between Barthes' mythological system and the language of membership resides in their double-layered character. For Barthes, the two semiological systems (language-object and metalanguage) overlap. The language-object is the mode of representation through which myth may be heard. It is the *denotative* system of sheer referentiality which consists of a symmetrical relation between sign and referent. The language-object is a vehicle for the reproduction of myth, but it is not myth itself. The metalanguage is that which is spoken *through* the language-object; that which appropriates the language-object in a *connotative* relation. It is the embedded meaning to which only well-versed members have access.

The first-order semiological system for Barthes has its parallel in the re-flexive, taken-for-granted world of denotative speech. The second-order semiological system, metalanguage, is paralleled by the reflective, connotative language of membership. It has an embedded meaning that may only be read from a position of achieved cultural acuity.

Fundamental Differences. The fundamental difference between Barthes' metalanguage and the language of membership resides at the level of in-tentionality. The language of membership is a form of discourse akin to the mode of mapping of the trained observer. It entails an ongoing involvement of the stranger as both actor and other in the continual reachievement of the definition of membership.

For Barthes, there is no room for recognition and negotiation, for the sign systems are not available on a second-order level to Everyperson. Their read-ing is a privileged activity. Actors go about living at the level of the language-object, innocently consuming myth. Barthes' system, by neglecting actor, neglects the willing participant in the constant restructuring of myth. The modern stranger must be seen in terms of his desire for membership and cultural proximity. Membership orientation *necessitates* the continuing cycle of exploratory gestures which allows the member to find his place in terms of an unwritten language.

The reflective search for meaning which is the linguistic activity of the stranger becomes, like metalanguage, an unquestioned system itself. The critical point to be taken from Barthes is in regard to the "semiological chain", which demands that "that which is a sign ... in the first system, be-comes a mere signifier in the second" (p. 114). For the modern stranger, in the social transition from a denotative to a connotative language of member-ship, that which was once the cause for reflection − *i.e.* the reflexive crisis which forced actor and other to examine their heretofore trustworthy recipes − becomes a reflexive, taken-for-granted activity in the world where third-order mapping is a necessity. Aspects which once contravened hard and fast rules of membership − being from another place, speaking a different language − are no longer disruptive because such changes have come to pass in North American cities making heterogeneity the norm. *Because* the past taken-for-granted recipes are no longer sufficient, however, new ones have been created. The reflective, outward glance of the inside actor that characterizes the language of membership has become a reflexive, taken-for-granted system in its own right. As with the myth reader who thinks nothing of "reading behind the image", for whom such reading is in fact the only possible reading, the modern stranger has adopted a reflexive stance toward the second-order language of membership such that it, too, has become second nature.

If the modern stranger is a willing participant in the ongoing restructuring of membership criteria, and the mode taken is one of a habitual language of membership, then it remains to be shown how such a language is possible, and what form it takes.

3.2. Communicative Competence: Recognition and Negotiation

In suggesting that membership and exclusion are grounded in language, I take with Habermas (1970) that there are certain preconditions or "competencies" which must be met before an ideal speech situation is achieved; that it is only in an ideal speech situation that nondistorted communication may occur; and finally that a group defines itself according to its ability to engage in nondistorted communication, that is, according to its consciousness of itself as a speech community; as possessing a language of membership.

I also take with Mead (1934) the need to go back to language to establish that which is the fundament of the social; that it is the possession of the key to a universe of discourse which provides the tool to articulate desire; that desire being one of sharing "that I exist", "that I act", and "that I choose"; in other words, of affirming "authentic" being-in-the-world through the recognition of others.

In working toward a language of membership I am assuming, therefore, an intersubjectively produced "communicative competence" which supercedes the genetically granted, instrumental and monological "linguistic competence" described by Chomsky (1968), Gumperz (1971) and Hymes (1972b). Habermas maintains that

in order to participate in normal discourse, the speaker must have – in addition to his linguistic competence – basic qualifications of speech and of symbolic interaction (role-behavior) at his disposal, which we may call communicative competence. Thus, communicative competence means the mastery of an ideal speech situation. (1970:138).

The ideal speech situation which must prevail before nondistorted communication may occur is preeminently intersubjective. Communicative competence, it follows, is only open to those who already share meanings within a cultural context; who experience "complete reciprocity". The communicatively competent actor must, in turn, be a member of a speech community.

Membership within a speech community is therefore considered to be the precondition for intersubjectivity by Habermas. It must be shown, however, to what extent the groupness of the community is established through or prior to language. To use Habermas' language, a speech community is predicated on "semantic universals" which may be either *a priori* or *a posteriori*: either precultural universals or culturally-specific universals.

Some meanings are a priori universal, inasmuch as they establish the conditions of potential communication and general schemes of interpretation; others are a posteriori universal in the sense, [sic] that they represent invariant features of contingent scopes of experience which, however, are common to all cultures. (p. 134)

A priori semantic universals are made possible because humans have the physical capacity and the desire to communicate. Mead's usage may be taken further to suggest two implications for the stranger. First, *strangers are able to recognize that they do not speak the same language.* Second, *they may attempt to rectify it by generating significant symbols.* These in turn may be designated as two stages in the communication between strangers: first, that of *recognition*; and second, that of *negotiation*. The social organizational changes which have produced the particular world into which the modern stranger is thrown necessitate that the first stage, of recognition, take place at the *illocutionary level* — and it is only once recognition has occurred that negotiation, which constitutes the basis for further communication (either locutionary or illocutionary), may proceed.[4]

To say that strangers realize that they do not speak the same language appears to be a facile claim. However, it speaks to the inherent self-consciousness of membership. Membership is not entirely taken-for-granted, because it is predicated on an *initial having joined*. The "having joined" of each current member establishes that at one time he was a non-member who did not speak the same language and who therefore had to fulfil both the steps of recognition and negotiation in order to achieve the current state of membership in the group's universe of discourse. Membership is not entirely taken-for-granted because it is predicated on the continuing possibility that the other may fail, may show a lack of fluency in the language, may "lose one's footing" (Dreitzel, 1983).[5]

Encounters between strangers are oriented to the possibility of nondistorted communication and the concomitant likelihood that it is not a given, yet will have to be achieved. One encounters the other and on the basis of minimal indicators makes certain assumptions regarding the likelihood that he will be party to one's universe of discourse. Such minimal indicators are contextual and culturally enhanced, existing within a particular "social structure" (Habermas, 1970), which is composed of meaning-endowed relations between actors, others, and the environment. It allows, for example, the following discourse to occur between two strangers:

The scene is a fast-food outlet across from a stadium. A man walks into the store, places his order, and while waiting strikes up a conversation with the male employee who is preparing his food.

Customer: So, do you think old John is going to get his way?
Employee: Naw, can't see all of East City bending over for him.
Customer: Bet you'd be pretty happy if they moved here.

Employee: Yeah (smiles knowingly). Extra cheese on both?

One approach to making sense of this interaction might look like a typical ethnomethodological deconstruction of the taken-for-grantedness of the universe of discourse in which they are engaged (Garfinkel, 1967). By "filling in the blanks" it would provide the reader with a key to the unwritten but shared meaning system which allows complete strangers to carry on such a conversation. It might look something like this:

The scene is a fast-food outlet across from a stadium [the university football stadium which has recently been the center of controversy in the sports news. John Doe, owner of the East City Sharks, a football team, has threatened to move the team to this stadium if he does not get a larger share of concession profits at the Sharks games. John Doe, is well known among sports fans as a man who likes to get his way]. *A man walks into the store, places his order, and while waiting strikes up a conversation* [contingent only upon "openings" in the "main involvement" of the situation — food trans-action — and thus constituting a "side involvement" (Goffman, 1963a)] *with the male employee* [presenting himself as young, tanned, well-built and athletic looking] *who is preparing the food.*

Customer: So, do you think old John [Doe] is going to get his way [and get a share of the concession profits at East City Sharks Games]?
Employee: Naw, can't see all of East City bending over for him.
Customer: Bet you'd be pretty happy if they [Sharks] moved here [the stadium].
Employee: Yeah [smiles knowingly because they both understand that such a move would be great for business]. Extra cheese on both? [end of side involvement, return to main involvement]

Such an analysis is helpful in that it may illuminate for the reader that which is taken for granted. It points to the ability of a third member (the trained observer) to engage in third-order mapping by imagining that this talk is being heard by a non-member, and to impute the problematic nature posed by attempting to "get in" to a universe of discourse. The analysis is made from the standpoint that there are privatized meanings shared by members, and that it is possible for members to take the "sociological stance", to dis-tanciate themselves from their own situatedness and imagine that they are strangers faced with what the actors engaged in the discourse maintain to be a trustworthy recipe.

But where ethnomethodology ends, an analysis of the language of member-ship must begin. Rather than work back from a discourse to reveal the layers of assumptions which make it possible for the actor to *take the viewpoint of the other*, I intend rather to look at the initial encounter between strangers as a situation which demands that the member *take the viewpoint of the outsider* in order to establish what degree of familiarity to assume in the encounter. This is the "outward glance" available only to the insider. It is a reading of the situation, and of the other, as one who speaks one's language or not. This is essential before any conversation may take place. Fishman (1972a) notes that topics, domains, role-relations and locales are all important factors in defining what language variety will be selected at any one time.

To illustrate the impact of this initial contextual glance on the discourse, simply change any one of the structural variables which frame the encounter: the fast-food outlet is conducive to a high level of turnover of patrons in a highly impersonalized and hence universalized setting; the proximity to the stadium produces a strong likelihood that both clientele and employees will be conversant in the language of football; the "jock-like" appearance of the employee, sustained through the culturally valued signs of youthfulness, a tanned and highly muscular body, hint at the likelihood of his fluency in "sports talk". The four variables of importance – the immediate physical environment of the encounter (locale); its location within a meaning-endowed milieu (domain); the prelinguistic signs of membership displayed by the approached other (role-relations); and the availability of "sports talk" (topic) – all combine to set the stage for contextualized discourse. They produce a setting in which the discourse is most logical and taken-for-granted. The setting as an event is influenced by the perceived confluence of environment and actor; negotiation (second stage) results, therefore, from the initial recognition (first stage).

The presentation of self of the employee, and the customer's "correct" reading of the illocutionary messages conveyed, are critical in framing this interaction. The elements which hint at communicative competence determine the degree of familiarity to be employed: the preliminary recognition of the other as one who would be fluent in "sports talk" enables one to make the choice as to whether to engage in such sports talk. Even more critical, however, is the ability of the third party (observer) to note the factors present in the preframing recognition which facilitate further interaction.

The perception by the actor that the other is a member of his universe of discourse (in this case, the overarching speech community that might engage in "sports talk") is not, therefore, a completely unreflective activity. It is not, that is to say, taking place solely at the reflexive, prelinguistic level of habit, of the unchallenged habitus, of the taken-for-granted world of competent membership, of "linguistic competence". It is reflective activity which has *become* habitual; an ongoing technique of adjustment which speaks to the member's capacity to come to terms with the problematic in a reflexive way. It is a process of assessing the frame and choosing how to proceed on the basis of the recognition of the other as either a member or a non-member;

it is a reflective activity which produces the context for subsequent reflexive action.

This presituational reading entails taking the position of being "in between". A certain amount of detachment is called for when one is engaged in assessing the potential communicative competence of the other. It is a probabilistic "exploratory" (Cohen, 1955) evaluation which *must be made*. Each actor must not fail to evaluate the membership orientation of others in encounters; indeed, such evaluation is a precondition for engaging in an encounter. It is the discovery, at the level of the *a priori* semantic universals, of the degree to which one shares membership in a universe of discourse.

How is this evaluation to be made? How is it possible for strangers to recognize that they do or do not speak the same language? The first step of recognition produces a social moment which calls for negotiation on the basis of the thing discovered. This negotiation may take an illocutionary or a locutionary form, but it is nevertheless oriented toward establishing the grounds for commonality and further communication. The exploratory stage of the encounter is by definition an illocutionary precursor to further communicative action. It takes place at the stage of establishing each other's universe of discourse. Strangers know that they do not speak the same language. They know this because the most important conversation takes place not in the encounter but before it; not in the completion of the frame but in setting it up.

To know that the other does not speak one's language is, paradoxically, to be fluent in a vacuum of discourse. It is to know that the conditions of membership preclude strangers; that one's failure to be communicatively competent in one group's universe of discourse implies a fluency in another, on the one hand; and secondly, as Mead has pointed out, the need to establish an intermediary space, the space "in between" language varieties, in which communication is made not only possible but necessary.

If strangers recognize each other on the basis of unfamiliarity, that is also to say that they recognize that they are not familiar. But what is there that is familiar in the world of the modern stranger? Is the encounter with the strange always, as Geertz claims for the ethnographer, an exercise in "finding our feet" (1973:13)? Insofar as the trained observer is to take interest in everything and everyone that presents itself (to him) as strange: yes. The modern stranger engages in a constant assessment — the outward glance — of the approached other's potential comembership. But the observer engages every strange situation in an in-depth mapping of the third-order because he is not membership oriented and treats every stranger as a potential "informant". For the modern stranger, on the other hand, the recognition of strangeness is not always followed by a *reflective* placing of other as one requiring a deeper getting-to-know.

Upon recognition of the other as strange, negotiation may take one of two paths. The first, based upon the recognition that the other is *not* a potential member, entails continuing the unbroken reflexive stream of silence. The second, based upon the recognition of the other as a potential member, entails taking reflective action toward passing from the realm of unfamiliarity to that of familiarity. So it is at the juncture between recognition and negotiation – between apprehension and action – between second-order and first-order codes – that the language of membership may shift from usage in a reflexive to a reflective manner.

The reflexive (habitual) recognition of strangers is the fundamental organizing activity of modern urban society. This is the realm of the "once over", the "first impression". Others are either accepted or dismissed on the basis of unwritten, unspoken codes of membership which manifest themselves in external presentations of self. Members internalize the codes such that they engage in a reflexively sustained dialogue of acceptance or rejection with encountered others, until that stream of silence is broken by only two anomalous cases: the other who is recognized as being a potential other; and the other who is recognized as being culturally illiterate or linguistically incompetent (a true "stranger" to the language of membership). Reflexivity may only be sustained among "normal" strangers; those content with the second-order publicization of privacy as their mode of discourse. The smooth flowing of encounters between strangers entails every other being an explicit and willing informant at the level of the second-order code.

The difference between the modern stranger and the trained observer in this regard involves the embedded *familiarity* of the strange. Whereas the observer of another culture is forced to learn to read an "other" tongue (including both written and unwritten codes), the modern stranger moves in a world whose strangeness is his mother tongue; where language varieties become the rule, not the exception. The continuous stream of strangeness for the ethnographer is a situation he seeks to overcome; to transform to the familiar. For the modern stranger, however, the continuing stream of strangeness is itself familiar in its self-evidence. Strangers are preconstituted as "informants" at the level of the silent language of membership. They offer up to the potential other all he needs to know to make the choice to stop or to continue on. And it is ironically the stopping that causes trouble to the continuing stream of strangeness.

To stop – to choose to act on the basis of other's compelling "information" – is to risk the possibility that (1) the informant is lying; (2) the informant does not know how he is presenting himself; or (3) the informant does not see the actor as a potential other as well. Each of these risks demands that negotiative action take the form of a series of "exploratory gestures".

(1) Appearance that "lies" remains presented and read as "truth" in the language of membership. As Wittgenstein has said, "lying is a language game that needs to be learned like any other one" (1976:90). The externals which silently present clues to internals are not lies as long as they are read at the level of recognition. Presentation of self is never contested until the member is stopped by another and asked to account for himself. Until that time, the "truth" – what one "is" – is only what is read. The lie can not be *misread*, for it is *true*. It is only in the transition from second-order recognition to first-order negotiation that the presentation may be discovered to be a lie. It is in the transition from unfamiliar to familiar; from public to private; from external to internal that it may be claimed of the other that "he lied".

(2) The possibility that the informant does not know how he is presenting himself always exists. Yet he may well be *read* as knowing the meaning of his self-presentation. The presentation exists independently of the intention of the actor because the actor is assumed to have intended it.

(3) There is always the possibility that the recognition of other as a potential co-member may be one-sided. This is likely to be the case when self-presentation is unintended as read; as in the case of the stranger who embodies a different code, or as in the case of the visibly "stigmatized" whose social identity, imputed on the basis of his visible stigma, is regarded as inseparable from his personal identity (Goffman, 1963b).

The recognition between strangers that they do not speak the same language may not occur immediately. It may be that their respective languages have varying connotations to different others; that an other from a different speech community may read actor's silent utterance as one which has a valid meaning, yet that is not necessarily a shared meaning. The lie, the misrepresentation, or the one-sided apprehension of other, all of which may be masked by the apparently nondistorted communication occurring at the "completely reciprocal" level of the silent language of membership, emerge as misunderstandings in subsequent negotiative discourse.

So the public presentation of self of the modern stranger is predicated on the assumption of *intention*, of *cultural fluency*, and of an *identity between public and private selves*. If any of these features is lacking in encounters between strangers, then misunderstanding, which is to say unaware speaking of different language varieties, will occur. This possibility of misunderstanding underscores the trouble with langue, any language: that it is *not* self-evident; that it does *not* reveal all; that there is need for further exploration in the realm of gestures before the risk of "incorrent" imputation of private identity on the basis of public presentation disappears.

The paramount assumption of the language of membership that strangers can recognize that they do not speak the same language only works *because they can also recognize when they do*. That members are willing participants in the co-information transmission through exploratory gestures is the fundament of the continuous flow of strangeness in modern society. It is assumed that no one will act on misinformation; or will misread information; or that they will be unversed in the correct conduct of exploratory gestures. As Goffman has demonstrated again and again, the underlying agreement between actors in public situations itself constitutes a normative order.

Habermas would have his reader believe that nondistorted communication is the outcome of an ideal speech situation. Yet the least distorted communication takes place only at the prelinguistic, illocutionary level of establishing difference. Speech is invoked to confuse, to solidify difference. Speech is negotiative action which is predicated on a prior recognition of difference. Indeed, it might be claimed that the only true form of nondistorted communication is that which establishes that self and other are not the same. From then on, as Mead has taught, actor uses language to assert self; to deal with the intersubjective world into which he has been thrown. But it is an intersubjectivity predicated on an acute awareness that membership decisions have already been made at the illocutionary level.

There is a metalanguage which frames future discourse and makes it possible, necessary, and successful as a tool for asserting difference. It is the metalanguage of prelinguistic recognition which does the exploratory work of placing actors in particular settings and scripting the subsequent scenes.

If this is the case, then it is not to Schutz's four linguistic propositions but rather to the semantic universals which make particular speech communities (to which the propositions then apply) possible, that the analysis of the stranger should turn. That is to say, the real question concerning the modern stranger should be regarding what it is about membership orientation *per se* — the desire for recognition which produces an attempt at recognition — which produces speech communities. This takes place at the recognition stage. Any subsequent negotiation which may take place as a result of the establishment of membership is contingent upon perceived communicative competence. That perceived competence may be confirmed by action, particularly along the lines of Schutz's four propositions. But these propositions are only invoked *after* difference/similarity has been established.

Certain questions which might arise from Habermas' work on communicative competence now lose relevance. One might ask, when addressing the "ideal speech" situation, whether it is possible for strangers to become communicatively competent; what processes are involved; or whether strangers are the ones who produce systematically distorted communication by lacking knowledge of the *a posteriori* semantic universals of the community to which they are strange. None of these, however, looks to the question which has animated this work: what it is that makes strangers to begin with.

The ideal speech situation suggested by Habermas is tautological. As constituted, one may only work toward it while already within it. Nondistorted communication is a contradiction in terms if communication is taken with Mead as only possible around a set of shared significant symbols. The locutionary is the key to communicative competence, with the illocutionary supplementing meaning. Rousseau's claim that one does not know where a man comes from until he has spoken still may stand. There are things which further distinguish self from other that do not present themselves in the illocutionary mode. But what do they matter when the possibility of speech is curtailed by the pre-emptive function of the recognition of membership — of the exploratory gesture? The individual's potential speech may remain just that, forever, if the precursory level of recognition does not produce a mutual desire to proceed toward talk.

For the modern stranger, the framing activity of the illocutionary recognition serves as an initial context in which to establish membership. The subtle ways in which members articulate their orientation become vastly more significant in determining subsequent communication than a blatant speaking of interests.

Whereas exclusion once took place on the basis of *cultural distance* which was evident in the denotative aspects of language, the modern stranger finds himself potentially excluded *within* a world of culturally proximate signs. While accomplished at the fluency of cultural "fringes", polysemy, colloquiality, and historical embodiment that once distinguished the stranger from the host on the basis of a referential language, the second-order, illocutionary language of membership heightens the sensitivity of the member to within-cultural distanciation and the hidden meanings which may only be decoded as a result of studied and longstanding membership in a culturally discursive community.

Derrida's "trace" is suggestive of the change which has taken place in the language of membership. First-order referential speech, for which the sign = referent, and for which understanding was a reflexive activity, prevailed in a tradition-directed world. The language of membership for the modern stranger entails the deconstruction of a second-order code in which the "traces" — the implied, culturally contextualized meaning which lies *beyond* the sign — and one's skill at recognizing it is the measure of one's communicative competence.

The dual demand placed upon the modern stranger is one that confronts both publicity and privacy as being hopelessly intertwined. For the first time, a person's social identity is predicated on how one chooses to present oneself, while one's personal identity is much more a product of the reflections perceived through the fragments of the broken mirror. One has control only over the package of symbols that one puts together — not their reading. The reflected "image" is the product of others' readings of the "traces" evident in one's speech. The confluence between intended meaning and received meaning is critical, and points to the paradoxical ascendancy of shared cultural experience, history, and consequently meaning in a time which is being touted as highly alienating.

The language of membership for the modern stranger is Cooley's looking-glass self taken to the limit: the self has *become* the looking-glass; the reflection has come to carry more weight than the object reflected. In semiological terms, the meaning embedded in the sign has taken it far beyond the referent in its communicational implications. For the modern stranger, authenticity is commensurate with the constant rearticulation of self through the language of membership. The unique quality of that articulation, however, lies in the stranger's accomplished ability *to read* other. The language has become a silent one.

Notes

1. In his well-known study of delinquent subcultures, Cohen happened upon this principle of communication which may apply generally when there is little consensus regarding the conditions of membership in a group.

   Cohen's example of innovation, in the context of delinquent subcultures, refers to an individual's attempts to engage in behavior which is not within the code of membership of the group.
2. Adam Smith, in *The Theory of Moral Sentiments* (1966 [fp 1759]), identified many of the reflective processes which later came to ground symbolic interactionism.
3. More recent work by Becker (1963) and Lemert (1951) allows for the *equivocality* of the mirror image through the possibility of a "breakdown in communications".
4. The notion that strangers recognize that they do not speak the same language, and Habermas' concept of *a priori* linguistic universals, provide a starting point for subsequent research on the interface between biological recognition of like-others, and the cultural recognition of like-others which is the focus of this study.
5. My translation.

Chapter V
Toward the Modern Stranger

I have tried to suggest how the language of membership is a silent one: an unwritten, unspoken language that can only be used by members who are culturally fluent and seek to pre-empt the verbal with the non-verbal. In public settings, the silent language has far greater exclusionary and inclusionary significance for the member than mere words.

In *The Silent Language* (1973), Hall brings attention to the gaps "in between" cultures and the strategies used for filling them in. His forays at cultural proxemics, despite their lack of theoretical grounding, compel the reader to muse over the kind of actor that could step in between and be totally adaptable. The acute perception of the modern stranger to the unspoken which underlies the spoken makes it possible for him to move in and out of worlds and elicit "welcome" responses both at home and away. For home is away. For the modern stranger, home resides in the daily accomplishment of yet another cultural setting; of membership in yet another speech community.

The modern stranger is an historical actor *par excellence.* He is living in a world whose normative structure governing membership and exclusion is not one which may be learned once and used forever after as a trustworthy recipe, as Riesman claims is characteristic of tradition-direction. Instead, he learns to be a perpetual reader of changing definitions of membership. As a member-reader he actively participates in that defining, because his reading becomes a form of speaking. His ability or inability to fit in, to "go with the flow", itself speaks to his fluency in the language of membership.

The modern stranger as he has been formulated is the one who can cope with a world which has taken us very quickly away from tradition-directed forms of establishing and maintaining membership. He has been made responsible for his own self-actualization in a world in which the expression of that accomplishment has become a full-time preoccupation. His struggle is with the authentic use of a very limited set of tools of that expression — what Simmel called "externals" — to convey what can only develop "internally". He must give, but not too much; he must walk a tightrope of dignity in a hall of broken mirrors. The tightrope itself will give, but we think — we must think — that it will hold him. It is the thin path that connects the past with the future; that makes into myth the world of sheer privacy which once prevailed — that holds the threat, conveyed in literature such as Orwell's *1984* (1961), of sheer publicity which might transpire. The tension produces, if nothing else, the desire to find out what it means to be truly human — to achieve recognition and acceptance for the accomplishment of fluency in the language of membership. The paradox is that fluency once achieved removes the threat of either end of the rope encroaching upon the midpoint. He can manage, he can cope. And he can willingly engage in the collective search for identity because he has found his end in the search.

1. Implications

If the modern stranger is the professional navigator, the one who is perpetually situated "in between", who perpetually seeks to accomplish distance through membership and membership through distance, then what are the implications of this conclusion for modern society and sociology's ability to confront it? The study of the modern stranger provides a basis for returning to issues which are current for sociologists. I will look at both the empirical and theoretical issues which have grounded this study, and suggest how the concept of the modern stranger may now contribute to their furtherance.

1.1. Empirical Issues

The empirical context which has grounded this study is one of *cosmopolitanism*. Chapter Two showed how the three forces of urbanization, mobility, and sophisticated global communications have contributed to produce a world in which questions of community, membership, home, authentic culture, and public and private identity have become problematic for the producers of culture as well as for the consumers of culture. This study has sought to explore the conditions of membership which have come to prevail in such a world. It was found that the tradition-directed myth of home has set a standard which the modern stranger has found difficult to replicate in a world of acquaintances rather than friends; of temporary domiciles rather than permanent homes; of mass media production of familiarity through the conventionally alienating objectification of the other.

In a world in which information-transmission and rapid technological change have forced the common-sense member into a passive position of consumption rather than production, survival has become a search for authenticity by struggling to produce a self in the face of the barrage of reflections which the modern stranger meets in every social contact. He fights the tendency to become a consumer of himself; this entails objectifying and reading other. The objectification of other constitutes the only productive relationship he has; and implicates himself, ultimately, as product of other – as the reflections that he gives off become the source of other's objectification of him.

This new form of objectification, which I have called "discursive strangeness", makes members willing participants in an ongoing reaffirmation of the group and the criteria for membership. At the same time, it forces the anonymity which theorists have noted as accompanying the empirical changes in social organization to manifest itself at the level of appearance. It preserves the strangeness, the autonomy, of members while giving them a place. It constitutes a form in which others may be interchangeable – as members who are totally fluent in navigating the city, the corporation, the globe. The new world is the world of the modern stranger: the impediments to finding a place and making it one's own have all but disappeared because this is the one activity which seems to unite the world of strangers.

In liberating the stranger from being an outsider, the application of the "modern stranger" has potential for the rethinking of the "marginality" which has been imputed to certain social types of actors. In particular, the category of the "homeless" must be seriously rethought. The modern stranger as the trained observer in the city, as the "urban man" who invokes categories to define and order the city according to an ongoing process of recognition and negotiation, does so "in between" a mythology of "home" in which publicity and privacy are discrete modes of involvement, and an empirical reality in which that "home" is rapidly slipping from the grasp of the majority of members. In such a world, how can the category of "homelessness" have any meaning in defining the boundaries of "homefulness"; in suggesting how the modern stranger as the taxonomist categorizes others in such a way as to find his own place?

"Homeless women" is a social type that has recently been produced by the unwitting conspiracy of imputational specialists and the mass media, and incorporated categorically into the urban way of seeing others in the form of the construct, "bag lady". The production of this social type when "homefulness", as has been demonstrated, is an increasingly ambiguous term, speaks to the desperation with which members cling to the myth of home. Homeless women are formulated as "strangers" in Simmel's sense, whose existence is predicated on an alien normative structure yet who are so spatially proximate as to constitute part of the ecological makeup of any large metropolis in North America. It is because these women depict, as does any "freak", that which members most fear (Fiedler, 1978), that they are excluded from membership. Their marginal existence epitomizes a bit too closely the changing conditions of membership which affect us all (Harman, 1987).

Another example of homelessness which could be examined has to do with the effects of socialization into cosmopolitanism which is, as Musgrove predicted, becoming increasingly the norm for the generation growing into an other-directed world. Children of transient families (e.g. diplomats, armed forces personnel, and multinational business people) have always been subjected to competing definitions of "home" and "away"; of community. One consequence of rampant cosmopolitanism in North American society is that these children are no longer in a minority. For them, "home" has become much more like "away" because internationalism, in producing modern strangers, has become the dominant normative condition. It is this change at home, however, that can no longer be ignored. How long can we continue to sweep other-direction under the carpet of mythological tradition-direction? Subsequent research must be devoted to the ability of the institutions of socialization — family, school, mass media — to let go of the myths and educate for other-direction.

In focusing on modes of social interaction, I have not attempted to address the other side of the modern stranger — that is, the internal realm of identity. Clearly, much of the reason for the need to develop a new sociology of the stranger is to pave the way for the important work yet to be done by social psychology. How much room is there for "self" as a self-actualizing and "authentic" unit of the larger whole? What kinds of struggles are individuals enduring in order to find a place, to define their world — to be subjects in a world which is satisfied, for its own ends, in keeping them objects?

1.2. Theoretical Implications

In the current study, I have attempted to sketch out a social world that has made these empirical conditions of paramount importance for subsequent research. Yet it seems as though the tools available to sociology, in the form of the existing literature on the stranger and marginality, have not adequately responded to the promise of the interpretative theoretical approaches which attempt to find the place of meaning — for actor and other, as produced and consumed — in coming to terms with the world of strangers.

By preserving the primacy of the desire to articulate self and to be accepted as a member, I have sought to overcome the bleak portrait sketched by many who see only the decline of the individual in the current state of society. There is yet room for optimism. It is true that we walk the tightrope between past and future, but that does not mean that we need to cringe from either. The modern stranger can make his own dance, within the limits imposed by the space in which each member may construct a world.

In speaking to social interaction, however, I have invoked the macro-sociological structure suggested by Riesman. If the appropriation of Riesman's typologies of modes of ensuring conformity has been somewhat uncritical, it has been for two reasons. First, as the theorists discussed in Chapter Two have demonstrated, modernity has produced a shift in social organization which generally conforms to Riesman's categories. Second, the two inter-actional-level axes around which the stranger has been formulated correspond in their subtypes to the orientations of Riesman's three actors. The tradition-directed stranger was typified according to spatial proximity and non-member-ship orientation (in the case of Simmel, and membership orientation in the case of Park's marginal man); the inner-directed stranger was typified accord-ing to social and cultural proximity and non-membership orientation; and the other-directed stranger according to cultural proximity and membership orientation.

The three "mappers" generated in the discussion on modes of observation also conform to Riesman's paradigm. First-order mapping is the mode of the tradition-directed stranger; second-order mapping is that of the inner-directed stranger; and third-order mapping — being "in between" — is the mode of the other-directed stranger.

There are several limits to the applicability of Riesman's categories, how-ever. First, although the inner-directed mode has a definite place in the analysis, it is useful more in terms of providing a mid-point in the transition from tradition-direction to other-direction than in terms of having much theoretical import on its own. The tension is essentially between the two polarities of tradition-direction and other-direction: between Simmel's stranger and the modern stranger; between Wright's "folk" and "urban" cultures.

The polarity which has been expressed between tradition-direction and other-direction is embodied at the level of society in the semiological chain of language-object and metalanguage. The critical effect the shift from tradition-direction to other-direction has had on the actor, however, is on his ability to adapt to the accompanying assaults to his taken-for-granted world. The semiological chain is paralleled in a double-layered reflective relationship. Whereas the tradition-directed stranger could be accounted for by Cooley's reflexive looking-glass self, the modern stranger has evolved a second-order reflexive system that involves the *habitualization* of the reflexive crisis that would have led Schutz's stranger to reflection.

The set of parallelisms spinning off from Riesman's system is summarized in Figure 3. In order to construct a typology of the modern stranger, I have demonstrated how the mode of orienting to membership in the taken-for-granted world has shifted, with accompanying shifts in modes of relating proxemically, membership orientation, and mapping.

Figure 3. Typological Parallels in the Modern Stranger

Type of Actor	Mode of Proxemic Relation	Mode of Membership Orientation	Mode of Mapping	Mode of Reflexivity/ Reflectivity
Tradition-directed stranger	Spatial/ social	Non-membership orented (Simmel's stranger)/ (Park's marginal man)	First-order (traveller/ explorer)	Reflexive crisis
Inner-directed stranger	social/ cultural	Non-membership oriented	Second-order (journalist/ conquistador)	Reflective search for authenticity
Other-directed stranger ("The Modern Stranger")	Cultural	Membership-oriented	Third-order (ethnographer/ trained observer)	Internaliza-tion of reflexive crisis (language of membership)

The democratization of reading meaning that has accompanied the spread of mass communications and the accompanying creation of mass culture has a two-tiered effect on the relation between the creators of meaning and the readers of meaning. First, the generation of a critical public who "see" behind attempts to perpetrate images has forced the creators to engage in second-order myth production which may be critically consumed in the ongoing structuring of habitus from within the system of the silent language of membership. Second, and crucial for the success of the first condition, is that members have risen in response to the challenge by willingly participating in this ongoing discourse. Recognition and negotiation through the silent language of membership has become the most significant mode of communication in other-directed society.

There are implications for the ease with which sociologists invoke terms of "normative order" and "deviance" which stem from this new articulation of the stranger. Fundamental to the sociology of deviance is the assumption that outsiders may be identified on the basis of their failure to comply with normative standards which are shared by all members in an unquestioning fashion. The exclusionary rules which informed Simmel's writing continue to underlie contemporary theories of deviance. What happens when marginality becomes a condition for membership? When all members are seen as implicated in the constant regeneration of norms, the place of institutionalized power and authority is questionable. Is it coincidental that with greater urbanization there has been a phenomenal increase in grassroots approaches to the maintenance of social order? To the extent that city-dwellers feel their property and welfare threatened by an unidentified enemy — is that a fear of normlessness or the collective definition of norms?

2. Conclusion

I have shown that the defining characteristics of the modern stranger are cultural fluency and membership orientation. The expert navigator of the cultural world is the one who may "fit in" anywhere by being acutely aware of the cultural nuances which are embodied in every culture, as Schutz has shown with his propositions of cultural contextualization, cultural polysemy, colloquiality, and historical embodiment. In seeking to "free the stranger from being an outsider", I have demonstrated that the stranger is no longer an exception but the rule. Where once he was relegated to the margins, he has taken over the page. There are no margins; perhaps there is no longer a definable page either.

The monumental task for members is to seek beyond societal prescriptions to the way in which the *choice* to conform gives freedom for the unfettered pursuit of authentic self, and to see that "choice", even if it is a choice between cultural forms which already exist and define the member that appropriates them, is *all we have*. Whereas in the past the mandate to conform to tradition-direction was an end in itself, today the "freedom from" the authority of tradition-direction constitutes the possibility of "freedom to" be a stranger — be autonomous — *within* the denotatively conformist world of objectification of other.

The crucial issue now is, as at every point of drastic social change, to let go of the myths which force the actor to crawl blindly along the tightrope at a snail's pace, forever looking over his shoulder. The myth of home in particular prevents an entire culture from revelling in the chance for each member to become a professional navigator. It cannot continue to be perpetrated in a world which increasingly prohibits its actualization. The ball is squarely in the court of a re-education for strangeness in order that the *good* of home might be preserved, or at this point, at least salvaged. The task which faces us today is to evolve a stronger sense of the humanization of a potentially dehumanizing trend. But that humanization is not to be found in the past. We must productively utilize the unfailing desire of *homo faber* to find meaning in his work, to reproduce self in his world. It would seem that today the route to sustained meaning is a clear distinction between the reflexive and the reflective modes of communication. We are learning to be reflexive about strangeness. This is hard. It is hard to relearn what to take for granted. But once accomplished, there is tremendous room for the creative interpretation of each other through the development of the reflective mode. The broken mirror may never be repaired. But that does not spell the end of each member's creative relation to the world. Perhaps it is merely a beginning.

Appendix A
Some Political Implications of the Modern Stranger

1. The word "choice" appears with disconcerting frequency in the literature on modernity. Fromm's picture of "automaton conformity" paints a bleak view of the loss of choice but even more sadly of a loss of will. The city is a caricature of the "choices" and limits open to the modern stranger. To the noncity dweller, it offers the "lifestyle" choices of anonymity, wealth, a vast array of consumer goods, virtually endless leisure activities.

The modern stranger is free to "consume" what the city has to offer. This is his choice. Yet choice is limited to those who have access. Resources — such as education, employment opportunities, gender, racial origin, lifestyle skills — are allocated disproportionately and clearly have a critical impact on an individual's "freedom" to consume.

But the unequal opportunities for consumption tend to feed the city rather than hinder it. Desire for "more" and "better"; to comply with what is "there" to be had, makes consumption an end in itself. And it is the fundamental *lack of choice* regarding whether one consumes which is the political condition of the modern stranger. There is no politics when there is no real choice. And choice in the city is always *between predefined alternatives*, never choice between conditions of choice.

For the modern stranger is the consummate consumer. To choose not to choose is to remove oneself from the category of "urban culture". In *Channels of Desire*, Ewen and Ewen suggest:

Mass imagery, such as that provided by AT&T, creates for us a memorable language, a system of belief, an ongoing channel to inculcate and effect common perceptions, explaining to us what it means to be part of a "modern world". It is a world defined by the retail (individualized) consumption of goods and services; a world in which social relations are often disciplined by the exchange of money; a world where it increasingly *makes sense* that if there are solutions to be had, they can be bought .... Consumption is our way of life. (1982: 42)

2. Gramsci's (1971) term, "hegemony", is applicable to the assumption in urban culture that "choice of what" is the only choice. By hegemony is meant the embedded ideology which is produced and legitimized by the cultural elite and which causes members to coexist in the "false consciousness"

that they have no ideology. Gramsci notes two "functions" of hegemony: (i) "The 'spontaneous' consent given by the great masses of the population to the general direction imposed on social life by the dominant fundamental group"; and (ii) "The apparatus of state coercive power which 'legally' enforces discipline on those groups who do not 'consent' either actively or passively" (p. 12). Hegemony is thus the *legitimate* manipulation of a society by its "intellectuals".

Hegemony for the modern stranger is the cultural fundament of capitalism that the accumulation of private property, the worship of "the new", and the consumption of "experiences" are not choices but accepted modes of authentic being. It follows that the conflict between the cultural goals and their achievement is the mechanism which enables the system to feed upon itself.

3. The hegemony of modern culture is restrictive, to be sure. And as with any set of material conditions, human society adapts. This study, which could have examined those material conditions; which could have called for ways in which they might be changed; looks to them as a given world in which actors have adapted a peculiarly modern sensibility and authenticity – that of the modern stranger.

In recognizing the consumer culture as the basis for the modern stranger, I have neither accepted it nor rejected it; neither have I taken a purely relativist view. The struggle of the modern stranger to find a niche, to establish membership, to live passionately and authentically, is a human struggle that deserves more than cultural relativism. It should at least provoke wonder. My wonder has made me ask, "How is it possible for humans to adapt socially to changing conditions of membership?". How, indeed, when the tools for communicating membership have become the very commodities, novelties, and experiences that confer authenticity in modern life? We would get nowhere by dismissing an entire culture for wallowing in commodity fetishism or for existing in a reality that is greatly removed from the suffering of human existence. To call for a universal human condition that the modern stranger denies, or defies, is to call an entire mode of being false. No. It exists, and members aspire, as they always do, to manage, to get by, *to live*.

4. This is not to say that change is not needed. The first step, it would seem, is for society to catch up with itself. The yawning gap between existing conditions of community and the mythologization of community must be filled. Perhaps by a third way – the *possibility* of community. Yet the "choices" available to modernity do not include a return to the past. Spatial proximity – a grounding to place and things – is increasingly being obviated by images, messages, and fantasy of the most fleeting nature. Is it a paradox that the growing obsolescence of industries of production is met with an ever in-

creasing rate of consumption? There are no contradictions in an age of such rapid change. The faster the signs appear indicating a loosening of our hold on the material ground to membership, the more desperately we cling to it. To imagine the demise of the thing is to open limitless possibilities for allaying the inequalities and injustices that property produces; just as it is to imagine a rootlessness which we have so far displaced with a second-order language of membership.

The modern stranger, in looking to membership to provide a hint of authenticity in such a world, has to his advantage a growing adaptability to the displacement of traditional modes by the new. The question is, how will that adaptability be used in a self-conscious way to make "choice" a real choice rather than a choice between predefined alternatives?

References

American Psychological Association
  1977   "Guidelines for Nonsexist Language in APA Journals." *Publication Manual Change Sheet* 2 (June).
Antonovsky, Aaron
  1956   "Toward a Refinement of the 'Marginal Man' Concept." *Social Forces* 35 (Oct): 57-62.
Arendt, Hannah
  1958   *The Human Condition.* Chicago: University of Chicago Press.
Austrom, Douglas, and Kim Hanel
  1980   "Looking for Companionship in the Classified Section." Unpublished Study, Department of Psychology, York University, Canada.
Barth, Frederik
  1970   "Introduction." Pp. 9-38 in Frederik Barth (ed.), *Ethnic Groups and Boundaries: The Social Organization of Culture Difference.* London: George Allen and Unwin.
Barthes, Roland
  1976   *Mythologies* (Annette Lavers, trans.). Paladin.
Baudelaire, Charles
  1947   *Paris Spleen, 1869* (Louise Varese, trans.). New York: New Dimensions.
Becker, Howard
  1963   *Outsiders.* New York: Free Press.
Bell, Daniel
  1976   *The Cultural Contradictions of Capitalism.* New York: Basic.
Benedict, Ruth
  1934   *Patterns of Culture.* Boston: Houghton Mifflin.
Benjamin, Walter
  1969   "The Task of the Translator." Pp. 69-82 in *Illuminations* (Hannah Arendt, ed., Harry Zohn, trans.). New York: Schocken.
Berger, Peter, Brigitte Berger, and Hansfried Kellner
  1973   *The Homeless Mind: Modernization and Consciousness.* New York: Vintage.
Bernstein, Basil
  1972   "Social Class, Language and Socialization." Pp. 157-178 in Pier Paolo Giglioli (ed.), *Language and Social Context.* Harmondsworth: Penguin.
Bittner, Egon
  1983   "Technique and the Conduct of Life." *Social Problems* 30 (3): 249-261.
Boas, Max, and Steve Chain
  1976   *Big Mac: The Unauthorized Story of McDonald's.* New York: Methuen.
Bodley, R.V.C.
  1944   *Wind in the Sahara.* New York: Coward-McCann.
Boorstin, Daniel
  1961   *The Image: A Guide to Pseudo-Events in America.* New York: Harper and Row.

Boughey, Howard
  1978   *The Insights of Sociology.* Toronto: Allyn and Bacon.
Bourdieu, Pierre
  1977   *Outline of a Theory of Practice* (Richard Nice, trans.). Cambridge: Cambridge
          University Press.
Bowen, Eleanor Smith
  1964   *Return to Laughter.* New York: Doubleday.
Bruyn, Severyn T.
  1966   *The Human Perspective in Sociology.* Englewood Cliffs, N.J.: Prentice-Hall.
Bugental, J.F.T.
  1976   *The Search for Existential Identity.* San Francisco: Jossey-Bass.
Burgh, Chris de
  1980   *"The Traveller,"* lyrics.
Buscaglia, Leo
  1982   *Living, Loving and Learning.* New York: Fawcett Columbine.
Chomsky, Noam
  1968   *Language and Mind.* Cambridge, Mass.: MIT Press.
Cohen, Albert
  1955   *Delinquent Boys.* Glencoe, Ill.: Free Press.
Cooley, Charles Horton
  1964   *Human Nature and the Social Order.* New York: Schocken.
Coser, Lewis
  1956   *The Functions of Social Conflict.* New York: Free Press.
Cressey, Paul Goalby
  1983   "A Comparison of the Roles of the 'Sociological Stranger' and the 'Anony-
          mous Stranger' in Field Research." *Urban Life* 12 (1): 102-120.
Daniels, Arlene Kaplan
  1967   "The Low-Caste Stranger in Social Research." Pp. 267-296 in Gideon Sjoberg
          (ed.), *Ethics, Politics, and Social Research.* Cambridge: Schenkman.
Defoe, Daniel
  1975   *Robinson Crusoe: An Authoritative Text, Backgrounds and Sources, Critic-
          ism* (Michael Shinagel, ed.). New York: W.W. Norton.
Derrida, Jacques
  1974   *Of Grammatology* (Gayatri Chakravorty Spivak, trans.). Baltimore: Johns
          Hopkins University Press.
Dickie-Clark, H.F.
  1966   "The Marginal Situation: A Contribution to Marginality Theory." *Social
          Forces* 44 (March): 363-370.
Dickson, Lovat
  1973   *Wilderness Man: The Strange Story of Grey Owl.* Toronto: Macmillan.
Dreitzel, Hans Peter
  1977   "On the Political Meaning of Culture." Pp. 83-129 in Norman Birnbaum
          (ed.), *Beyond the Crisis.* New York: Oxford University Press.
  1981   "The Socialization of Nature: Western Attitudes towards Body and
          Emotions." Pp. 205-223 in Paul Heelas and Andrew Lock (eds.), *Indigenous
          Psychologies: The Anthropology of the Self.* London: Academic Press.
  1983   "Peinliche situationen." *Unpublished manuscript.*
Durkheim, Emile
  1933   *The Division of Labor in Society* (George Simpson, trans.). New York: Free
          Press.

Eliot, T.S.
1944   *Four Quartets*. London: Faber and Faber.
Erikson, Kai T.
1966   *Wayward Puritans*. New York: Wiley and Sons.
Ewen, Stuart
1976   *Captains of Consciousness: Advertising and the Social Roots of Consumer Culture*. New York: McGraw-Hill.
Ewen, Stuart, and Elizabeth Ewen
1982   *Channels of Desire: Mass Images and the Shaping of American Consciousness*. New York: McGraw-Hill.
Fiedler, Leslie
1978   *Freaks: Myths and Images of the Secret Self*. New York: Simon and Schuster.
Fishman, Joshua A.
1965   "Who Speaks What Language to Whom and When." *La Linguistique* 2: 67-88.
1972   "The Relationship between Micro- and Macro-Sociolinguistics in the Study of Who Speaks What Language to Whom and When." Pp. 15-32 in J.B. Pride and J. Holmes (eds.), *Sociolinguistics: Selected Readings*. Harmondsworth: Penguin. (a)
1972   *The Sociology of Language*. Rowley, Mass.: Newbury House. (b)
Fortes, Meyer
1975   "Strangers." Pp. 229-253 in Meyer Fortes and Sheila Patterson (eds.), *Studies in African Social Anthropology*. New York: Academic Press.
Foucault, Michel
1972   *The Archaeology of Knowledge and The Discourse on Language* (A.M. Sheridan Smith, trans.). New York: Harper.
Frake, C.O.
1964   "How to Ask for a Drink in Subanun." *American Anthropologist* 66(6): 127-132.
Franck, Karen A.
1980   "Friends and Strangers." *Journal of Social Issues* 36 (3): 52-71.
Fromm, Erich
1947   *Man for Himself*. New York: Rinehard.
1955   *The Sane Society*. New York: Fawcett.
1969   *Escape from Freedom*. New York: Avon.
Fuentes, Carlos
1978   *The Hydra Head* (Margaret S. Peder, trans.). New York: Farrar, Straus and Giroux.
Gans. Herbert J.
1975   *Popular Culture and High Culture: An Analysis and Evaluation of Taste*. New York: Basic.
Garfinkel, Harold
1967   *Studies in Ethnomethodology*. Englewood Cliffs, N.J.: Prentice-Hall.
Geertz, Clifford
1973   *The Interpretation of Cultures: Selected Essays*. New York: Basic.
Glaser, Barney G., and Anselm L. Strauss
1967   *The Discovery of Grounded Theory: Strategies for Qualitative Research*. Chicago: Aldine.
Goffman, Erving
1961   *Encounters: Two Studies in the Sociology of Interaction*. New York: Bobbs-Merrill.

1963   *Behavior in Public Places: Notes on the Social Organization of Gatherings.* New York: Free Press. (a)

1963   *Stigma: Notes on the Management of Spoiled Identity.* Englewood Cliffs, N.J.: Prentice-Hall. (b)

Goldberg, Milton M.

1941   "A Qualification of the Marginal Man Theory." *American Sociological Review* 6 (Feb): 52-58.

Golovensky, David I.

1952   "The Marginal Man Concept: An Analysis and Critique." *Social Forces* 30 (Dec): 333-339.

Goodenough, Ward

1957   "Cultural Anthropology and Linguistics." Pp. 167-173 in P.L. Garvin (ed.), *Report of the Seventh Annual Round Table Meeting on Linguistics and Language Study.* Washington D.C.: Georgetown University Press.

Gramsci, Antonio

1971   *Prison Notebooks* (Quintin Hoare and Geoffrey Nowell Smith, eds. and trans.). New York: International Publishers.

Green, Arnold W.

1947   "A Re-examination of the Marginal Man Concept." *Social Forces* 26 (Dec): 167-171.

Greene, Graham

1980   *A Journey without Maps.* Penguin.

Greifer, Julian L.

1945   "Attitudes to the Stranger: A Study of the Attitudes of Primitive Society and Early Hebrew Culture." *American Sociological Review* 10 (Dec): 739-745.

Grey Owl

1935   *Pilgrims of the Wild.* London: Lovat Dickson.

Gumperz, John J.

1971   *Language in Social Groups.* Stanford, Ca.: Stanford University Press.

1972   "Sociolinguistics and Communication in Small Groups." Pp. 203-224 in J.B. Pride and J. Holmes (eds.), *Sociolinguistics: Selected Readings.* Harmondsworth: Penguin. (a)

1972   "The Speech Community." Pp. 219-231 in Pier Paolo Giglioli (ed.), *Language and Social Context.* Harmondsworth: Penguin. (b)

Habermas, Jürgen

1970   "Toward a Theory of Communicative Competence." Pp. 115-148 in Hans Peter Dreitzel (ed.), *Recent Sociology No. 2: Patterns of Communicative Behavior.* Toronto: Macmillan.

1971   *Knowledge and Human Interests* (Jeremy J. Shapiro, trans.). Boston: Beacon Press.

1979   "What is Universal Pragmatics?" Pp. 1-68 in *Communication and the Evolution of Society.* Boston: Beacon Press.

Haley, Alex

1976   *Roots.* Garden City, N.Y.: Doubleday.

Hall, Edward T.

1973   *The Silent Language.* New York: Anchor.

1977   *Beyond Culture.* New York: Anchor.

Harman, Lesley D.

1985   "Acceptable Deviance as Social Control: The Cases of Fashion and Slang." *Deviant Behavior* 6: 1-15.

1986   "Sign, Symbol, and Metalanguage: Against the Integration of Semiotics and Symbolic Interactionism." *Symbolic Interaction* 9 (1): 147-160.

1987   "The Creation of the 'Bag Lady': Rethinking Home for Homeless Women." *Human Affairs* 12.

Hegel, G.W.F.

1967   *Philosophy of Right* (T.M. Knox, trans.). New York: Oxford University
[1821]   Press.

Hemingway, Ernest

1964   *A Moveable Feast.* New York: Charles Scribner's Sons.

Hughes, Everett C.

1945   "Dilemmas and Contradictions of Status." *American Journal of Sociology* 50: 353-359.

1949   "Social Change and Status Protest: An Essay on the Marginal Man." *Phylon* 10 (1): 58-65.

Hymes, Dell

1972   "Models of the Interaction of Language and Social Life." Pp. 35-71 in J.J. Gumperz and D. Humes (eds.), *The Ethnography of Communication.* New York: Holt, Rinehart and Winston. (a)

1972   "On Communicative Competence." Pp. 269-293 in J.B. Pride and J. Holmes (eds.), *Sociolinguistics: Selected Readings.* Harmondsworth: Penguin. (b)

Inkeles, Alex

1964   *What is Sociology?* Englewood Cliffs, N.H.: Prentice-Hall.

Kerckhoff, Alan C., and Thomas C. McCormick

1955   "Marginal Status and Marginal Personality." *Social Forces* 34 (Oct): 48-55.

Klapp, Orrin E.

1969   *Collective Search for Identity.* New York: Holt, Rinehart and Winston.

Krause, Charles

1978   *Guyana Massacre: The Eyewitness Account.* New York: Berkley.

Labov, W.

1966   *The Social Stratification of English in New York City.* Washington, D.C.: Center for Applied Linguistics.

Lasch, Christopher

1977   *Haven in a Heartless World: The Family Beseiged.* New York: Basic.

1978   *The Culture of Narcissism: American Life in an Age of Diminishing Expectation.* New York: W.W. Norton.

Lemert, Edwin

1951   *Social Pathology.* New York: McGraw-Hill.

Levine, Donald N.

1979   "Simmel at a Distance: On the History and Systematics of the Sociology of the Stranger." Pp. 21-36 in William Shack and Elliott Skinner (eds.), *Strangers in African Societies.* Berkeley: University of California Press.

Lifton, Robert Jay

1968   "Protean Man." *Partisan Review* 35: 13-27.

Lofland, John

1969   *Deviance and Identity.* Englewood Cliffs, N.J.: Prentice-Hall.

Lofland, Lyn H.

1973   *A World of Strangers: Order and Action in Urban Public Space.* New York: Basic.

MacCannell, Dean

1976   *The Tourist: A New Theory of the Leisure Class.* New York: Schocken.

Mann, John W.
    1948   "Group Relations and the Marginal Personality." *Human Relations* 11 (Jan):
            77-92.
Mannheim, Karl
    1940   *Man and Society in an Age of Reconstruction* (Edward Shils, trans.). New
            York: Harcourt, Brace and World.
Marx, Karl
    1964   *Early Writings* (T.B. Bottomore, trans. and ed.). New York: McGraw-Hill.
Maslow, A.H.
    1954   *Motivation and Personality.* New York: Harper and Row.
May, R.
    1953   *Man's Search for Himself.* New York: Delta.
McLemore, S. Dale
    1970   "Simmel's 'Stranger': A Critique of the Concept." *Pacific Sociological Re-
            view* 13 (2): 86-94.
Mead, George Herbert
    1934   *Mind, Self and Society* (Charles W. Morris, ed.). Chicago: University of
            Chicago Press.
Mead, Margaret
    1928   *Coming of Age in Samoa: A Psychological Study of Primitive Youth for
            Western Civilization.* New York: Morrow Quill.
Merton, Robert K.
    1968   *Social Theory and Social Structure.* New York: Macmillan.
Meyer, Julie
    1951   "The Stranger and the City." *American Journal of Sociology* 56 (March):
            476-483.
Musgrove, F.
    1963   *The Migratory Elite.* London: Heinemann.
Naipaul, V.S.
    1969   *The Loss of El Dorado: A History.* Suffolk: Penguin.
Nash, Dennison
    1963   "The Ethnologist as Stranger: An Essay in the Sociology of Knowledge."
            Southwestern Journal of Anthropology 19: 149-167.
Nash, Dennison J., and Alvin W. Wolfe
    1957   "The Stranger in Laboratory Culture." *American Sociological Review* 22 (4):
            400-405.
Orwell, George
    1961   *1984.* New York: New American Library.
Packard, Vance
    1972   *A Nation of Strangers.* New York: McKay.
Park, Robert E.
    1928   "Human Migration and the Marginal Man." *American Journal of Sociology*
            33 (8): 881-893.
Park, Robert E., and Ernest W. Burgess
    1924   *Introduction to the Science of Sociology.* Chicago: University of Chicago Press.
Pitt-Rivers, Julian
    1968   "The Stranger, the Guest and the Hostile Host." Pp. 13-30 in J.G. Peristiany
            (ed.), *Contributions to Mediterranean Sociology.* The Hague: Mouton.
Polo, Marco
    1953   *The Travels of Marco Polo* (Manuel Komroff, ed., Marsden, trans.). New
            York: Modern Library.

Powdermaker, Hortense
  1966   *Stranger and Friend: The Way of an Anthropologist.* London: Secker and
         Warburg.
Raskin, Jonah
  1971   *The Mythology of Imperialism.* New York: Random House.
Riesman, David
  1951   "Some Observations Concerning Marginality." *Phylon* 12 (2): 113-127.
  1961   *The Lonely Crowd* (Abr. Ed.). New Haven: Yale University Press.
Rodgers, Bruce
  1972   *The Queens' Vernacular: A Gay Lexicon.* San Francisco: Straight Arrow Books.
Rose, Peter I.
  1967   "Strangers in their Midst: Small-town Jews and their Neighbors." Pp. 463-
         479 in Peter I. Rose (ed.), *The Study of Society: An Integrated Anthology.*
         New York: Random House.
Rousseau, Jean-Jacques
  1966   "Essay on the Origin of Languages." Pp. 5-74 in *On the Origin of Language:
         Two Essays by Jean-Jacques Rousseau and Johann Gottfried Herder* (John
         H. Moran and Alexander Gode, trans.). New York: Frederick Ungar.
Said, Edward
  1978   *Orientalism.* New York: Pantheon.
Saussure, Ferdinand de
  1966   *Course in General Linguistics* (Wade Baskin, trans.). New York: McGraw-Hill.
Schleiermacher, Fr. D.E.
  1959   *Hermeneutik* (Heinz Kimmerle, ed.). Heidelberg.
Schnall, Maxine
  1981   *Limits: A Search for New Values.* New York: Potter.
Schutz, Afred
  1944   "The Stranger: An Essay in Social Psychology." *American Journal of Soci-
         ology* 49 (6): 499-507.
  1945   "The Homecomer." *American Journal of Sociology* 60 (5): 369-376.
  1967   *The Phenomenology of the Social World* (George Walsh and Frederick
         Lehnert, trans.). Evanston: Northwestern University Press.
  1970   *On Phenomenology and Social Relations* (Helmut R. Wagner, ed.). Chicago:
         University of Chicago Press.
Sennett, Richard
  1978   *The Fall of Public Man.* New York: Vintage.
Shack, William, and Elliott Skinner (eds.)
  1979   *Strangers in African Societies.* Berkeley: University of California Press.
Shaffir, William B., Robert A. Stebbins, and Allan Turowetz
  1980   *Fieldwork Experience: Qualitative Approaches to Social Research.* New
         York: St. Martin's.
Simmel, Georg
  1968   *Soziologie: Untersuchen uber die Formen der Vergesellschaftung.*
  [1908] Berline: Duncker und Humblot.
  1971   "Fashion." Pp. 294-323 in Donald N. Levine (ed.), *On Individuality and
         Social Forms.* Chicago: University of Chicago Press. (a)
  1971   "The Stranger." Pp. 143-149 in Donald N. Levine (ed.), *On Individuality and
         Social Forms.* Chicago: University of Chicago Press. (b)
Siu, Paul C.P.
  1952   "The Sojourner." *American Journal of Sociology* 58 (1): 34-44.

Slater, Philip
1970   *The Pursuit of Loneliness: American Culture at the Breaking Point.* Boston: Beacon Press.
Smith, Adam
1966   *The Theory of Moral Sentiments.* New York: Augustus M. Kelley.
[1759]
Stonequist, Everett V.
1937   *The Marginal Man: A Study in Personality and Culture Conflict.* New York: Russel and Russel.
Tarde, Gabriel
1969   *On Communication and Social Influence* (Terry N. Clark, ed.). Chicago: University of Chicago Press.
Tönnies, Ferdinand
1955   *Community and Association.* London: Routledge and Kegan Paul.
Trilling, Lionel
1972   *Sincerity and Authenticity.* Cambridge: Harvard University Press.
Veblen, Thorstein
1953   *The Theory of the Leisure Class.* New York: Mentor.
Wardaugh, Ronald
1986   *An Introduction to Sociolinguistics.* Oxford: Basil Blackwell.
Wax, Rosalie
1971   *Doing Fieldwork: Warnings and Advice.* Chicago: University of Chicago Press.
Weber, Max
1949   *The Methodology of the Social Sciences* (Edward A. Shils and Henry A. Finch, trans.). New York: Free Press.
White, Leslie
1959   "Four Stages in the Evolution of Minding." In Sol Tax (ed.), *The Evolution of Man, vol. 2 of Evolution after Darwin.* Chicago: University of Chicago Press.
Whyte, William H., Jr.
1956   *The Organization Man.* New York: Touchstone.
Willener, A.
1976   *The Action-Image of Society: On Cultural Politicization.* London: Tavistock.
Wilson, H.T.
1977   *The American Ideology: Science, Technology and Organization as Modes of Rationality in Advanced Industrial Societies.* London: Routledge and Kegan Paul.
Wirth, Louis
1938   "Urbanism as a Way of Life." *American Journal of Sociology* 44 (1): 1-24.
Wittgenstein, Ludwig
1976   *Philosophical Investigations* (G.E.M. Anscombe, trans.). Oxford: Basil Blackwell.
Wood, Margaret Mary
1934   *The Stranger: A Study in Social Relationships.* New York: Columbia University Press.
Wright, Rolland H.
1971   "The Stranger Mentality and the Culture of Poverty." Pp. 315-337 in Eleanor Leacock (ed.), *The Culture of Poverty.* New York: Simon and Schuster.

Index

Bent Preisler

Linguistic Sex Roles in Conversation

1986. 14,8 x 22,8 cm. XVIII, 350 pages. With 29 illustrations. Cloth
ISBN 3 11 011081 4
(Contributions to the Sociology of Language, 45)

This large-scale empirical investigation, based on socially stratified data recorded in England and a comprehensive theory of linguistic tentativeness, throws new light on the nature and extent of sex roles in linguistic interaction.

It contributes not only to sociolinguistic theory, but to discourse analysis and to the description of the pragmatics of English modal expressions as well.

A distinction between linguistics and pragmatic tentativeness is established, and it is shown that women's more frequent use of linguistic tentativeness signals is a general style feature which transcends age, social class, socio-psychological role and group composition, although manifestations of these signals vary according to age and social class.

mouton de gruyter

Berlin · New York · Amsterdam

Analyzing Intercultural Communication

Edited by Karlfried Knapp, Werner Enninger, and
Annelie Knapp-Potthoff

1987. 14,8 x 22,8 cm. VIII, 320 pages. With 1 illustra-
tion and numerous tables. Cloth
ISBN 3 11 011246 9

(Studies in Anthropological Linguistics 1)
Series Editors: **Florian Coulmas** and **Jacob L. Mey**

This collection of 12 papers focuses on problems of
communication across cultural boundaries.
Based on material from contacts among speakers of a
wide variety of linguistic and cultural backgrounds,
each paper presents a different approach to the
analysis of intercultural communication. The articles are grouped in five sections: 1. Socio-political
contexts of intercultural communication; 2. Socio-
psychological perspectives; 3. Language choice;
4. Discourse processes; 5. Selected elements of discourse.
The main focus is on revealing typical misunderstandings in intercultural communication in relation
to characteristics of the social context, psychological
expectations of the participants, and elements of linguistic structure.

mouton de gruyter
Berlin · New York · Amsterdam